DISCOVER DAYTON
COOKBOOK

PUBLISHED BY

THE JUNIOR LEAGUE
OF
DAYTON, OHIO, INC.

18 WEST FIRST STREET • DAYTON, OHIO 45402

DISCOVER DAYTON COOKBOOK

First Printing   September, 1979   10,000 copies
Second Printing   April, 1980   10,000 copies

Library of Congress Cataloging in Publication Data
Main Entry under title:

Junior League of Dayton.
Discover Dayton Cookbook

Includes index.
1. Cookery, American — Ohio.   2. Historic sites — Ohio — Dayton
3. Dayton, Ohio — History — Miscellany. I. Title.
TX715.J97313   1979   641.5   79-66297
ISBN 0—9603082-1-0

Printed by Drury Printing

Manufactured in the United States of America

FOREWORD

The Junior League of Dayton, Ohio, Inc., is delighted to bring you DISCOVER DAYTON.

From the nineteen people who first settled Dayton in 1796 to the present 835,000 (and the ninety-minute, air-transportation market which serves 62% of the total United States population), Dayton has been ever changing and ever improving. We are an upbeat, positive city of which the Junior League is proud to be a part, and through the money realized from our projects such as Town Hall and DISCOVER DAYTON, we can contribute our share to Dayton's continued growth and vitality.

DISCOVER DAYTON is a unique book. Dayton Junior League members and friends have submitted over 1200 recipes for consideration, and we have tested and tasted each one to select only the best for you. Some of the recipes have been modified by the cookbook committee, and we have edited them with the goal of creating a book which is easy to read and consistent in form — a book on which even a bride can always depend for success. DISCOVER DAYTON is a bright, happy book filled with colorful pages, salutes to our city's landmarks and historical sites, and delicious recipes. We invite you to take a tour through both the book and the city with our whimsical cover character. Our first four sections will help you enhance your family meals, impress your friends, and rejuvenate your culinary talents. The fifth section is a bonus of gourmet tidbits: microwave and food processor tips, Town Hall celebrity recipes, recipes from our members' favorite restaurants (in Dayton's ninety-minute surface-transport market), and a wine guide designed to educate you about both cooking with and serving wine.

Dayton Junior League members have logged many thousands of woman hours with our impetus being a desire for you to be consistently proud to serve each recipe. We think our cookbook will give you and yours many happy times. So, settle back, relax, and enjoy — discover Dayton!

PREFACE

The purpose of the Junior League is exclusively educational and charitable and is to promote voluntarism, to develop the potential of its members for voluntary participation in community affairs, and to demonstrate the effectiveness of trained volunteers.

Proceeds from the sale of DISCOVER DAYTON go into the Community Trust Fund, which finances the League's community programs.

Built in the 1830's in Greek Revival architecture, the Fowler-Parrott house is one of the oldest existing downtown buildings. Located at 18 West First Street, the building was owned by the Fowler-Parrott family for 119 years, from 1844 to 1963. Now an office building the Fowler-Parrott house has been nominated for the National Register of Historic Places. In 1979 the Junior League of Dayton moved its office into the building which had proudly housed the Junior League Shop from 1937 to 1949.

ORIGINAL DISCOVER DAYTON
STEERING COMMITTEE

CHAIRMAN
Mrs. William R. Thompson

ASSISTANT CHAIRMAN
Mrs. Stephen G. England

EDITOR
Mrs. Robert L. Deddens

FINANCIAL MANAGER
Mrs. Ronald L. Petersen

PROMOTIONS COORDINATOR
Mrs. James C. Medford

EXECUTIVE COMMITTEE LIAISONS
Mrs. Earl F. Pritchard

Mrs. William M. Kasch

COMMITTEE CHAIRMEN

ART AND ILLUSTRATIONS
Mrs. Alfred J. Weisbrod

COVER DESIGNERS
Mrs. Richard C. Cammerer

Mrs. George M. Murray, III

DISTRIBUTION
Mrs. Kieran M. Devery

LAYOUT
Mrs. Richard C. Shelton

PROOFREADING AND INDEX
Mrs. Stephen R. Elling

RESTAURANT
Mrs. William T. Mayhew

TESTING
Mrs. Robert C. James

TYPING
Mrs. Eugene J. Cassella

TABLE OF CONTENTS

Hawthorn Hill

Beautiful Beginnings

HAWTHORN HILL

The dreams and hopes of a machine that could fly were brought into reality by Orville and Wilbur Wright in a bicycle shop in Dayton. Hawthorn Hill, completed in 1914, two years after Wilbur's death, became the home of Orville and his sister Katherine. The name Hawthorn Hill was inspired by the Wrights' childhood home on Hawthorn Street and by the beautiful trees on the 17 acre estate. The mansion, located in Oakwood on Harman and Park Avenues, was acquired by the National Cash Register Company to be used as a guest house following Orville's death in 1948. Although Hawthorn Hill is not open to the public, it does stand in tribute to the men who made Dayton the "birthplace of aviation."

SPINACH DIP

Easy and creamy make-ahead dip with pleasant blend of seasonings. Use with raw vegetables, crackers, or chips.

1	10-ounce package frozen chopped spinach
1	cup mayonnaise
1	cup sour cream
1½	tablespoons lemon juice
1	cup fresh parsley, chopped (or flakes)
1	tablespoon dill weed
1	teaspoon fines herbs (we use Spice Islands)
½	cup onions, minced (or dehydrated)
1	teaspoon salt

Thaw and thoroughly drain chopped spinach. Combine all ingredients and refrigerate, covered, for 24 hours before serving.

VARIATION: Parsley, dill weed, and fines herbs may be omitted or quantities reduced with fine results.

YIELD: 3½ cups

Mrs. R. James Heikes
(Bonnie Bright)

MARINATED MUSHROOMS AND ARTICHOKE HEARTS

Great change-of-pace appetizer!

2/3	cup red wine vinegar
½	cup vegetable oil
¼	teaspoon garlic salt
1	tablespoon sugar
1½	teaspoons salt
	Dash of pepper
2	tablespoons water
	Dash of tabasco sauce
1	medium onion, sliced
1	14-ounce can artichoke hearts
1	pound fresh mushrooms

In a small bowl, mix together all ingredients except mushrooms. Place mushrooms in a medium-size glass bowl. Add marinade mixture to the mushrooms. Prepare 2 to 3 days ahead. Store covered in refrigerator. Serve cold with toothpicks.

YIELD: 8 to 10 servings

Mrs. Alfred Weisbrod
(Gracey Potter)

SPICED WALNUTS

Super speedy! This makes a delicious and different appetizer to serve along with drinks or just as a snack. Everyone will love it. It is truly SPICY!!!

¼	cup vegetable oil
2	teaspoons chili powder
½	teaspoon cumin
½	teaspoon tumeric
	Pinch cayenne
½	teaspoon sugar
3	cups walnut halves or large pieces

In a heavy skillet, heat oil, chili powder, cumin, tumeric, cayenne, and sugar. When very hot, remove from heat. Add walnuts to oil mixture, and stir until coated. Line a shallow baking pan with paper towels; spread walnuts on paper towels. Bake in a preheated 300º oven for 10 minutes; salt to taste. Cool and pack in an airtight container.
YIELD: 3 cups

Mrs. Siavosh Bozorgi
(Bonnie Hughes)

MARINATED SHRIMP

Terrific tangy taste to titillate the tongue!

3	pounds shrimp, cooked, cleaned, and drained
1	cup mayonnaise
1	tablespoon Durkee's Famous Sauce (dressing)
½	small onion, grated
	Juice of ½ lemon
¼	teaspoon salt

Mix together all ingredients except for shrimp. Add shrimp; cover, and marinate for 24 hours in refrigerator. Stir occasionally.
YIELD: 16 to 20 servings

Mrs. Jonathan P. Shelton
(Nancy Garst)

SHRIMP STUFFED BAGUETTES

Good combination of flavors.

3   deli or French rolls, baked
½   cup butter, softened
1½   cups shrimp, cooked and ground fine in grinder or food processor
3   eggs, hard boiled and chopped
¼   to ½ cup chopped walnuts
1   8-ounce package cream cheese, softened
     Salt to taste

In a small bowl, blend butter with a little salt. Cut off ends of rolls, and hollow out to make a tube. Spread tubes with butter; cover, and refrigerate. In a large mixing bowl, beat together shrimp, eggs, walnuts, and cream cheese. With a spatula, stuff rolls with filling until tube is filled full. Wrap airtight, and chill well (May be frozen.). At serving time, using a sharp knife, cut rolls into ¼-inch thick slices.

VARIATION: Tuna, chicken, or ham may be substituted for shrimp.

YIELD: 24 to 36 slices

Mrs. James Garrison
(Lesli Janacshek)

3

LAYERED CREPE WEDGES

**Prepare the cream cheese filling the night before.
Assemble crepes the next morning. Collect compliments that evening!**

1	8-ounce package cream cheese, softened
2	teaspoons milk
5	green onions, diced
¼	teaspoon white pepper
1	teaspoon monosodium glutamate MSG (we prefer Accent)
¼	teaspoon garlic powder
2	tablespoons sour cream
1	3-ounce package dried beef, chopped finely
¼	cup diced green pepper
¾	cup chopped pecans
½	teaspoon salt
2	tablespoons butter
6	crepes — use your favorite crepes recipe

In a medium-size mixing bowl, beat the cream cheese until smooth and creamy. Add milk, onions, pepper, MSG, garlic powder, sour cream, dried beef, and green pepper; mix well. Cover and refrigerate at least 2 hours, or overnight. In a small skillet, combine pecans, salt, and butter. Cook and stir over medium heat until golden brown; remove from heat, and set aside. About 1½ to 2 hours or longer before serving, remove cream cheese mixture from refrigerator, and allow to soften to a spreading consistency. Spread 1/6 of the cream cheese mixture on one side of each crepe. Make 2 stacks of 3 crepes each. Sprinkle the toasted pecans around the outside edge of the top of each stack. Cover and refrigerate for at least 1 hour. Cut into wedges, and serve.

YIELD: 16 appetizers

Mrs. William Kasch
(Sonnie Kern)

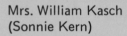

COLD FILET APPETIZER WITH SOUR CREAM SAUCE

Prepare ahead; always perfect!

1   carrot, chopped
1   stalk celery, chopped
1   medium onion, chopped
2   tablespoons butter
2   pounds filet of beef
     Salt and pepper to taste
1   teaspoon fresh chopped parsley
4   tablespoons butter

SOUR CREAM FILLING

½   pound bacon, cut in small pieces
1   clove garlic, minced
1   cup sour cream
2   tablespoons pan juices reserved from filet
1   tablespoon grated onion
1   tablespoon chopped chives
1   teaspoon chopped fresh parsley
½   teaspoon horseradish (optional)
¼   teaspoon tarragon
¼   teaspoon dill weed
     Salt and white pepper to taste

In a small roasting pan, saute the carrot, celery, and onion in 2 tablespoons of the butter until the vegetables are soft and the onion transparent. Sprinkle the filet with salt, pepper, and chopped parsley. Place the filet on top of the vegetables and dot with the remaining 4 tablespoons butter. Roast in preheated 500° oven for 20 to 25 minutes. Remove from the oven and cool in the pan for at least 1 hour. Transfer the meat to a serving platter. Strain and reserve the pan juices. Cut a V-shaped piece 1-inch deep the entire length of the filet. Fill the resulting trough with Sour Cream Filling. Cover filet with a foil tent and refrigerate for ½ hour. Trim the removed V of meat by cutting off the point of the V, leaving a flat piece of filet. Place the flat piece on top of the filling and refrigerate until ready to serve. To serve, slice the chilled filet into ½ to ¾-inch slices and garnish the platter with fresh parsley.

SOUR CREAM FILLING

In a skillet, saute the bacon with the garlic until the bacon is crisp. Remove the bacon bits with a slotted spoon and drain on paper toweling. In a bowl, combine the sour cream with bacon and all remaining ingredients. YIELD: 10-12 slices

Mrs. Stephen G. England
(Katherine Benham)

ENGINEERED HORS D'OEUVRES

These evolved over years of study and self denial!

EDITOR'S NOTE: Don't let the lengthy directions discourage you from preparing these delicious hors d'oeuvres . . . only about 20 to 30 minutes preparation time. Beware: you must follow directions, or your guests will drop their pickles.

2   3-ounce packages of thin-sliced dried beef squares (Kahn's is easy to handle; Buddig is okay.)

14   to 16 sweet midget pickles

1   8-ounce package of cream cheese.

Three hours to 1 week ahead of serving time stack slices of dried beef and press down on stack to "iron" beef. Place cream cheese in top of a covered double boiler over hot water, or on low power in microwave oven. Heat thoroughly until very warm and soft like sour cream. Select longest and straightest pickles, and place on paper toweling to dry. With a knife, trim off about the last 1/8-inch from each end of the pickles so that they will butt together. Lay a sheet of waxed paper, about 18-inches long, vertically to edge of work surface.

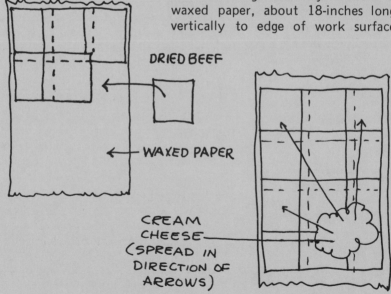

DRIED BEEF

WAXED PAPER

CREAM CHEESE (SPREAD IN DIRECTION OF ARROWS)

recipe continues . . .

BEGIN ROLLING HERE.
LIFT PAPER TO AID YOU.

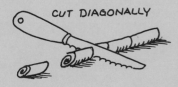

CUT DIAGONALLY

FINISHED HORS D'OEUVRE

Working on waxed paper across from left to right, arrange 3 beef slices at top of paper overlapping each other about 1/3-inch. Repeat, overlapping second row about 1/3-inch over bottom of top row. Likewise, add third and fourth rows of beef. With firm rubber or plastic spatula, scrape one-half (4 ounces) of the very warm, very soft, cream cheese onto the bottom right square of beef. Spread cream cheese over entire beef surface always spreading from the bottom right upwards or toward the left only — one stroke in the wrong direction, and you're in trouble! You may need to spread some cream cheese off the beef surface and recommence with it back at the bottom right. Along bottom edge of beef, line up a single row of pickles touching end to end. Using waxed paper to help you lift up bottom of roll evenly, firmly roll up beef from bottom. Tear off another sheet of waxed paper about 18-inches long, and roll it around your still fragile beef roll. Twist ends to make a "cast," and place it in refrigerator to set. Repeat with remaining ingredients. Unwrap beef roll, and place on same waxed paper (only a knife to wash!) over cutting surface. With sharp, serrated knife *diagonally* cut slices about 1/3-inch thick (designed so the pickle doesn't fall out). Arrange cut side up on a serving plate.
YIELD: about 24 bite-size appetizers

Mrs. Alan Meckstroth
(Betty Lutz)

7

STRAWBERRY CHEESE MOLD

Need a quick but tasty appetizer? This is super easy to prepare,
and the strawberry preserves add just the right touch!
For "Mom's Strawberry Preserves" (see index).

½ pound sharp cheddar
cheese, grated
½ pound mild cheddar
cheese, grated
2 tablespoons mayon-
naise
1 small onion, finely
chopped
½ to 1 cup finely chop-
ped pecans
Fresh parsley for
garnish
1 16-ounce jar straw-
berry preserves; try
"Mom's Strawberry
Preserves" (see index)

In a large mixing bowl, combine
grated cheese, mayonnaise, onion, and
nuts. Press into a slightly oiled 5-cup
mold, and refrigerate. About 15
minutes before serving, unmold and
surround with fresh parsley. Top with
strawberry preserves, and serve with
your favorite cracker.
YIELD: 10 to 12 servings

Mrs. Donald J. May
(Brenda Amburgey)

"SIMPLE" DIP OR CRACKER SPREAD

This dip was created out of desperation when a cocktail party
suddenly came to my house, and these things were available.
Serve with corn chips or spread on unseasoned crackers.

2 8-ounce packages
cream cheese, or low
calorie cream cheese,
softened
½ to 1 cup thousand
island dressing, to
moisten
2 to 3 eggs, hard boiled
and coarsely chopped

In a medium-size mixing bowl, beat
cream cheese until smooth and
creamy. Beat in ½ cup salad dressing;
stir in eggs. If desired, add up to ½
cup more salad dressing to obtain
spreading or dipping consistency.
YIELD: about 3½ cups

Mrs. E. James Buckley
(Patricia Weyer)

SAZIKI

Easy and refreshing dip! Greek-Turkish origin.

4   cucumbers
3   cloves garlic
1   tablespoon olive oil
     Salt and pepper to
     taste
1   pint sour cream

Clean cucumbers, seed as necessary, and put through a fine grater (not blender). Allow to drain in colander until juices have stopped running. In a small bowl mash garlic with olive oil, salt, and pepper. Stir in cucumbers and sour cream. Chill. Serve with crackers.
CHEF'S NOTE: Try garnishing squash or baked potatoes with this tasty dip.
YIELD: 6 to 8 servings

Mrs. Samuel G. Sava
(Elizabeth Tsourounis)

ARTICHOKE DIP

Super easy. Good combination of texture and flavor.

1   8½-ounce can (drained
     weight) artichoke
     hearts
1   cup mayonnaise (we
     prefer Hellman's)
1   cup grated Parmesan
     cheese
     Juice of ½ lemon
     Cayenne pepper to
     taste

Drain, rinse, and mash artichokes. Mix together all ingredients. Turn into small buttered baking dish. Bake in preheated 350° oven for about 30 minutes or until bubbly and brown on top. Serve in a baking dish which is put on a large platter and surrounded by small, stone-cut wheat thins or any favorite crackers.
VARIATION: Double recipe and serve in chafing dish.
YIELD: 2½ cups

Mrs. R. James Heikes
(Bonnie Bright)

9

SHRIMP PRELUDE

One of my favorite party dips.

1   pound boiled shrimp, chopped and drained
1   tablespoon minced onion
1   tablespoon minced celery
1   teaspoon minced green pepper
1   to 2 teaspoons lemon juice
4   drops tabasco sauce
¾   cup mayonnaise
    Salt and pepper to taste.

Use paper towels to pat cooked shrimp dry. In a medium-size bowl, combine all ingredients until well mixed. Season to taste. Refrigerate covered. Serve with crackers.
YIELD: 2 to 2½ cups; serves 8

Mrs. Henry Wagner, Jr.
(Suzanne Canny)

SHRIMP SPREAD OR DIP

A light snack with a nice shrimp flavor.

1   8-ounce package cream cheese, softened
1/3   cup mayonnaise
1   teaspoon lemon juice
½   teaspoon minced onion
¼   teaspoon salt
2   tablespoons dry white wine
1   7-ounce can shrimp, chopped and drained (reserve juice)

Combine all ingredients except shrimp; mix well. Stir in chopped shrimp. Thin with reserved juice if necessary. Serve with crackers.
YIELD: 2 cups

Mrs. William R. Thompson
(Sally Decker)

10

CRABMEAT SPREAD

This is as attractive to serve as it is delicious!
Layers of white, red, and pink — must prepare ahead.

1   8-ounce package cream
     cheese, softened
     Juice of 1 lemon
3   tablespoons mayon-
     naise (we prefer Hell-
     man's)
1   to 2 teaspoons worces-
     tershire sauce, to taste
1   tablespoon grated
     onion
     Garlic powder to taste
1   6-ounce package
     frozen Alaskan King
     crab, thawed, drained,
     and shredded (we
     prefer Wakefield)
6   ounces chili sauce
     Parsley flakes, for
     garnish

In a small mixing bowl, beat together all ingredients except crab, chili sauce, and parsley flakes; beat until smooth. Spread mixture into one or several shallow glass serving dishes. Spread chili sauce on cream cheese mixture; top with shredded crabmeat. Cover and refrigerate for at least 24 hours. Sprinkle with parsley flakes before serving. Serve with Triscuits.
YIELD: 10 servings

Mrs. Earl F. Pritchard
(Judy Elliot)

HOT CHEESE DIP

Great to serve on wintry evenings; it's so simple!

4   strips lean bacon,
     chopped
2   cups cubed sharp
     cheddar cheese
1   10¾-ounce can cream
     of mushroom soup
8   green onions, chopped
     fine

Fry chopped bacon; do not drain. Add remaining ingredients to pan, and cook over medium heat until mixture is bubbly. Serve hot in a fondue pot with French bread cubes.
CHEF'S NOTE: Serve with a tossed green salad for a quick and easy Sunday night supper.
YIELD: 2½ cups, serves 8

Mrs. Gayle B. Price, Jr.
(Rita Fanget)

CRABMEAT APPETIZER

Easy and delicious.

1   6½-ounce can crab-
     meat
½   cup butter, melted
8   ounces sharp cheddar
     cheese, grated
1   teaspoon sour cream
1   teaspoon onion juice
     Dash each of worces-
     tershire sauce, salt,
     tabasco sauce and
     pepper

In a small bowl, combine all ingredients except bread, and spread on
party rye bread or English muffins
which have been cut into quarters.
Place on a cookie sheet, and broil
for 5 minutes.
CHEF'S NOTE: The mixture may be
frozen. Thaw in a covered container,
and then spread as above.
YIELD: 40 rounds

Mrs. Richard Prigozen
(Roberta Richmond)

HOT CRAB DIP

Tasty . . . Fast!

8   ounces cream cheese,
     softened
1   tablespoon milk
1   6½-ounce can flaked
     crabmeat, drained
2   tablespoons finely
     chopped onion
½   teaspoon white horse-
     radish
1   teaspoon chives
     Salt and pepper to
     taste

In a small bowl, combine all ingredients until well blended. Turn into
1½-pint baking dish. Bake uncovered
in preheated 375° oven for 15
minutes. Stir often. Serve warm with
crackers.
YIELD: 6 to 8 servings

Mrs. William Weprin
(Barbara Beerman)

PITA BREAD HORS D'OEUVRES

Super easy!

1 package Pita Bread (whole wheat, onion, or sesame)
Ground oregano, to taste
Parmesan cheese, to taste
Butter

Cut piece of bread in half, then in half again, opening up the "pocket" so that each piece of bread yields 8 "quarters." Butter each piece and sprinkle with ground oregano and Parmesan cheese. Place on a cookie sheet, and broil until lightly browned. Watch closely! Serve immediately.
YIELD: Each piece of bread makes 8 appetizers.

Mrs. Richard F. Paolino
(Beth Maloney)

ASPARAGUS BITES

Both men and women will enjoy this appetizer's bacon flavor.

2 pound loaf sandwich bread, about 24 slices (we prefer Pepperidge Farm)
8 ounces cream cheese, softened
3 ounces bleu cheese, mashed
1 egg
6 ounces canned bacon flavored bits (we prefer Bacon Bits or Bacos)
24 asparagus spears, canned
12 tablespoons butter or margarine, melted

Roll bread flat with a rolling pin. Set aside. In a small mixing bowl, combine cream cheese, bleu cheese, and egg. Beat until smooth. Spread cheese mixture on bread. Sprinkle bacon-flavored bits over cheese mixture. Drain asparagus spears. Place one spear lengthwise on each slice of bread. Roll up like a jelly roll around spear. Pinch closed. Place 12 rolls on heavily greased 10 x 16 x 1-inch jelly roll pan or cookie sheet. Drizzle melted butter over each roll. Cut each roll into thirds and separate into 36 bite size pieces. Bake in preheated 400° oven for 15 minutes. Repeat for remaining 12 rolls. Serve hot.
YIELD: 72 bite-size appetizers

Mrs. Richard B. Pohl
(Carol Crabill)

SAUSAGE DIP

Very unusual and tasty!

1 pound bulk sausage
½ cup finely chopped onions
½ pound mushrooms, thinly sliced
1½ tablespoons flour
1 cup sour cream
1 cup milk
1 tablespoon worcestershire sauce
1 teaspoon soy sauce
1 teaspoon paprika

In frying pan, cook sausage, crumbling with fork until browned. Remove sausage with slotted spoon onto paper towels to drain. To the remaining fat, add onion and mushrooms, and cook rapidly, stirring often until onion is light brown. Drain fat; return sausage to pan. In a small bowl, combine flour and sour cream. Add milk, worcestershire sauce, soy sauce, and paprika; add to sausage. Bring to a boil over medium heat, stirring constantly. Serve hot in fondue dish — corn chips are especially good for dipping.
YIELD: 12 to 16 servings

Mrs. E. H. Decker
(June Hendrickson)

DAYTON DIP

Delicious spicy taste. May be frozen.

2 pounds hot sausage
1 13-ounce can evaporated milk
2 pounds American processed cheese spread (we prefer Velveeta or Old English chunk cheese)
1 4-ounce jar pimentos, drained and chopped
Tabasco sauce, to taste

In a skillet, brown sausage over medium heat, and drain. Add milk, cheese, pimento, and tabasco sauce; simmer until cheese melts, stirring occasionally. Serve with Nachos, Fritos, or Dorito Chips.
VARIATION: For a less spicy dip, use 1 pound of hot sausage and 1 pound of mild sausage.
YIELD: 20 servings

Mrs. William Kasch
(Sonnie Kern)

14

HOT CHEESE HORS D'OEUVRES

Can vary cheese — Swiss and cheddar good, too.

1   8-ounce loaf of party rye bread (we prefer Pepperidge Farm)
1   8-ounce package (10 thin slices) American process sharp cheese, cut in fourths
3   medium red onions, very thinly sliced
    Mayonnaise (we prefer Hellman's)
    Grated Parmesan cheese

Layer each slice of rye bread with ¼ slice of cheese and a slice of red onion. Top with about a teaspoon of mayonnaise and sprinkle generously with Parmesan cheese. Place on a cookie sheet, and broil for 1 to 2 minutes. Serve hot with napkins.
YIELD: 40 appetizers

Mrs. Charles Simms
(Ann Harlamert)

HOT CHEESE CANAPE

Keep this in the freezer for those unexpected occasions, when appetizers are needed.

½   pound sharp cheddar cheese
8   slices uncooked bacon
2   small onions
1   teaspoon dry mustard
½   teaspoon worcestershire sauce
2   teaspoons mayonnaise
1   or more packages of party rye

Put cheese, bacon, and onions through a meat grinder or food processor. In a medium-size mixing bowl, combine cheese mixture, dry mustard, worcestershire sauce, and mayonnaise. Mix thoroughly. Place mixture on a large piece of plastic wrap. Shape into a log so that when sliced it will fit onto a piece of party rye. Wrap and freeze until ready to serve. At serving time, cut frozen log into ¼-inch slices. Place cheese slice on a piece of party rye. Place on cookie sheet. Place under the broiler until browned. Serve immediately.
YIELD: 30 to 40 servings

Mrs. William Thompson
(Sally Decker)

ITALIAN TREATS

Children love these.

1	pound Italian sausage
1	pound ground beef
1	pound Velveeta cheese
1	tablespoon oregano
½	teaspoon garlic salt
½	teaspoon worcester-shire sauce
1	8-ounce can tomato sauce
2	loaves party rye bread

In a large skillet, brown sausage and beef; drain excess fat. Melt cheese in saucepan, and add meat. Stir in oregano, garlic salt, worcestershire sauce, and tomato sauce. Cook for 5 minutes; cool slightly. Cover and refrigerate until serving time. Mound on party rye bread slices; place on ungreased cookie sheet. Bake in a preheated 400° oven for 10 minutes. Serve warm.
YIELD: 6 dozen

Mrs. Ronald Petersen
(Sherry Hess)

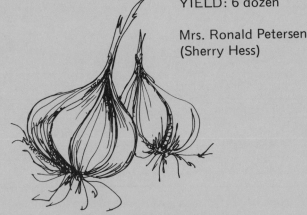

CHEDDAR MUFFIN PUFFS

A favorite hors d'oeuvre at dinner parties.

1½	cups shredded cheddar cheese
1	cup mayonnaise
5	green onions, chopped
1	teaspoon mashed capers
6	whole English muffins, split and quartered

In a small bowl, combine all ingredients. Spread on muffin quarters. Bake on cookie sheet in preheated 400° oven for 6 to 8 minutes. Serve warm.
YIELD: 48 appetizers

Mrs. Charles Sutherland
(Joyce Jehl)

CRAB PUFFS

A gourmet delight that may be prepared ahead and frozen.

2	8-ounce cans crescent rolls
1	8-ounce package cream cheese, softened
2	tablespoons soft herb-flavored bread crumbs
½	teaspoon monosodium glutamate, MSG (we prefer Accent)
1	6-ounce can crabmeat
2	drops sesame oil
¼	cup finely chopped celery
½	teaspoon grated scallions
1	tablespoon Dijon style mustard
	Peanut oil for frying

Press perforation line of one square (2 triangles) of rolls together to seal. Cut into 6 equal squares (18 squares per can). Combine cream cheese, bread crumbs, MSG, crabmeat, sesame oil, celery, scallions, and mustard. Place ¾ teaspoon of the cream cheese mixture into the center of each dough square, sealing dough around the mixture (will be in a ball shape). Fry in hot (375°) peanut oil for 3 minutes, turning after 1 minute. Serve hot.
YIELD: 3 dozen

Mrs. William H. Otte
(Linda Bruggeman)

BACON ROLL-UPS

Can be made ahead and frozen.

12	slices white sandwich bread
½	pound boiled ham, thinly sliced
½	pound American cheese, thinly sliced
1	pound bacon, uncooked

Cut crusts off bread and roll flat with a rolling pin. Put one slice of ham and one slice of cheese on each piece of bread, cutting ham and cheese to fit. Roll and cut each roll into thirds. Wrap ½ slice bacon around each section and secure with wooden pick. Place on broiler pan. Bake, turning once, in preheated 400° oven for about 30 minutes, or until bacon is done. Broil for a few minutes to brown if necessary.
YIELD: 36 appetizers

Mrs. Kieran Devery
(Carol Stefan)

HOT CHEESE STRAWS

Spicy hot!

15	ounces extra sharp cheddar cheese, grated
¾	cup margarine
2	cups flour
½	teaspoon salt
1¼	teaspoons baking powder
4	to 5 dashes tabasco sauce
1	to 2 teaspoons cayenne pepper

Allow cheese and margarine to come to room temperature. Work with hands to mix well. Sift together flour, salt, and baking powder. Add with tabasco and cayenne; mix well. Using hands, roll individual straws about 4 inches long and about as big around as a pencil. Place on ungreased cookie sheet. Bake in a preheated 300° oven for 10 minutes. Lower temperature to 225°, and bake until crisp. May be frozen; no reheating necessary.
YIELD: 4½ dozen

Mrs. Ramon L. Scott
(Patti Krygier)

SPINACH QUICHE BITES

Easy to prepare ahead; may be kept in freezer until needed.

1	8-ounce can refrigerated crescent rolls (we prefer Pillsbury)
1	8-ounce package Swiss cheese slices, cut into thin strips (we prefer Kraft)
½	cup grated Parmesan cheese
3	tablespoons flour
1¼	cups milk
4	eggs, beaten slightly
¼	teaspoon salt
1/8	teaspoon pepper
1/8	teaspoon nutmeg
1	10-ounce package frozen chopped spinach, cooked and well drained

Cover bottom and ¼-inch of sides of greased 9 x 13-inch pan with rolls. Flatten out the crescent rolls, and press against bottom of pan to form flat crust for quiche; set aside. In a large bowl, toss together cheeses and flour. Mix in milk, eggs, salt, pepper, and nutmeg; stir in spinach. Pour into prepared crust. Bake in preheated 350° oven for 50 minutes. Cut into small squares (approximately 40). May be served immediately as hot hors d'oeuvres, or made ahead and reheated on hot tray. May be frozen after baking; reheat in preheated 400° oven for 20 minutes.
YIELD: 40 bite-size appetizers

Mrs. Richard B. Pohl
(Carol Crabill)

MICKEY'S MUSHROOMS

The beefy-wine sauce makes this easy appetizer deliciously different.

1   pound butter
4   pounds medium-size
     whole fresh mush-
     rooms (about 100)
1   quart Burgundy or
     port wine
1½   tablespoons worcester-
     shire sauce
1   teaspoon dill weed
1   teaspoon fresh pepper,
     coarsely ground
1   teaspoon garlic powder
1   tablespoon mono-
     sodium glutamate
     (MSG)
2   cups water
3   cubes beef bouillon
3   cubes chicken bouillon
3   cubes vegetable
     bouillon
     Salt to taste

In a large kettle combine all ingredients except salt. Bring to a boil. Reduce heat; cover and simmer for 5 to 6 hours. Remove cover and continue cooking for 3 to 5 hours, or until liquid has been reduced to barely cover mushrooms. Add salt to taste only if needed. Freeze. When ready to serve, reheat to boiling. Serve warm in chafing dish with cocktail picks. YIELD: about 100 bites

Mrs. R. James Heikes
(Bonnie Bright)

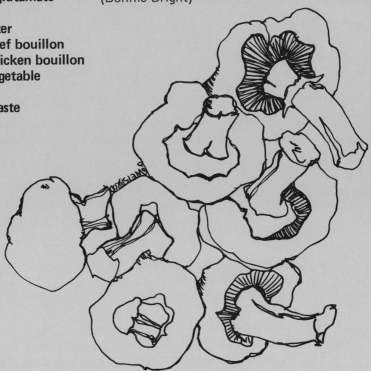

BROILED OR BAKED STUFFED MUSHROOMS

Excellent garnish for roasts or steaks, or serve as an appetizer.

20	large mushrooms
2	tablespoons minced scallions
1½	tablespoons butter
2	tablespoons flour
¼	cup half and half (more if needed)
½	teaspoon salt, or to taste
¼	teaspoon pepper, or to taste
¼	teaspoon nutmeg, or to taste
½	cup grated Swiss cheese, or ¼ cup bread crumbs mixed with ¼ cup crumbled bleu cheese
2	to 3 tablespoons butter, for dotting

Wipe mushrooms clean; remove stems, and set caps aside. Chop the stems finely. Saute chopped mushroom stems and minced scallions in butter. Sprinkle with flour. Stir in half and half. Cook and stir over medium-low heat until sauce thickens. Add salt, pepper, and nutmeg to taste. Remove from heat. Put cream sauce mixture into mushroom caps. Sprinkle with grated Swiss cheese OR bread crumbs mixed with bleu cheese. Place caps in an 8 x 12-inch baking dish. Dot with butter. Bake in preheated 350° oven for 15 to 20 minutes; then brown under broiler for a minute or so. Serve hot.

VARIATION: May be broiled without baking for 10 to 15 minutes.

YIELD: 6 servings

Mrs. R. Stephen Gresham
(Martha Boyd)

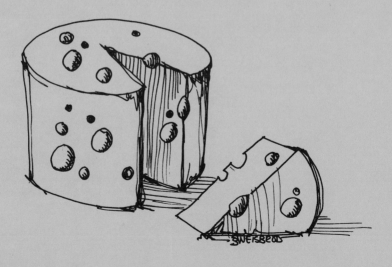

MUSHROOMS IN TOMATO SAUCE

Spicy!

2 pints fresh mushrooms
1 pound hot, loose
  sausage
4 tablespoons butter
½ cup white wine
1 15-ounce can tomato
  sauce

Wash and stem mushrooms; chop stems, and set aside. Stuff caps with sausage, and arrange on a foil-lined cookie sheet. Bake in a preheated 325° oven for 35 to 45 minutes, or until sausage is done. Meanwhile, in a large skillet, saute chopped stems in butter. Add wine and tomato sauce; simmer for 30 to 45 minutes. Add mushrooms to sauce. May be prepared the day before serving or frozen and reheated. Serve in a chafing dish with wooden picks.
YIELD: 8 to 10 servings

Mrs. Hugh Thurnauer
(Eileen Babcock)

MUSHROOM-BACON ROULADES

Appetizer or luncheon dish.

1 2-pound loaf of soft
  sandwich bread
1 10¾-ounce can cream
  of mushroom soup,
  undiluted
2 pounds thinly sliced
  bacon

Remove bread crusts. Cut each piece of bread into 4 squares. Spread undiluted mushroom soup on each slice of bread. Roll each square from point to point. Wrap with ½ piece of bacon. Secure with a wooden pick. Place appetizers on a large pan, and bake in a preheated 375° oven for 25 to 30 minutes.
VARIATION: To serve as a luncheon main dish, leave bread slices whole and wrap with a whole strip of bacon. Luncheon yield: Serves 10.
YIELD: 80 bite-size appetizers

Mrs. Charles D. Ross
(Lois Huston)

STUFFED CABBAGE ROLLS WITH CRANBERRY SAUCE

This recipe was sent to me from my "Aunt Cele." She wrote: "Good luck and good eating." These delicious cabbage rolls may be used as a main course, an appetizer, or a side dish. They are a wonderful addition to a cocktail buffet served in a chafing dish. They may be made in advance and frozen.

2   medium heads of cabbage

CRANBERRY SAUCE:

1   1-pound can jellied cranberry sauce
1   8-ounce can tomato sauce
1   cup water
2   tablespoons lemon juice
¼   cup sugar
½   cup raisins

MEAT MIXTURE:

2   pounds lean ground beef
3   saltines, soaked in water and squeezed dry
1   medium onion, grated
3   tablespoons uncooked rice
¼   cup water, mixed with 2 tablespoons ketchup
1   egg, beaten
   Salt and pepper to taste

Core the cabbages, and place in a large kettle. Cover with boiling water, and cook for 10 minutes. Remove from heat, and run cold water over cabbages. Separate leaves, and reserve the best leaves from each cabbage. To make Cranberry Sauce, combine all ingredients except raisins in a saucepan, and bring to a boil. Add raisins and simmer for 5 minutes. Remove from heat, and set aside. Combine all meat mixture ingredients in a large bowl. Fill cabbage leaves with 2 to 3 heaping teaspoons of the mixture (as much as the leaves can take, but not so much that meat escapes when leaves are rolled). Trim off any excess cabbage on either side of the meat. Place filled and rolled leaves in a roasting pan; cover with Cranberry Sauce, and simmer on top of the stove, covered, for 1 hour. Then bake in a preheated 350° oven, uncovered, for 1 hour, or until the cabbage is tender. Baste occasionally. It is best to refrigerate the rolls for several hours before serving so the fat will congeal and can be removed. Before serving, return to room temperature. Reheat in a preheated 350° oven for 30 to 40 minutes. The cabbage rolls will keep several days in the refrigerator, and they freeze well.

YIELD: 25-30 cabbage rolls

Mrs. Dennis Patterson
(Linda Epstein)

SOMBRERO SPREAD

Really yummy Mexican flavor; looks nice when served.

1 pound ground beef
½ cup chopped onion
½ cup extra hot ketchup
3 teaspoons chili powder
1 teaspoon salt
1 16-ounce can red kidney beans, with liquid
½ cup shredded cheddar cheese
¼ cup chopped stuffed green olives
¼ cup chopped onion Taco-flavored tortilla chips (we prefer Doritos)

Brown meat and ½ cup chopped onion in a skillet over medium heat. Stir in ketchup, chili powder, and salt. Mash beans in blender; add to meat mixture and heat through. Place in a chafing dish or a fondue pot. Garnish with cheese, olives, and ¼ cup chopped onion. Serve hot with Doritos or other taco-flavored tortilla chips. May be prepared ahead, except "garnish" ingredients, and reheated.
YIELD: 3 cups

Mrs. Bruce A. Triplett
(Leslie Conway)

HOT SAUSAGE DOG

Makes a quick, meaty appetizer.

1 pound Polish sausage, cut into 1-inch pieces
1 pound hot dogs, cut into 1-inch pieces
2 tablespoons vegetable oil
1 cup beer
¼ cup brown sugar, packed
4 teaspoons cornstarch
½ cup cider vinegar
¼ cup prepared mustard
4 teaspoons prepared horseradish

In a large skillet, brown sausage and hot dog pieces in hot oil; drain excess fat. Add beer; cover, and simmer for 10 minutes. In a small bowl, combine brown sugar and cornstarch. Blend in vinegar, mustard, and horseradish. Add to sausages; cook, and stir until thickened. Turn into a fondue pot or chafing dish; keep warm. Serve with toothpicks.
YIELD: 5 dozen

Mrs. Peter J. Kaufmann
(Cynthia MacFadden)

23

SWEET AND SOUR MEATBALLS

What makes these meatballs good and special is the Italian sausage.

1   pound ground beef
1   pound Italian sausage (spicy)
2   eggs
½   cup dry bread crumbs
½   cup water
    Salt, pepper, and garlic salt to taste
1   12-ounce bottle chili sauce
½   cup grape jelly
    Juice of 1 lemon

In a large bowl, combine beef, sausage, eggs, bread crumbs, water, salt, pepper, and garlic salt until well mixed. Form mixture into small meatballs, and place in a large skillet. In a small saucepan, combine all remaining ingredients, and heat until jelly melts. Pour over meatballs; cover, and simmer for 45 minutes (Do not stir.). Cool slightly; cover, and refrigerate overnight, or until grease rises to the top. Remove excess grease, freeze in sauce or heat to serving temperature. Serve hot.
YIELD: about 4 dozen meatballs

Mrs. William H. Broad, III
(Corinne Crabill)

LUZ'S MEXICAN MEATBALLS

Good spicy flavor.

2   pounds ground beef
1   egg, slightly beaten
1   teaspoon salt
½   cup dry bread crumbs

SAUCE:
2/3   cup chopped Spanish onion
3   cloves garlic, crushed
¼   cup cider vinegar
½   cup tarragon vinegar
¾   cup ketchup
1/3   cup vegetable oil
1/3   cup sugar
1   teaspoon salt
½   teaspoon cayenne pepper
½   teaspoon dry mustard
2   tablespoons dill seed

In a large bowl, mix together all ingredients. Form into meatballs; arrange on a broiler pan, and broil until lightly browned and fat is cooked off, turning once. In a Dutch oven, combine all sauce ingredients; add meatballs. Bake uncovered in a preheated 325° oven for 2 hours. CHEF'S NOTE: May also be cooked in a slow cooker or on slow speed in a microwave (Follow manufacturer's instructions.).
YIELD: about 4 dozen meatballs

Mrs. Alan R. Merrill
(Lynn Wagner)

SEAFOOD BAKE APPETIZER

I developed this recipe from several similar recipes
for a dinner party at which the guest of honor did not eat cheese.
It is delicious and great since it can be prepared
several hours in advance.

1   6-ounce can small
     shrimp, drained
2   6-ounce cans, or
     frozen packages of
     crabmeat (thawed)
½   cup toasted, herb-
     seasoned croutons,
     crushed fine
     Salt to taste
1   teaspoon paprika
¼   teaspoon pepper
½   cup dry vermouth (or
     dry white or red wine)

Mix all ingredients thoroughly, and place in individual baking dishes (Shell dishes look pretty.). Bake in preheated 400° oven for 20 minutes.
CHEF'S NOTE: If appetizer is prepared ahead of time and refrigerated, bake an extra 5 minutes.
YIELD: 12 servings

Mrs. William Stephens
(Pam Swartzel)

CAVIAR MOLD

Rave reviews!

1   beef bouillon cube
1   cup boiling water
1½   teaspoons unflavored
     gelatin (½ envelope)
6   hard boiled eggs,
     grated
1   cup mayonnaise
3½   ounces black caviar
3   tablespoons chopped
     green onions
5   dashes worcestershire
     sauce
     Fresh ground pepper,
     to taste
1   hard boiled egg, sliced
     thinly for garnish
     Plain crackers

Dissolve bouillon cube in one cup boiling water. Measure ¼ cup bouillon (Remaining ¾ cup bouillon is not used in this recipe.). Soften 1½ teaspoons unflavored gelatin in hot ¼ cup bouillon; stir well, and set aside. In a medium-size mixing bowl, combine 6 grated eggs, mayonnaise, caviar, chopped onions, worcestershire sauce, and pepper. Add bouillon-gelatin mixture to caviar mixture. Stir until thoroughly mixed. Pour into 4-cup mold. Chill at least 4 hours or until firm. Unmold caviar, and garnish with egg slices. Serve with plain (bland) crackers.
YIELD: 8 to 10 servings

Mrs. Alexander Williams
(C. Sue Seifert)

OVEN-DRIED BEEF JERKY

Great when camping.

1½ to 2 pounds, lean, boneless flank or round steak
¼ cup soy sauce
1 tablespoon worcestershire sauce
¼ teaspoon pepper
¼ teaspoon garlic powder
½ teaspoon onion salt

Trim and discard all fat from meat. Slice meat in long, ¼-inch thick strips (This is easier if meat is partially frozen.). In a glass bowl, combine remaining ingredients. Stir until seasonings are dissolved. Add meat strips, coating all surfaces thoroughly. The meat will absorb most of the liquid. Cover tightly and refrigerate meat in marinade for at least 1 hour or overnight. Drain all excess liquid. Arrange meat strips together, but not overlapping, directly on oven racks. Dry meat at lowest oven temperature, 150° to 200°, until it turns brown, is dry, and feels hard (about 4 to 7 hours). Cool thoroughly before storing in airtight containers. Beef jerky keeps indefinitely at cool room temperatures or in refrigerator.
YIELD: ½ pound

Mrs. William Coyne
(Linda Augaitis)

ONION SALT

GARLIC POWDER

SAGANAGA STINGERS

Delightful on a summer evening!
Super easy. Tastes like a whiskey sour.

1   12-ounce can beer
1   6-ounce can frozen
    lemonade concentrate
6   ounces bourbon

Pour beer into blender. Empty frozen lemonade concentrate into blender; add bourbon (Use lemonade can to measure bourbon.). Blend and enjoy the frothy, sweet nectar.
YIELD: 4, 6-ounce servings

Mrs. Denis Thomas
(Barbara Butt)

CHANTAGAF

A great after-tennis drink!

4   ounces ginger ale (we
    prefer Schweppes or
    Canada Dry)
4   ounces beer (we prefer
    Tuborg)

Chill ginger ale and beer. Serve in a frosted glass or mug.
YIELD: 1, 8-ounce drink

Mrs. Charles Ballard
(Patti Davis)

AMARETTO COOLER

Easy!

9   ounces Amaretto
27 ounces orange juice,
    ice cold
13½ ounces soda water, ice
    cold

Mix all ingredients together; stir briskly. Serve over ice.
YIELD: 8, 6-ounce servings

Mrs. Robert R. Wieland
(Sara Gerhart)

HOT SPICED CIDER

Great for Halloween parties!

2	quarts cider
½	cup brown sugar, packed
1	teaspoon whole cloves
1	teaspoon allspice
1	teaspoon ground cinnamon
3	3-inch sticks of cinnamon
1/8	teaspoon nutmeg

Place cider in a 2-quart capacity electric percolator. Place all remaining ingredients in percolator basket. Perk for 7 minutes. Serve hot in mugs — with doughnuts of course!
YIELD: 2 quarts

Mrs. Gerald Westerbeck
(Judy Richardson)

RUSSIAN TEA

Real taste change from regular tea.

1	cup granulated sugar
	Juice of 2 oranges
	Juice of 1 lemon
1	cup grape juice
2	quarts strong tea
1	teaspoon cinnamon or 1 cinnamon stick
1	teaspoon whole cloves

Combine all ingredients in a large kettle. Simmer for 1 hour or more and serve hot.
YIELD: 12 cups

Mrs. Ramon L. Scott
(Patti Krygier)

PINEAPPLE-ORANGE COOLER

This is especially nice for brunch.

1	46-ounce can pineapple juice, chilled
2	6-ounce cans frozen lemonade, undiluted
1	6-ounce can frozen orange juice, undiluted
4	cups cold water
1	cup sugar
2	32-ounce bottles ginger ale, chilled
1	32-ounce bottle soda water, chilled

Mix together all ingredients except ginger ale and soda water. Chill until serving time. Turn into punch bowl, and add ginger ale and soda water. Garnish with ice ring if desired. (I use fresh orange slices frozen in water in a ring mold.).
YIELD: 20, 8-ounce servings

Mrs. Donald C. Woods
(Peggy A. White)

28

ALTE ENTE (COLD DUCK)

**My father-in-law recalls that this was always served
at Christmas time when he was growing up in Germany.**

3 bottles Rhine or Mosel
     wine, chilled
1 bottle inexpensive
     champagne, chilled
     Splash Cognac (about
     1/8 to 1/4 cup)
2 to 3 tablespoons sugar
1 lemon, sliced for
     garnish
1 orange, sliced for
     garnish

In a large punch bowl, mix together all ingredients with 2 tablespoons sugar. Wait 10 to 15 minutes. Taste and add more sugar if desired. Surround bowl with crushed ice to keep cool.
YIELD: 20 servings

Mrs. Herwig Baumann
(Vickie Overholzer)

SANGRIA

Refreshing!

1   lemon
1   lime
1   orange
4   ounces brandy
¼   cup sugar
     Bottle Lambrusco
     wine (4/5 quart)
2   tablespoons lemon
     juice
     Ice cubes
16 ounces club soda

Slice the lemon, lime, and orange. Place citrus slices in a large non-metal container. Stir in brandy and sugar. Let stand at room temperature for one hour. Add wine and lemon juice. Stir thoroughly. Let stand at room temperature for one more hour. Just before serving, add lots of ice cubes and club soda. Stir briskly until cold. Serve in chilled glasses.
YIELD: 12 servings

Mrs. Bruce A. Triplett
(Leslie Conway)

CHAMPAGNE PUNCH

This champagne punch is very smooth and very potent!
Always serve with food accompaniment.

3 fifths champagne (we prefer dry white, but pink may be used)
1 fifth gin
2 quarts ginger ale
1 quart club soda
12 ounces frozen lemonade concentrate

Thoroughly chill champagne, gin, ginger ale, and soda. Just before serving pour all liquids into a large punch bowl. Slice the lemonade concentrate and add to the punch. Ice may be added last, if desired.
CHEF'S NOTE: If a sweeter punch is preferred, add powdered sugar, 1 tablespoon at a time, until desired sweetness is obtained.
VARIATION: A fresh strawberry in the bottom of each cup is a festive touch.
YIELD: 68, 3-ounce punch cups

Mr. James E. Benham

EGG NOG

This recipe has been in the family for several generations.
We frequently had a batch in the cupboard that was several years old.
This is a real "make-ahead" recipe!

9 eggs
1½ pounds powdered sugar, sifted
1½ cups brandy
1½ cups light rum
1 tablespoon nutmeg

Beat eggs until light and foamy. Beat in the powdered sugar, one-half cup at a time until thick and creamy. Blend in the liquors alternately with sprinklings of nutmeg. The liquor must be added in a small stream, no more than a cup at a time. Beat at medium to slow speed constantly. Pour the base mixture into empty liquor bottles; cork. For each serving, use 1/3 to ½ cup glass of the base mixture; fill the glass with cold milk, and stir well.
YIELD: ½-gallon of base mixture; 1 to 1½-gallons egg nog

Mrs. William R. Thompson
(Sally Decker)

DAYTON CREME DE MENTHE

This makes a great homemade holiday gift when packaged in a pretty glass container.
We rate this better than commercial, and it keeps for years!

8   cups sugar
8   cups water
1   tablespoon essence of peppermint (available at pharmacies)
3   tablespoons vanilla
1   tablespoon green food coloring
1   pint 190-proof clear alcohol (available at liquor stores)

Mix all ingredients in a 1-gallon glass jar. Secure lid tightly. Place in a dark, cool place and let age for at least 3 weeks.
YIELD: 1 gallon

Mrs. James Garrison
(Lesli Janacshek)

FROZEN RUM PUNCH

This smooth and refreshing punch will conveniently keep in the freezer for months!

1   fifth light rum (we prefer Bacardi)
12 ounces frozen lemonade concentrate
6   ounces frozen orange juice concentrate
6   ounces frozen limeade concentrate
7   cups water

Mix all ingredients in a glass or plastic large-mouth jar or a bowl with a lid. Freeze for at least 24 hours before serving. Stir occasionally during first 24 hours. Remove from freezer ½ hour before serving. Serve in champagne glasses.
YIELD: 3 quarts

Mrs. James Brown
(Ann Nye Guthrie)

APRES SKI SPICED WINE

The best way to relax after a day on the slopes!

½   cup sugar
1½   cups water
      Peel from ½ lemon
10   whole cloves
1   stick cinnamon,
      broken up
¼   cup brandy
1   bottle sweet or dry red
      table wine, according
      to sweetness desired
5   cinnamon sticks for
      garnish

In a large pan, boil the sugar, water, lemon peel, and spices for 10 minutes. Strain. Add brandy and wine to strained mixture. Heat gently over low heat (Do not boil.). Serve in small mugs with a cinnamon stick for stirring.

CHEF'S NOTE: Use real cinnamon spice sticks, not cinnamon candy. If necessary ground cinnamon may be substituted to taste.

YIELD: 5 servings

Mrs. Frank Welsh
(Rosemary Dahlen)

WINE SLUSH

Smooth, sweet, and refreshing!

1   6-ounce can limeade
      concentrate, thawed
1   6-ounce can lemonade
      concentrate, thawed
1   6-ounce can orange
      juice concentrate,
      thawed
1½   cups ginger ale
1   bottle dry red, dry
      white, or rose wine,
      chilled
1   each orange, lemon,
      and lime, cut in slices

Combine juice concentrates and ginger ale; turn into freezer trays and freeze firm. Scoop frozen mixture into a small serving bowl. Fill a larger bowl with ice. Place slush bowl in larger ice bowl. Surround with fruit slices. To serve, spoon slush mixture into glasses; pour in red, white, or rose wine, and garnish with fruit.

YIELD: 4 cups slush

Mrs. Peter J. Kaufmann
(Cynthia MacFadden)

RED RASPBERRY BOUNCE

Great after-dinner drink!

1   quart fresh whole red
    raspberries
2   cups sugar
1   bottle vodka (4/5
    quart)

Combine all ingredients in 1-gallon glass jug; cap tightly. Store in a cool dark place and let ferment for 5 to 6 months. Strain berries before serving or gift giving.
VARIATION: Frozen raspberries may be substituted for fresh. If berries are sweetened, reduce sugar accordingly.
YIELD: about ½ gallon

Mrs. James Garrison
(Lesli Janacshek)

ITALIAN KISS

I was given this recipe by the owner of an Italian restaurant in Annandale, Virginia, where they serve it as a dessert. I serve it as a very rich and refreshing drink.

12 ounces of half and half, very cold
2 ounces white Creme de Menthe
4 scoops orange sherbert, frozen, not melting

Place all ingredients in a blender, and whirl until smooth. Pour into champagne glasses. Serve immediately.
YIELD: 4 servings

Mrs. Paul D. Hawn
(Mary Moore)

KAHLUA FIZZ

This drink is terrific after dinner. It's sweet, yet light.

Ice
2 ounces Kahlua
2 ounces half and half
6 ounces club soda

In a tall glass filled with ice, add all the ingredients in the order given. Stir lightly.
YIELD: 1 drink

Mrs. William Coyne
(Linda Augaitis)

THE WHISPER

After-dinner drink or dessert!

2 large scoops coffee ice cream
1 ounce dark creme de cacao
1 ounce cognac

Place all ingredients in blender. Blend until mixed and thick (Do not over-blend.). Serve as a delicious after-dinner drink or as a dessert accompanied by brownies.
YIELD: 2 servings

Mrs. Richard C. Shelton
(Louise Wittenmyer)

HERBED BEER BREAD

Sliced thinly and spread with cream cheese, this moist and
mild bread is excellent for a cocktail buffet.
It is quick and easy to make.

3   cups self-rising flour
3   tablespoons sugar
2   tablespoons dried
     parsley flakes
1½   teaspoons dill weed
½   teaspoon rubbed sage,
     optional
1   12-ounce can beer

In a large bowl, combine the dry
ingredients. Add beer and stir only
until mixed (The beer will foam while
stirring.). Spoon into a greased 9 x 5 x
2½-inch loaf pan. Smooth the top of
the loaf. Bake in preheated 350° oven
for 30 to 40 minutes until lightly
browned. Cool before slicing.
YIELD: 1 loaf

Mrs. Frank Welsh
(Rosemary Dahlen)

SOUR CREAM SWEET BUNS

Quick and easy yeast buns. These are so delicious!

1	cup sour cream
2	tablespoons vegetable oil
3	tablespoons sugar
1/8	teaspoon baking soda
1	teaspoon salt
1	large egg, slightly beaten
1	cake compressed yeast
3	cups sifted flour
3	tablespoons butter, melted
3	tablespoons brown sugar, firmly packed
3	tablespoons granulated sugar
¼	teaspoon nutmeg
¾	teaspoon cinnamon
1	cup confectioners sugar, optional
1	to 2 tablespoons milk, optional

In a large saucepan, heat sour cream over low heat just to lukewarm. Remove from heat, and stir in oil, 3 tablespoons sugar, baking soda, and salt. Cool; add egg, and crumble in compressed yeast cake; stir to dissolve. Mix in flour with a wooden spoon. Turn onto a lightly floured board or pastry cloth. Knead lightly for about 30 to 60 seconds to form a smooth ball. Cover with a thin, damp cloth, and let stand 5 minutes to tighten up dough. Roll dough into a ¼ x 6 x 24-inch rectangle on a lightly floured board or cloth, using a lightly floured rolling pin. Melt 3 tablespoons butter, and spread over surface of rectangle. Mix 3 tablespoons brown sugar and 3 tablespoons granulated sugar together with nutmeg and cinnamon; sprinkle evenly over rectangle. Roll up rectangle beginning with wide side, and seal by pinching edge of dough into roll. Cut into 1½-inch thick slices. Arrange buns, cut side down, in greased 7 x 11-inch baking pan. Cover with damp cloth, and let rise in warm (85 to 90°), draft-free place until about double (approximately 1 hour). Bake in preheated 375° oven for 15 to 20 minutes or until light brown. In a small bowl, combine confectioners sugar and milk. Drizzle over buns while they are still warm.
YIELD: 16 buns

Mrs. Thomas B. Talbot, Jr.
(Elma Carey)

ANNA SAND'S CHRISTMAS BRAID

Lovely to look at, delightful to taste.
Takes time, but not too difficult.

2 packages active dry yeast
1/3 cup very warm water (110°)
1 cup milk
½ cup granulated sugar
½ cup shortening
1½ teaspoons salt
5 to 5-1/3 cups sifted flour
2 eggs
½ teaspoon ground cardamon

GLAZE

1 cup confectioners sugar, sifted
2 teaspoons milk
1 to 2 teaspoons maraschino cherry juice
6 to 10 maraschino cherries, well-drained, diced fine

Dissolve yeast in very warm (not hot) water. Set aside. In a saucepan, scald milk. Add sugar, shortening, and salt. Cool to lukewarm. Stir in 2 cups flour. Add eggs; beat well. Stir in yeast mixture, cardamon, and enough remaining flour to make a soft dough. Turn onto lightly floured surface; knead until smooth and elastic (about 10 minutes). Put into greased bowl. Turn greased side up. Cover with a slightly damp cloth. Let rise in a warm place (85°) until double in bulk (about 2 hours). Punch down; divide dough in half. Let rest 10 minutes. Divide one portion into three equal parts. Shape each part into a strand about 1 to 1½-inches around. Place three strands on lightly greased baking sheet. Braid loosely. Tuck ends under. Repeat to prepare second braid. Cover with a slightly damp cloth. Let rise in a warm place until double in bulk (about one hour). Uncover. Bake in preheated 350° oven for 25 minutes or until done. Cool and glaze.

In a small bowl, moisten confectioners sugar with milk and cherry juice until a good glaze consistency. Add well-drained, minced cherries. Glaze cooled braids.
YIELD: 2 braids

Mrs. James W. Clark
(Patricia Jones)

"REFRIGERATED" HUNGARIAN COFFEE CAKE

**This recipe is a time-saver when made ahead
and baked just before serving.**

1 cup milk, scalded
½ cup vegetable oil
½ cup sugar
1 teaspoon salt
2 cakes compressed yeast,
or 2 envelopes of
active dry yeast
2 eggs, beaten slightly
4¼ to 4½ cups flour,
sifted
½ cup butter, melted
¾ cup sugar
2 teaspoons cinnamon
½ cup chopped nuts
1 cup raisins

Scald milk. Pour in a large mixing bowl. Add oil, ½ cup sugar, and salt. Stir to dissolve, and then cool to luke-warm. Crumble yeast cakes or pour dry yeast into milk mixture. Stir to blend; then let stand until yeast is dissolved. Add beaten eggs. Stir in 3 cups flour with a wooden spoon. Stir in remaining 1¼-1½ cups flour until dough leaves the sides of the bowl. Turn onto lightly floured board or pastry cloth. Knead 5 to 10 minutes until smooth and elastic. Place in a greased bowl; turn once to bring greased side up. Cover with a thin, damp, cloth, and let rise in a warm, draft-free place 1½ hours or until double in bulk (If cloth dries, dampen again.). Punch dough down; turn over, and grease top lightly. Cover with plastic wrap or waxed paper. Tie securely around top of bowl with a rubber band (Do not use an aluminum bowl for storage.). Store in refrigerator until needed — no longer than 2 days. Three hours before serving, melt butter in a sauce-pan. Combine ¾ cup sugar, cinnamon, and nuts in a small bowl. Shape dough into small balls, 1 to 1½-inches in diameter. Roll each ball first in butter then in cinnamon-sugar mixture. Place balls in bottom of a greased 9-inch tube pan so they do not touch each other. Sprinkle layer with half of the raisins. Arrange next layer of balls;

recipe continues . . .

sprinkle with remaining raisins. Cover with a final layer of balls. Cover and let rise in a warm place until double in bulk (1½ to 2 hours). Bake in a pre-heated 375° oven for 35 to 40 minutes. Turn upside down on a wire rack to let hot cinnamon-sugar syrup run over ring as it cools. Serve by breaking balls apart with 2 forks.
YIELD: 1 large cake

Mrs. Thomas B. Talbot, Jr.
(Elma Carey)

STRAWBERRY NUT BREAD

Very moist. Using individual loaf pans makes a nice Christmas gift. In the summer it's delicious with fresh strawberries on the side.

3   cups flour
1   teaspoon soda
1   teaspoon salt
3   teaspoons cinnamon
2   cups granulated sugar
2   10-ounce packages frozen strawberries, thawed and undrained
4   eggs, well beaten
1¼   cups vegetable oil
1¼   cups chopped pecans or walnuts
      Powdered sugar for garnish

In a large bowl, stir together dry ingredients (except powdered sugar). Combine all remaining ingredients (except powdered sugar) in a separate bowl. Add liquid mixture to the dry mixture. Stir carefully, just enough to blend all ingredients. Fill five 6 x 3 x 2½-inch greased loaf pans no more than ¾ full. Bake in preheated 350° oven for 45 to 50 minutes, or until bread tests done. Cool in pans. Sprinkle with powdered sugar.
VARIATION: Use two 9 x 5 x 3-inch loaf pans. Bake in preheated 350° oven for 55 to 60 minutes, or until bread tests done.
YIELD: 5 small loaves

Mrs. Donald May
(Brenda Amburgey)

RHUBARB BREAD

A nice, moist quick bread;
a pleasant change from many sweet breads.

2   eggs, beaten
1½   cups brown sugar,
       firmly packed
2/3   cup vegetable oil
1   teaspoon vanilla, or
       1 teaspoon brandy
2½   cups sifted flour
1   teaspoon baking
       soda
1   teaspoon salt
1/8   teaspoon baking
       powder
1   cup buttermilk
1½   cups diced raw rhubarb
1   cup chopped walnuts
1   tablespoon butter
½   cup sugar
1   drop lemon extract

In a large bowl, beat eggs until light; add brown sugar, oil, and flavoring. Sift together flour, soda, salt, and baking powder; add to egg mixture alternately with buttermilk, blending after each addition. Stir in rhubarb and nuts. Divide evenly between two greased 4½ x 8½-inch loaf pans. In a small bowl, mix together butter, sugar, and lemon extract until crumbly. Sprinkle half on each loaf. Bake in a preheated 325° oven for 60 minutes, or until bread tests done.
YIELD: 2 loaves

Mrs. William Bell
(Kathy Smith)

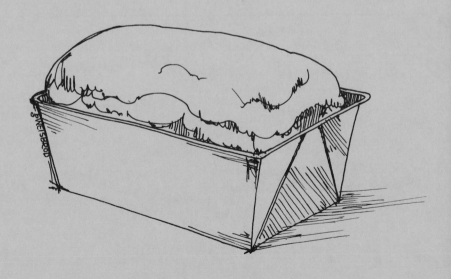

LEMON BREAD

Very moist and lemony. A refreshing change.

½ cup margarine
1 cup sugar
2 eggs, slightly beaten
1¼ cups flour
1 teaspoon baking
  powder
¼ teaspoon salt
½ cup milk
½ cup finely chopped
  walnuts
  Grated rind of 1
  lemon
¼ cup sugar
  Juice of 1 lemon,
  strained

In a bowl, cream together margarine and 1 cup sugar. Beat in the eggs. Sift together flour, baking powder, and salt. Add dry ingredients, alternately with milk, to the creamed mixture. Stir in nuts and grated lemon rind. Pour the batter into a greased 9 x 5-inch loaf pan. Bake in preheated 350° oven for 1 hour. Remove the bread from the oven and pierce the top with a skewer to make small holes. Combine ¼ cup sugar and lemon juice; pour over the hot bread. Cool; cover, and refrigerate until ready to serve or serve immediately. YIELD: 1 loaf

Mrs. H. Brockman Anderson
(Margy Todd)

HERB SPREAD

**This mild herb spread can be made and stored in the refrigerator like butter.
It is handy for a quick, special bread to complement any dinner.**

2 teaspoons parsley,
  dried
2 teaspoons chives, dried
1 teaspoon sweet basil
1/8 teaspoon marjoram
¼ pound butter
1 teaspoon lemon juice
1 1-pound loaf white
  bread, thinly sliced

Cream together all ingredients (except bread). Spread on each slice of a 1-pound loaf of thinly sliced white bread. Put slices back together into loaf form, and wrap in foil. Bake in preheated 350° oven for about 20 minutes or until heated through. Store herb spread, covered, in refrigerator. May be reheated. YIELD: 12-14 slices

Mrs. William F. Miller
(Barbara Parkin)

RING OF ROLLS

Super easy and very tasty.
Very good for a luncheon or a dinner. Excellent for calorie counters who usually avoid breads: they can break off a tiny piece for a "taste."

2 to 3 tablespoons butter
Salad seasoning (we prefer McCormick's Salad Supreme)
1 8-ounce package refrigerated butter-flake rolls

Melt butter in bottom of 2-cup ring mold. Sprinkle salad supreme seasoning, according to taste, over the butter. Place refrigerator rolls around the mold. Bake in preheated 375° oven for 12 to 15 minutes, or until rolls test done. Invert mold on a serving plate immediately. Serve hot. CHEF'S NOTE: Recipe may be doubled using a 4-cup ring mold. Do not double butter.
YIELD: 6 servings

Mrs. Charles Sutherland
(Joyce Jehl)

HEARTY WAFFLES

Really hearty!

4 eggs
1¾ cups buttermilk
1 teaspoon baking soda
1½ cups sifted flour
2 teaspoons baking powder
1 teaspoon salt
¼ cup bacon drippings and/or vegetable oil
1 tablespoon honey
Dash of cinnamon
1 cup quick-cooking oatmeal

Beat eggs until light. Add all other ingredients except oatmeal, beating until well blended. Stir in oatmeal. Bake in preheated, prepared waffle iron until steaming stops or until done to your taste. Serve steaming hot with butter and warm syrup.
VARIATION: ½ cup chopped pecans is a tasty addition. This batter may also be used for pancakes — reduce oatmeal to ½ cup.
YIELD: 8 to 10 waffles

Mrs. Robert L. Deddens
(Ruth Carey)

SUZIE'S SWEET ROLLS

Easy, tasty, and attractive! Especially nice for a luncheon.

1 cup shortening
4 cups flour
½ cup granulated sugar
½ teaspoon salt
1 envelope active dry yeast
1 cup warm water
2 eggs, beaten
½ cup butter, melted
¾ cup granulated sugar
1 tablespoon cinnamon
1 cup walnuts or pecans, chopped

In a non-metal bowl, cut shortening into flour, sugar, and salt as you would for a pie crust. Add yeast which has been dissolved in very warm, not hot, water (105 to 115⁰) and the beaten eggs. Mix well. Cover and refrigerate 6 hours or overnight. Remove from refrigerator about 1½ hours before baking. Divide dough into four equal balls. Roll each dough ball out to about ¼-inch thick and a 12-inch round, like a pie crust. Spread with cooled, melted butter; sprinkle with sugar, cinnamon, and nuts. Cut each circle into 12 wedges; roll each wedge from wide part to the point. Place rolls point side down on a greased cookie sheet. Cover lightly; let rise in a warm place (85⁰) until doubled in bulk (about 1 to 1½ hours). Bake in preheated 350⁰ oven for 12 to 15 minutes, or until done.
YIELD: 4 dozen rolls

Mrs. Frank Holloway
(Suzie Headley)

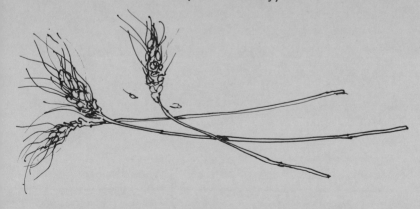

CARROT BREAD

May be used as a dessert bread; just add a dollop of whipped cream.

2½ cups flour
2 cups sugar (scant)
2½ teaspoons baking soda
2½ teaspoons cinnamon
½ teaspoon salt
1 8-ounce package chopped dates (we prefer Dromedary Chopped Dates)
¾ cup coconut, not packed
1 cup chopped pecans
4 large eggs, beaten
2½ teaspoons vanilla
2½ cups grated carrots
1¼ cups vegetable oil

Into a large bowl, sift together flour, sugar, baking soda, cinnamon, and salt. Stir in dates, coconut, and pecans. Using a wooden spoon, stir in all remaining ingredients (Mixture will be quite thick—do not use electric mixer.). Turn mixture into four 3¾ x 7½ x 2-inch greased loaf pans. Let pans stand at room temperature for 20 minutes before baking. Bake in a preheated 350° oven for 55 minutes, or until cake tests done. Cool completely before wrapping for freezing. YIELD: 4 loaves

Mrs. Naim Balta
(Frances Gantt)

ONION BREAD

This mildly tangy yeast bread is simple to make. It requires no kneading.

1½ cups very warm water (110°)

1 package active dry yeast or 1 cake compressed yeast

2 tablespoons shortening

1 tablespoon instant minced onion

2 tablespoons sugar

2 teaspoons salt

½ teaspoon oregano

3½ cups sifted flour

2 tablespoons butter, melted

In a medium-size mixing bowl, combine warm water and yeast. Stir until dissolved. Stir in shortening. Add onion, sugar, salt, oregano, and 2 cups flour. Blend 2 minutes at medium speed on mixer. Stir in remaining 1½ cups flour — batter will be sticky. Cover with a damp cloth, and let rise in a warm place (85°) until double in bulk (about 1 hour). Beat batter with a spoon for 30 seconds. Spread in a greased 9 x 5 x 2½-inch loaf pan. Cover and let rise 40 minutes or until double. Brush top of loaf gently with melted butter. Bake in preheated 375° oven for 35 to 40 minutes, or until bread tests done.
YIELD: 1 loaf

Mrs. James W. Clark
(Patricia Jones)

CORN SPOON BREAD

Very tasty — good texture.

2 eggs, slightly beaten

1 8½-ounce box corn muffin mix

1 8-ounce can creamed corn

1 8-ounce can whole kernel corn

1 cup sour cream

½ cup butter or margarine, melted

1 cup shredded Swiss cheese

In a medium-size bowl, combine all ingredients, except the Swiss cheese. Spread in a buttered 7 x 11-inch baking dish. Bake in a preheated 350° oven for 35 minutes. Sprinkle shredded cheese on top of casserole, and bake for an additional 10 to 15 minutes, or until inserted knife comes out clean.
YIELD: 9 to 12 servings

Mrs. Glenn A. Mosier
(Katherine Koenig)

GANG-GANG'S "BROWN" (GRAHAM) BREAD

All my senses are peaked by just writing the name of this recipe. I remember the sweet aroma of bread baking in a wood stove, the acrid smell of wood burning, and the quick crackling of burning kindling contained within the stove. A short, stooped lady stood at the sink with her back toward me, gray hair knotted at her head and apron strings around her middle. What a wonderful grandmother she was! And when the bread was cooled, she would slice it paper-thin and spread a mound of fresh, sweet butter on it and hand this morsel to an eager little girl. How I love to make this bread just to recall those moments and to miss a great lady. . . .

1½	cups milk, scalded
½	cup brown sugar, firmly packed
2	teaspoons salt
1	egg, beaten
6	tablespoons margarine, melted
1	compressed yeast cake or envelope active dry yeast
½	cup warm water
3	cups graham flour
3	cups white flour

Pour scalded milk into a small bowl; stir in sugar, salt, egg, and margarine; cool until lukewarm. In a large mixing bowl, crumble or sprinkle yeast cake into warm water; stir until combined. Stir milk mixture into yeast. Add half of each of the flours, and beat until smooth; stir in remaining flour. Turn dough out onto a floured board, and knead until elastic and smooth — as a baby's bottom. Place in a greased bowl and brush with oil. Cover and let rise in a warm place for about 1½ to 2 hours, or until double in bulk. Punch down and put into two 9 x 5 x 2½-inch greased loaf pans. Let rise for about 30 minutes to 1 hour, or until double in bulk. Bake in a preheated 350° oven for 35 to 40 minutes.
YIELD: 2 loaves

Mrs. George L. Word
(Paige Early)

TALBOT HOUSE CRACKERS

These homemade crackers have a light and delicate flavor
that will not interfere with your favorite garnishments.

2 cups flour
1 tablespoon sugar
½ teaspoon salt
¼ teaspoon baking
powder
¼ cup butter
About ½ cup milk

Sift dry ingredients together. Cut in butter with a pastry blender until mixture resembles meal. Stir in enough milk to make a stiff dough. Roll out 1/16 to 1/8-inch thick on a well-floured cloth. Cut with floured, round cookie cutter, or any cutter desired. Prick entire surface with tines of a fork, and brush lightly with milk. Place on an ungreased cookie sheet. Bake in a preheated 425° oven for 10 to 15 minutes (depending on cutter size), or until light, golden brown.
YIELD: 2 to 3 dozen (depending on cutter size)

Mrs. Thomas B. Talbot, Jr.
(Elma Carey)

SAUERKRAUT RELISH

Great replacement for coleslaw at a summer picnic.
Best when made a day ahead.

1 32-ounce jar sauerkraut,
drained
1 green pepper, diced
finely
1 onion, chopped finely
1 2-ounce jar pimentoes,
chopped
½ cup sugar

Mix together all ingredients. Serve on a bed of lettuce, or add to a relish tray. Refrigerate in the original sauerkraut jar. May be stored almost indefinitely.
YIELD: 2 pounds

Mrs. David R. Taylor
(Carole Fitzpatrick)

GRANDMA MAC'S CINNAMON TOAST

No redeeming features except you can get your children to eat whole wheat bread this way. I often keep a bowl of this in the refrigerator for a special treat on cold winter mornings. Great accompaniment to oatmeal. Quick and easy!

½   cup butter, softened
1   cup light brown sugar, firmly packed
2   teaspoons half and half or milk, optional
    Cinnamon to taste, about ½ teaspoon
    Dash of salt, optional
4   slices lightly toasted bread, any kind (we prefer whole wheat)

In a small mixing bowl, cream together butter and brown sugar until light and fluffy. Beat in half and half, cinnamon, and salt. Lightly toast 4 slices of bread, and spread entire top with the cinnamon-sugar mixture. Place on a cookie sheet, and broil briefly until mixture bubbles (Watch carefully as these will burn quickly.). Cool slightly on a rack; cut into triangles, and serve warm for breakfast toast. Cover and refrigerate remaining mixture for future use.

VARIATION: I often add (with a fork) brown sugar, cinnamon, and salt to the end of a bowl of whipped or soft-type margarine. Butter taste is better, margarine easier — no bowl or beaters!

YIELD: about 1 loaf

Mrs. Robert L. Deddens
(Ruth Carey)

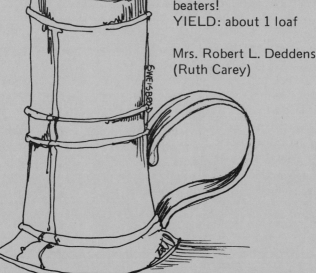

CARROT RELISH

**Couldn't be easier or more appropriate as a
tasty addition to most any meal.**

3   large, fat carrots or
     5 to 6 small ones,
     finely grated
½   cup sugar
     Juice of 1 lemon
1   teaspoon grated lemon
     rind

In a small bowl, stir all ingredients together. Put in glass container; cover, and store at least 12 hours before serving. Keeps well for several weeks.

Mrs. Fred G. Schantz
(Elspeth Hummel)

GREEN TOMATO MINCEMEAT

**Made by my grandmother in the fall to use all those green
tomatoes from her garden. This mincemeat does not contain meat!**

3   to 4 cups peeled and
     chopped cooking
     apples
4   cups chopped green
     tomatoes, peeled
2   cups white sugar
1   pound raisins
¼   cup vinegar
1   cup butter
1   teaspoon each: salt,
     cloves, and allspice
2   teaspoons cinnamon

Simmer all of the ingredients in a large kettle until thickened (about 2½ hours); stir occasionally. While still boiling hot, spoon into sterilized jars to 1/8-inch from top. Using two-piece lids, seal the jars. Invert the jars until all are filled. Turn right side up to cool.
YIELD: 3 pints

Mrs. Charles J. Roedersheimer
(Alice Murray)

BREAD AND BUTTER PICKLES

These pickles are sweet and very tender.

1 gallon firm, medium-
   size cucumbers
2 green peppers, seeded
8 small onions
½ cup salt, non-iodized
1 to 1½ quarts ice cubes,
   crushed

SYRUP

5 cups cider vinegar
5 cups sugar
1½ teaspoons tumeric
¼ teaspoon ground
   cloves
2 teaspoons mustard
   seed
1 teaspoon celery seed

Slice all vegetables thinly (about ¼-inch). Use a large (1½ to 2-gallon size) crock, plastic, or stainless steel bowl (never aluminum). Place vegetables in bottom of crock. Sprinkle with ½ cup salt. Cover with lots of crushed ice, weighted down with a plate. Refrigerate for at least 3 hours or overnight for crisper pickles. Add more ice as needed while in refrigerator. Remove ice and drain off all liquid. Do not rinse. Mix all ingredients for syrup together in a large kettle. Bring to a boil over medium heat, stirring constantly, and boil for 3 minutes. Add well-drained vegetables and cook over very low heat slowly and gently until scalded (simmering hot) — this takes about 30 to 40 minutes (Do not boil, just simmer.). While still simmering hot, place pickles in sterilized jars, then fill remaining space with syrup to ¼-inch from top edge of jars. Immediately screw scalded lids on tight. Set jars on wire rack to cool (Lids will pull down forming the seal as the jars cool.). If there is any syrup remaining, reserve it, and store in refrigerator, covered, until the next batch of cucumbers comes in.
YIELD: 5 quarts

Mrs. Edward J. Carey
(Eloise McLaughlin)

PLEASANT HILL ZUCCHINI RELISH

**From a good, home victory garden in the Midwest
come the ingredients for this relish.**

10	cups coarsely chopped zucchini (peel if over 2-inch diameter)
2	cups chopped onion
5	teaspoons salt
2¼	cups cider vinegar
3¼	cups sugar
1	teaspoon dry mustard
2	teaspoons celery seeds
2	teaspoons black pepper
1	tablespoon nutmeg
2	tablespoons tumeric
2	tablespoons cornstarch

Mix zucchini and onion with salt and let stand overnight. Drain, and rinse with cool water. Drain well. In a small bowl, stir together all remaining ingredients, except vinegar and sugar. Return vegetables to a large pan and stir in mixture of vinegar and sugar. Bring slowly to a boil; boil gently for about 5 minutes. Seal in hot, sterilized jars by filling jars with boiling hot relish to ¼-inch from the top edge of each jar and screwing sterilized lids on tight (As jars cool, seal is formed.).
YIELD: 3 quarts

Mrs. Thomas Shulman
(Ellie Arnovitz)

CHAMPAGNE JELLY

**Light and sweet — especially good at breakfast.
Makes a nice gift.**

1	cup orange juice, fresh, or reconstituted frozen
1	cup extra dry champagne
3	cups sugar
3	ounces pectin (we prefer Certo)
4	8-ounce jelly glasses, sterilized

Combine the first three ingredients in the top of a double boiler. Place over boiling water, and stir for 5 minutes, or until the sugar is dissolved. Remove the double boiler from the heat, but leave jelly over the hot water. Immediately stir in pectin (Be sure to use full measure.). Skim off the foam that forms. Pour hot jelly into prepared hot glasses and seal.
YIELD: 4, 8-ounce glasses

Mrs. Gene Hughes
(Julie Loeffel)

MOM'S STRAWBERRY PRESERVES

A delicious and easy way to bring summer into your house all year long. This is so fresh-like you'll use it for more than just toast. It's great over vanilla ice cream or used with "Strawberry Cheese Mold" (see index).

2	cups fresh strawberries, finely mashed
4	cups sugar
1	1¾-ounce package powdered fruit pectin
1	cup water

In a medium-size mixing bowl, mix strawberries and sugar well. Let stand for 20 minutes, stirring occasionally. In a saucepan, stir pectin into 1 cup water. Bring to a boil. Boil rapidly for 1 minute, stirring constantly. Remove from heat. Add strawberry mixture to the pectin and water and stir for 2 minutes. Pour into jelly jars or plastic containers and let stand at room temperature for 12 hours. Cover with tight-fitting lids when mixture has thickened slightly. Store in freezer or refrigerator.

CHEF'S NOTE: These preserves cannot be stored at room temperature. They may be served right from the freezer without thawing.

Mrs. H. H. Amburgey
(Geneva Ferguson)

HONEY BUTTER

Have you ever wanted something different to spread on rolls or biscuits? Here it is, and it is so simple.

| ½ | cup honey |
| ½ | cup butter, softened |

In a small mixing bowl, beat honey and butter together until fluffy. Put in a small, attractive serving dish; cover and chill for at least 30 minutes. Serve with warm bread, rolls, biscuits, or English muffins. Store leftovers in refrigerator.

YIELD: 1 cup

Mrs. Thomas B. Talbot, Jr.
(Elma Carey)

The Arcade

Savory Side Dishes

THE ARCADE

Even today's modern supermarkets cannot match the splendor that once belonged to Dayton's Arcade. In its myriad of shops and stands could be found every specialty imaginable — from luxury items to food specialties, in or out of season — and the upper floor apartments were always filled due to the central location. Built in 1902 at a cost of two million dollars, the Arcade was designed by Daytonian Frank M. Andrews. The two-building structure is Flemish in character featuring an interior dome that is three stories high and ninety feet in diameter while the Third Street entrance was inspired by an Amsterdam guild hall. The Arcade is listed in the National Register of Historic Places and is being restored to its past splendor as Dayton couples progress with preservation.

DRESSY GREEN GRAPE SALAD

A family favorite at my grandmother's. Serve as a salad or dessert.

4 egg yolks, beaten
½ cup milk
Juice of 1 lemon
¼ teaspoon dry mustard
½ pint whipping cream, whipped
8 ounces mini-marsh-mallows
1 20-ounce can crushed pineapple, drained
1 pound green grapes

In the top of a double boiler, combine egg yolks, milk, lemon juice, and dry mustard. Cook and stir until thickened; cool thoroughly. Fold in whipped cream, marshmallows, crushed pineapple, and green grapes. Turn into a 9x13-inch pan. Cover and refrigerate overnight.

YIELD: 9 to 12 servings

Mrs. William F. Miller
(Barbara Parkin)

CRONIN PINEAPPLE CASSEROLE

Delicious and really different and a special change of pace for holiday or party time. Serve with chicken, ham, or pork.

½ cup butter
7 slices white bread, torn into coarse crumbs
1 cup sugar
2 eggs, slightly beaten
3 tablespoons flour
1 20-ounce can crushed pineapple

In a large skillet, melt butter; add bread, and brown over medium-high heat until toast-like. In a 2-quart casserole, combine sugar, eggs, and flour; stir in undrained pineapple. Arrange buttered bread crumbs on top; press down, but do not stir. Bake uncovered in a preheated 350° oven for 45 minutes. Serve hot.

YIELD: 8 servings

Mrs. Anthony Rocco
(Gerry Anne Cronin)

CREAMY FRUIT SALAD

Easy to make ahead for a large group.

2   16-ounce cans fruit cocktail, drained
2   20-ounce cans chunk-style pineapple
3   11-ounce cans mandarin oranges, drained
2   pints sour cream
3   cups mini marshmallows
1   cup shredded coconut
1   banana, sliced
1   10-ounce jar maraschino cherries, drained

Combine all canned fruit with pineapple juice. Marinate at least 2 hours; drain. Mix marinated fruit with sour cream, mini marshmallows, and shredded coconut. Refrigerate until serving time. Garnish with sliced banana and cherries.

CHEF'S NOTE: Best when prepared a day ahead.

YIELD: 12 to 16 servings

Mrs. Charles Castle
(Susan Ohmer)

FROZEN FRUIT SALAD

Refreshing, make-ahead salad. Try serving this tasty salad with ham.

1   tablespoon unflavored gelatin (1 envelope)
¼   cup cold water
1   cup syrup from drained fruits (use mostly maraschino cherry syrup)
2   tablespoons lemon juice
½   cup salad dressing
½   pint whipping cream, whipped
1/8   teaspoon nutmeg
1/3   cup maraschino cherries, drained
1   29-ounce jar fruits for salads, drained

In a small saucepan, soften gelatin in cold water. Warm over low heat until dissolved. Remove from heat; add syrup and lemon juice; set aside. Fold salad dressing into whipped cream. Fold in cooled syrup mixture. Gently fold in nutmeg, maraschino cherries, and fruits. Turn into an 8 or 9-inch square cake pan. Cover and freeze until firm but not solid; cut into 9 squares. Cover and return to freezer until serving time. Serve on lettuce leaves; store leftovers in freezer.
YIELD: 9 servings

Mrs. Gerald Westerbeck
(Judy Richardson)

24-HOUR FRUIT SALAD

The fresh fruit makes this light, tasty, and refreshing!

2	eggs, beaten
4	tablespoons white vinegar
4	tablespoons sugar
2	tablespoons butter
½	pint whipping cream, whipped
1	cup fresh seedless green grapes
1	cup fresh strawberries
1	cup melon balls, drained
1	cup canned pineapple chunks, drained
12	large marshmallows, chopped
	Lettuce
¾	cup chopped pecans

Put eggs in a double boiler, over boiling water. Add vinegar and sugar. Beat constantly with an electric mixer set on medium speed (about 8 to 10 minutes or until smooth and thickened). Remove from heat. Stir in butter; cool. Fold whipped cream into cooled mixture. Fold in fruits and marshmallows. Cover and refrigerate overnight. Stir just before serving on lettuce. Garnish each serving with a sprinkling of chopped pecans.

VARIATION: Your favorite assortment of fresh or canned fruit (4 to 5 cups total) may be substituted for, or added to, those we recommend.

YIELD: 12 servings

Mrs. Harry G. Ebeling
(Martha Bowman)

HOT SPICED FRUIT

Good with chicken, ham, pork, or egg luncheon dishes.

1 11-ounce can mandarin oranges, packed in own juice
1 16-ounce can sliced peaches, packaged in own juice
1 13-ounce can pineapple chunks, packed in own juice
1 16-ounce can pear halves
1 16-ounce can light sweet cherries
   Juice of one lemon
¾ cup combined fruit syrup
¼ cup brown sugar
½ teaspoon nutmeg
1 teaspoon cinnamon
¼ teaspoon ground cloves
2 tablespoons butter

Drain all fruits, reserving ¾ cup of the combined syrups. Arrange fruit in a 2-quart casserole. Sprinkle with lemon juice. In a small bowl, combine ¾ cup reserved syrup with brown sugar and all the spices; pour over fruit. Dot with butter. Bake in a preheated 350° oven for about 25 minutes. Serve warm.
VARIATION: Garnish with sour cream sprinkled with nutmeg.
YIELD: 10 servings

Mrs. William Kasch
(Sonnie Kern)

HOT SHERRIED FRUIT

Easy to make!

1 29-ounce can sliced pears, drained
1 29-ounce can sliced peaches, drained
1 16-ounce can apricots, pitted and halved
1 16-ounce can plums, pitted and halved
¼ cup butter, melted
¼ cup dry sherry
¼ cup brown sugar
2 Curry powder, to taste

Combine all fruits in a 2-quart casserole. In a small saucepan, melt butter; add sherry, brown sugar, and curry powder to taste. Pour over fruit. Bake in a preheated 350° oven for about 40 minutes. Stir before serving.
YIELD: 12 to 16 servings

Mrs. James Deddens
(Marcia Kramer)

56

HEAVENLY APPLE SALAD

Refreshing fresh fruit flavor. Tasty dressing.

1½	cups boiling water
1	6-ounce box lemon gelatin
16	marshmallows, cut in small pieces (about 75 miniatures)
1	cup cold water
2	large apples, peeled and diced
½	cup chopped pecans
1	16-ounce can crushed pineapple, drained
2/3	cup granulated sugar
2	eggs, well beaten
2	tablespoons lemon juice
½	pint whipping cream, whipped

Sprinkle gelatin into a 9 x 13-inch dish; add boiling water, and stir until dissolved. Add marshmallows, and stir until melted. Stir in cold water. Refrigerate until gelatin thickens. Fold apples, pecans, and pineapple into thickened mixture. Refrigerate until set. In a small saucepan, combine sugar, eggs, and lemon juice. Cook over low heat, stirring constantly until thickened. Remove from heat and cool. Fold thickened egg mixture into whipped cream; spread over set gelatin. Refrigerate until serving time.
YIELD: 12 servings

Mrs. Charles D. Ross
(Lois Huston)

EVA'S BLUEBERRY JELLO MOLD

Refreshingly light taste and texture. Very pretty color.

2	cups boiling water
3	3-ounce packages of grape or black raspberry gelatin
2	15-ounce cans blueberries
1	8-ounce package cream cheese, softened
1	pint sour cream
1½	tablespoons lemon juice

Add 2 cups boiling water to gelatin; stir until dissolved. Drain blueberries into a bowl, and add enough cold water to make 2½ cups. Add cold liquid to gelatin. Refrigerate until beginning to set slightly. Meanwhile, beat cream cheese until smooth and continue beating while adding sour cream, lemon juice, and thickened gelatin. Stir in blueberries. Pour into mold, and chill until set.
YIELD: one 10 to 12-cup mold

Mrs. James Garrison
(Lesli Janacshek)

CHRISTMAS SALAD

Delicious with baked ham.

1 cup water
½ cup pineapple juice
1 tablespoon lemon juice
2 3-ounce packages
cherry gelatin
1 cup sugar
1 orange
1 cup ground cranberries
1 cup thinly sliced celery
1 cup well-drained,
crushed pineapple
½ cup chopped pecans

In a saucepan, heat water, pineapple juice, and lemon juice to boiling. Pour over gelatin and sugar in a large bowl; stir until dissolved. Chill until beginning to set. Squeeze orange and add juice to gelatin mixture. Remove all membrane from rind and put rind through fine blade of food chopper. Add orange rind and all remaining ingredients to gelatin mixture. Pour into lightly-greased and chilled 6-cup mold. Refrigerate.
OFF-SEASON VARIATION: Substitute one 10-ounce package of frozen cranberries with orange (we prefer Dean's Indian Trail) for the fresh cranberries. Omit the sugar.
YIELD: 8 to 10 servings

Mrs. Earl F. Pritchard
(Judy Elliott)

SOUR CREAM CRANBERRY SALAD

**Can be prepared in a matter of seconds.
Tart and creamy-light texture. Colorful!**

1 3-ounce package raspberry gelatin
1 cup boiling water
1 8-ounce can jellied cranberry sauce
1 cup sour cream
Fresh mint leaves for garnish, optional
Fresh raspberries for garnish, optional

In a small bowl, dissolve gelatin in boiling water. Cool slightly. Add all remaining ingredients except garnishes to a blender; blend. Pour into 8 individual 4 to 5-ounce gelatin molds. Chill until firm. Garnish with fresh mint leaves and/or fresh raspberries if desired.
YIELD: 8 servings

Mrs. Bruce A. Triplett
(Leslie Conway)

58

PORTOFINO MOLD

Excellent taste.

2	3-ounce packages raspberry gelatin
1¼	cups boiling water
1	20-ounce can crushed pineapple, undrained
1	16-ounce can whole cranberry sauce
¾	cup cranberry juice or port wine
1	cup chopped pecans
1	8-ounce package cream cheese, softened
1	cup dairy sour cream

Dissolve gelatin in boiling water. Stir in pineapple, cranberry sauce, and juice. Chill until mixture thickens slightly. Fold in pecans and turn into a two-quart serving mold or flat casserole. Chill until firm. When gelatin is set, beat the softened cream cheese until smooth; gradually beat in sour cream until the mixture is smooth. Spread over gelatin. Chill until serving time.
VARIATION: Nuts may be mixed into topping, instead of the gelatin.
YIELD: 12 to 15 servings

Mrs. Thomas D. Saunders
(Chris Derby)

RASPBERRY ASPIC

Recipe was given to me by a friend who promised that anyone who doesn't care for tomato aspic will love this. She was right.

5	cups V-8 juice
3	3-ounce packages raspberry gelatin
6	tablespoons mild horseradish (we prefer Kirkwood)
½	to 1 cucumber, sliced for garnish
½	to 1 avocado, peeled, pitted, sliced for garnish
	Parsley sprigs for garnish
	Mayonnaise or salad dressing for garnish

In a large saucepan, heat V-8 juice. Add gelatin and horseradish; stir until gelatin is dissolved. Pour into a greased, 6-cup ring mold (Fits perfectly into my Tupperware mold.). Chill until set; remove from mold. Garnish with cucumber, avocado, and parsley. Serve with mayonnaise or salad dressing in the center of ring.
YIELD: 10 to 12 servings

Mrs. Robert A. Pratt
(Beverly Lowe)

PINEAPPLE-CUCUMBER SALAD

This recipe was given to me by my mother many years ago.
This salad is very refreshing and attractive — nice for summertime.

2 envelopes unflavored gelatin
½ cup cold water
Reserved juice from drained pineapple
Juice of one lemon
1 cup sugar
1 15½-ounce can crushed pineapple, drained and save juice
1 large cucumber
Lettuce for serving
Mayonnaise for garnish

Soften gelatin in ½ cup water. In a small saucepan, combine pineapple juice, lemon juice, and sugar. Bring to a boil over medium heat stirring mixture. Refrigerate until thickened; then add pineapple and cucumber. Mix and pour into 6 to 8 individual molds or a 4-cup mold. Serve on lettuce with a dollop of mayonnaise.
YIELD: 6 to 8 servings

Mrs. A. Justin Smith
(Mary Elizabeth Marshall)

ROSY STRAWBERRY RING MOLD

An easy make-ahead dish with nice consistency and color.

1   6-ounce package
    strawberry gelatin
2   cups boiling water
8   ounces strawberry
    preserves
1   8-ounce can pineapple
    chunks in own juice,
    cut in halves
8   ounces sour cream
1   teaspoon sugar
¼   teaspoon ground ginger
½   cup slivered almonds
    Dash salt
½   to 1 quart fresh straw-
    berries, for garnish, if
    desired

In a large bowl, dissolve gelatin in boiling water. Add preserves. Stir in pineapple and juice, almonds, sour cream, sugar, ginger, and salt. Pour into oiled, 6-cup ring mold. Chill in refrigerator overnight or until firm. Unmold on serving plate. Fill the center of the ring with fresh strawberries as a garnish for a festive touch. YIELD: 8 servings

Mrs. Roy L. Hohman
(Judy Hoeltke)

STRAWBERRY HEART SALAD

An attractive buffet salad with a very tasty dressing.

1   12-ounce package,
    frozen, sweetened
    strawberries
1   6-ounce package
    strawberry gelatin
1   cup hot water
2   teaspoons lemon juice
1½ to 2 cups drained pine-
    apple chunks, or
    crushed pineapple
½   cup mayonnaise
1   3-ounce package cream
    cheese
    Dash of salt

Thaw strawberries, reserving juice. Dissolve gelatin in hot water and lemon juice. Add enough cold water to strawberry juice to make 2 cups; add to dissolved gelatin. Chill until mixture thickens; gently stir in fruit. Pour into a 6-cup ring mold which has been rinsed with cold water. Refrigerate. To serve, turn out on salad greens and fill cavity with blended mayonnaise, cream cheese, and salt. Garnish with whole strawberries if desired. YIELD: 10 to 12 servings

Mrs. William F. Miller
(Barbara Parkin)

COLD BROCCOLI SALAD

This is a very tasty salad.
It will take the place of a hot vegetable on a summer night,
or it is yummy as a side dish for a luncheon.

2   **10-ounce packages frozen broccoli spears**
½   **cup chopped onion**
½   **cup chopped olives**
1   **cup chopped celery**
3   **hard boiled eggs**
1   **cup mayonnaise (we prefer Hellman's)**
1   **tablespoon or more lemon juice**
½   **teaspoon salt**
     Pepper to taste

Thaw broccoli; drain and chop. In a salad bowl, combine all ingredients, and toss to mix. Cover and chill overnight.
YIELD: 8 to 10 servings

Mrs. John M. Cotner
(Cheryl Burcham)

CRUNCHY BROCCOLI SALAD

Crispy, fresh, clean flavor! Easy make-ahead salad.

1   **bunch tender, fresh broccoli**
½   **pound fresh mushrooms, sliced**
2   **tablespoons chopped onion**
1   **8-ounce bottle of Italian dressing (we prefer Wish-Bone)**
1   **tomato, chopped and drained**

Using the tender stalk and flowerettes, chop broccoli into bite-size pieces. Do not cook. Add mushrooms and onions. Toss to mix well. Pour all of the dressing over the broccoli mixture. Cover and marinate refrigerated for at least 12 hours. At serving time, drain dressing off broccoli. Add chopped tomato. Toss and serve.
YIELD: 6 servings

Mrs. Ronald Petersen
(Sherry Hess)

VEGETABLE MEDLEY

Vegetables stay crisp, and each flavor is preserved.

1 bunch broccoli, raw (flowerets only), cut into bite-size pieces
1 head cauliflower, raw (flowerets only), cut into bite-size pieces
½ pound fresh snow pea pods
2 zucchini, sliced
1 pound fresh mushrooms, sliced
1 8½-ounce can artichoke hearts, drained and cut into fourths
2 tablespoons chives
2 tablespoons pimento, chopped
1 1-pound package bacon, fried and crumbled, reserve ¼ cup for garnish
1 hard-boiled egg yolk, grated

DRESSING

1 package Italian dressing mix (we prefer Good Seasons)
3½ tablespoons olive oil
3½ tablespoons peanut oil
3½ tablespoons vegetable oil

In a large salad bowl, combine all ingredients except ¼ cup bacon and egg yolk. Cover and refrigerate. Pour dressing on right before serving. Garnish with bacon and grated egg yolk.

DRESSING

Follow directions on package *except* substitute oils listed instead of all vegetable oil. Pour over chilled, raw vegetables at serving time. Salt and pepper to taste.
YIELD: 12 servings

Mrs. James Weprin
(Barbara Davis)

MARINATED BRUSSELS SPROUTS

Doubles as vegetable dish or appetizer. Very easy; make ahead.

1   10-ounce package frozen Brussels sprouts (we prefer Birdseye deluxe baby Brussels sprouts)
½   cup bottled Italian salad dressing, shaken well
½   teaspoon dill seed
1   tablespoon sliced green onion
1   4½-ounce jar button mushrooms, drained

Cook Brussels sprouts according to package directions; drain. In a small bowl, combine all remaining ingredients. Pour over Brussels sprouts. Cover and refrigerate for at least 3 hours or overnight.

YIELD: 4 servings as a vegetable
6 servings as an appetizer

Mrs. Jonathan Wyant
(Barbara Jones)

ITALIAN DRESSING FOR TOMATO SLICES

Makes a very pretty platter with red, ripe tomatoes and green dressing on top.

1   bunch parsley
5   hard boiled eggs
2   anchovies
4   cloves garlic
1/3   cup vegetable oil
1/3   cup wine vinegar
Salt and pepper to taste
3   large ripe tomatoes, cut into ½-inch slices

Whirl first four ingredients in blender. In a small bowl, mix together oil and vinegar. Slowly add oil and vinegar until mixture becomes consistency of mayonnaise. Add salt and pepper to taste. Slice ripe tomatoes about ½-inch thick, and place on platter or serving plate. Put about a tablespoon of dressing on each slice. Cover and store remaining dressing in refrigerator for future use.

YIELD: 6 servings, 2-½ cups dressing

Mrs. William R. Thompson
(Sally Decker)

ANTIPASTO SALAD

Prepare in the morning or on the day before.

2   2-ounce tins anchovies, (optional)
2   tablespoons olive oil
2   tablespoons vegetable oil
1   tablespoon chopped parsley
1½ tablespoons wine vinegar (we prefer Heinz)
2   green peppers, cut in thin strips
3   tomatoes, peeled, cut into narrow wedges
3   green onions, minced
1   14-ounce can artichoke hearts, cut in half
30 black olives, pitted, cut in halves
2   garlic cloves

Drain oil from anchovies into bowl. Add olive oil, vegetable oil, parsley, and vinegar. Cut anchovies into pieces. Add anchovies, green peppers, tomatoes, minced green onions, artichoke hearts, and olives; toss to mix. Cut garlic cloves in half; put on toothpicks; bury in salad. Cover and refrigerate. At serving time remove garlic. Toss salad to mix.
YIELD: 4 to 6 servings

Mrs. Jonathan Wyant
(Barbara Jones)

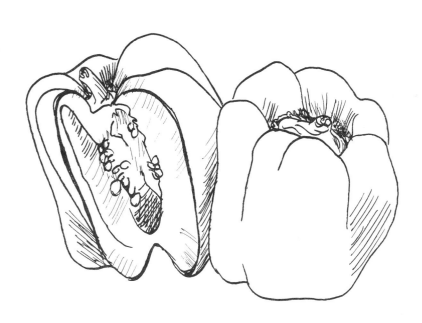

"VEGIE" SANDWICH

Very refreshing taste and good nutritional value.

¼ avocado, mashed
Garlic salt to taste
1 piece Pita (pocket bread)
2 to 3 tablespoons cream cheese with chives, softened
About 6 thin cucumber slices
About 3 thin tomato slices
Handful of bean sprouts

Mash avocado, and season to taste with garlic salt. Spread on one inner-side of pita bread. Spread the other side with cream cheese. Stuff with cucumbers, tomatoes, and bean sprouts.
VARIATION: Alfalfa sprouts may be substituted for bean sprouts.
YIELD: 1 sandwich

Mrs. Herwig Baumann
(Vickie Overholzer)

COLD VEGETABLE MEDLEY

Light, delicious marinade.

1 16-ounce can cut green beans
1 16-ounce can small whole white potatoes or boiled new potatoes, cubed
¼ cup vegetable oil
2 tablespoons vinegar
¼ teaspoon salt
¼ teaspoon pepper
1/8 teaspoon each of dry mustard, sweet basil, parsley, and garlic powder
1 16-ounce can pitted black olives, drained and chilled
2 small tomatoes, cut into wedges, chilled
2 small onions, cut into rings, chilled

In a small bowl, combine beans and potatoes. Mix together vegetable oil, vinegar, salt, pepper, dry mustard, sweet basil, parsley, and garlic powder. Pour over potatoes and green beans. Cover and refrigerate to marinate for 1 hour. Add olives, tomatoes, and onions. Toss together and serve.
YIELD: 6 servings

Mrs. Robert J. Gronek
(Veronica Toth)

GREAT COLD SALAD

Goes together easily.

3   16-ounce cans whole
    or cut green beans,
    drained
1   14-ounce can artichoke
    hearts, drained (8½
    ounces) and cut in half
1   8-ounce can water
    chestnuts, drained and
    sliced
½   pound fresh mush-
    rooms, cleaned and
    sliced
1   envelope onion soup
    mix
1   8-ounce bottle Green
    Goddess salad dressing
    Parsley sprigs, for
    garnish
    Tomato wedges, for
    garnish

Mix together all ingredients except parsley and tomatoes. Cover and chill overnight. Garnish with parsley sprigs and tomato slices when ready to serve. YIELD: 8 to 10 servings

Mrs. William Kasch
(Sonnie Kern)

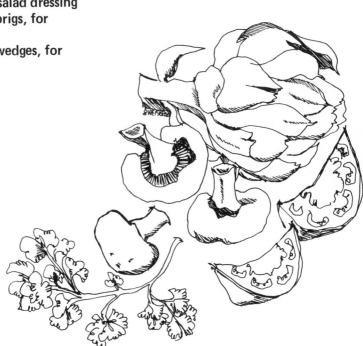

ARTICHOKES AND BEAN SPROUTS

Super quick and easy!

1 16-ounce can bean sprouts, drained
1 to 2, 14-ounce cans artichoke hearts, drained and quartered
1 16-ounce can cut green beans, drained
1 7-ounce can water chestnuts, drained and sliced
Your favorite herb or garlic dressing

Combine all salad ingredients with dressing. Cover and marinate in refrigerator for several hours.
YIELD: 12 servings

Mrs. Alan R. Merrill
(Lynn Wagner)

CARROT SALAD

Good combination of sweet and sour.

1 10¾-ounce can tomato soup
½ cup sugar
½ cup vegetable oil
¾ cup cider vinegar
1 teaspoon prepared mustard (we prefer French's)
1 teaspoon pepper
1 medium green or red pepper, chopped
4 cups sliced carrots, cook until JUST tender — do not overcook
1 medium onion, sliced and separated

In a small mixing bowl, beat all ingredients except green peppers, carrots and onions with mixer. Pour mixture over green peppers, carrots and onions in two 1-quart jars; cover and refrigerate for at least 24 hours before serving. (Will keep for 6 weeks; stir every day.) At serving time, drain and save dressing for other salads. Serve cold.
VARIATION: Remaining dressing makes a nice marinade for fresh zucchini or garbanzo beans.
YIELD: 8 to 10 servings

Mrs. R. James Heikes
(Bonnie Bright)

MERRY MARINATED TOMATOES

Flavors are fresh and subtle.
The colors are a natural at Christmas time.

4	to 6 plump tomatoes
6	tablespoons minced fresh parsley
6	tablespoons olive oil
2	teaspoons onion powder
½	teaspoon dried basil
¼	teaspoon pepper
½	teaspoon sugar
1	teaspoon salt
2	tablespoons vinegar

Peel and cut each tomato horizontally into 4 to 5 slices. In small bowl, combine all remaining ingredients. Spread about 1 teaspoon of the marinade on a cut side of each of the tomato slices. Place parsley side up in serving bowl. Pour any remaining marinade over all. Cover and refrigerate at least 3 hours before serving. May also be served individually, a few slices on lettuce. VARIATION: Thin slices of Provolone cheese under tomato slices are an enhancing contrast.
YIELD: 6 to 8 servings

Mrs. Alan Meckstroth
(Betty Lutz)

TOMATO COB

This is best made with vine-ripened tomatoes.

1	large tomato, peeled and diced
	Salt, to taste
	Pepper, to taste
	Onion juice, to taste
1	tablespoon mayonnaise
	Dash of curry powder
	Dash of chopped parsley

Place diced tomato in a bowl. Season with salt, pepper, and onion juice. Cover and refrigerate for the day so the juice will collect. Before serving drain well and top with mayonnaise, seasoned with curry powder and chopped parsley. Instruct guests to mix the tomatoes and mayonnaise sauce before eating.
YIELD: 1 serving

Mrs. R. Stephen Gresham
(Martha Boyd)

COTTAGE CHEESE TOMATO ASPIC

Different and tasty side dish; especially nice for summer.

1	3-ounce package lemon gelatin
1	cup tomato juice
1/3	green pepper, chopped
1	stalk celery, chopped
½	cup green olives, chopped (optional)
1	teaspoon grated onion
1	cup cottage cheese
½	cup mayonnaise

In a small saucepan, bring tomato juice almost to a boil. Remove from heat, and add gelatin; stir until dissolved. Add all remaining ingredients, and stir until well mixed. Pour into an oiled mold. Cover and refrigerate until firm.

YIELD: 6 servings

Mrs. Thomas C. Puthoff
(Linda Bates)

TOMATO ASPIC

Quick and easy!

1	8-ounce can tomato sauce with onion
1	3-ounce package lemon gelatin
1	cup boiling water
1	tablespoon cider vinegar
	Pinch of salt
	Grated onion to taste

In a small bowl, dissolve gelatin in the boiling hot water; cool. Stir in all remaining ingredients. Pour into 5 individual molds. Chill until set.

YIELD: 5 servings

Mrs. James Brown
(Ann Nye Guthrie)

SPINACH SALAD

Tasty combination — delicious dressing.

½   cup corn oil
¼   cup wine vinegar
     Juice of 1 lemon
¼   cup sugar
¼   cup ketchup
1   garlic clove, crushed
1   tablespoon worcester-
     shire sauce
½   teaspoon salt
1/8 teaspoon pepper
1/8 teaspoon dry mustard
1/8 teaspoon paprika
     Few drops tabasco
     sauce
1   pound fresh spinach
½   to 1 pound fresh
     mushrooms, cleaned
     and sliced (optional)
6   to 10 slices bacon,
     fried crisp, crumbled
6   hard boiled eggs, sliced

In a 2-cup jar with a tight-fitting lid, combine the first 12 ingredients. Shake well; set aside. Wash spinach carefully, removing tough stems. Drain (no need to dry). In a large salad bowl, tear spinach into bite-size pieces. Add mushrooms and reserved dressing; mix gently to distribute dressing well. Arrange salad on 6 serving plates; garnish with crumbled bacon, and top with egg slices.
yield: 6 servings

Mrs. P. Stanley Castleman
(Maria Preonas)

SPINACH SALAD AND CALIFORNIA DRESSING

Oranges add a new taste.

1   to 2 pounds fresh
     spinach, torn
1   medium onion, chopped
½   head lettuce, torn
2   11-ounce cans mandarin
     oranges, drained

DRESSING:

1½ cups sugar
1   teaspoon dry mustard
1   cup white vinegar
1   teaspoon salt
2   eggs, beaten frothy

Combine uncooked spinach, onion, lettuce, and oranges. Cover and refrigerate.

DRESSING

Combine sugar, mustard, vinegar, salt, and eggs in a saucepan. Bring to a boil. Boil for 1 minute; cool. Cover and refrigerate. Toss together greens and chilled dressing just before serving.
YIELD: 8 to 10 servings

Mrs. John Williams
(Jo Ann Ferrante)

SPINACH CHUTNEY

Very different and tasty.

¼	cup white wine vinegar
¼	cup vegetable oil
2	heaping tablespoons chutney
2	teaspoons sugar
½	teaspoon salt
2	teaspoons curry powder
1	teaspoon dry mustard
1	pound fresh spinach, torn into bite-size pieces
1½	cups chopped unpared apple
½	cup light raisins
¾	cup almondized peanuts (we prefer Jump's)
3	tablespoons sliced green onion

In a blender or food processor, combine vinegar, oil, chutney, sugar, salt, curry powder, and mustard; blend well. Cover and chill well before serving. Combine all remaining ingredients in a large salad bowl; shake dressing well and toss with salad.
YIELD: 6 to 8 servings

Mrs. William Kasch
(Sonnie Kern)

HUNT BRUNCH MIXED GREEN TOSSED SALAD

Colorful with lots of textures. Serve with Ma Heck's Lasagne (see index).

1	pound fresh spinach, torn
1	head lettuce, torn
1	8-ounce package herb seasoned dressing (we prefer Pepperidge Farm)
1	cup large curd cottage cheese
2	tablespoons basil
2	tablespoons oregano
2	tablespoons rosemary
2	tablespoons carraway seed
	Italian dressing

Toss all ingredients together. Serve with Italian dressing.
YIELD: 8 to 10 servings

Mrs. Jack Heck
(Phyllis Fraser)

COLE SLAW WITH DRESSING

Cabbage — as well as any other leafy green — can be used with this versatile dressing which will keep refrigerated for two weeks.

DRESSING

1	cup light brown sugar
½	cup granulated sugar
1½	teaspoons paprika
1	teaspoon salt
1	large onion, grated
1½	cups vegetable oil
	Apple cider vinegar

COLE SLAW

1	large head cabbage, cored and sliced very thin (not grated)
3	carrots, scraped and grated
¼	cup finely chopped green pepper, optional
¼	cup finely chopped onion, optional
½	cup sliced toasted almonds, optional

To make the dressing, mix sugars, spices, onion, and oil in a quart jar and stir well. Fill to the top with vinegar and stir. Cover and refrigerate; stir before using.

In a large salad bowl, toss all cole slaw ingredients together. Pour all dressing over salad. Refrigerate until serving time.

YIELD: Slaw: 8 to 10 servings
1 quart dressing

Mrs. Frederick Young
(Joyce Canney)

POTATO SALAD

Easy and different way to make potato salad. Tasty.

2	pounds new potatoes
1½	cups sliced Bermuda onion
8	ounces chive cottage cheese
9	tablespoons mayonnaise
1½	teaspoons salt
	Dash of cayenne

Boil whole potatoes until tender. Drain, cool, peel, and slice. In a large bowl, layer ingredients in the order listed. Cover and refrigerate for 12 to 24 hours. Toss gently. Serve.

YIELD: 12 to 15 servings

Mrs. Robert Mittlestead
(Mitzi Benham)

OLD FASHIONED CREAMY POTATO SALAD

Make ahead; flavors blend well.

6   Idaho potatoes, cut in ½-inch cubes (about 6 cups)
3   to 4 quarts water
1   cup chopped celery
½   to 1 medium onion, diced fine
2   hard boiled eggs, chopped
2   to 3 tablespoons prepared mustard
1½   cups salad dressing
1½   teaspoons salt
Pepper to taste
Paprika for garnish
Fresh parsley sprigs for garnish
Stuffed olives, drained and sliced, for garnish

In a Dutch oven, cook potatoes in boiling water until tender (about 15 minutes — do not overcook, or potatoes will become mushy). Drain; cover and refrigerate until cool. In a large bowl, gently combine cooled potatoes, celery, onion and eggs. In a small bowl, mix together mustard, salad dressing, and salt. Pour dressing over potato mixture. Toss gently to cover each bite with dressing. If potato salad is not creamy enough, add 1 teaspoon mustard mixed with ¼ cup salad dressing. Add pepper to taste. Scoop into large serving bowl. Cover and chill thoroughly. At serving time, garnish with paprika, parsley sprigs, and sliced, stuffed olives.
YIELD: 8 servings

Mrs. Gerald Westerbeck
(Judy Richardson)

HOT POTATO SALAD

*"This seems to be my specialty, and I'm tired of making it.
So, I decided to share my recipe with the world."*

6	red potatoes, boiled
¼	pound bacon
½	cup chopped pimento
1	medium onion, chopped
3	stalks celery, chopped
2	hard boiled eggs, chopped (optional)
	Salt and pepper, to taste
4	tablespoons reserved bacon fat
4	tablespoons cider vinegar
½	teaspoon dry mustard
1	teaspoon garlic salt
1	teaspoon basil

Boil potatoes just until tender; cool, peel, chop, and set aside. Fry bacon until crisp; drain and reserve 4 tablespoons of the fat. Crumble the bacon, and mix it with the potatoes, pimento, onion, celery, eggs, salt, and pepper in a 2-quart casserole. In the same bacon skillet, heat 4 tablespoons reserved fat with all remaining ingredients. Pour hot dressing over potato mixture and bake uncovered in a preheated 350° oven for 45 minutes.

CHEF'S NOTE: This recipe contains no sugar.

YIELD: 6 servings

Mrs. Walter Cheslock
(Virginia Stout)

POTATO SALAD

The egg yolks in the dressing make the flavor different and better.

3	cups diced boiled red potatoes
1	tablespoon chopped onion
½	cup chopped green pepper
1	cup chopped celery
2	eggs, hard boiled
½	cup mayonnaise
½	cup sour cream
1	tablespoon prepared mustard
	Salt to taste

In a large salad bowl, combine potatoes, onion, green pepper, and celery. In a small bowl, mash egg yolks; add mayonnaise, sour cream, and mustard; mix well. Mix dressing into potato mixture, and add salt to taste. Cover and refrigerate overnight so that flavors blend.

YIELD: 4 to 6 servings

Mrs. Thomas Shulman
(Ellie Arnovitz)

SPAGHETTI SALAD

A favorite and best when made the night before.

1	pound spaghetti
1	quart Marzetti's Blendaise
1	large Bermuda onion, chopped
2	small cucumbers, seeded and chopped
2	2-ounce jars pimento, drained
½	to 1 pint coffee cream Seasoned salt and pepper
2	tablespoons dill weed, optional
¼	cup stuffed green olives

Break spaghetti into 2-inch pieces. Cook according to instructions on package; drain; then rinse with cold water; drain. Turn spaghetti into a large bowl; stir in Blendaise. Add onion, cucumbers (do not peel), and pimento; stir to mix well. Slowly blend in coffee cream to obtain desired consistency. Add seasoned salt, pepper, and dill to taste. Cover and refrigerate. Garnish with olives before serving.
YIELD: 12 to 16 servings

Mrs. Jonathan P. Shelton
(Nancy Garst)

DILLED MACARONI SALAD

Great salad for a warm, summer day.

1	pound elbow macaroni
1/3	cup chopped green onions
2	cups diced unpared cucumber (about 1 large)
½	cup mayonnaise
½	cup sour cream
1	tablespoon lemon juice
2	tablespoons dill (dried or fresh)
1	tablespoon salt (sounds like a lot, but use a whole tablespoon)
1/8	teaspoon white pepper Fresh dill to taste

Cook macaroni according to package directions; drain. In a large bowl, combine macaroni, onion, and cucumber. In a small bowl, blend together mayonnaise, sour cream, lemon juice, dill, salt, and pepper. Toss dressing with macaroni mixture. Chill. Garnish with fresh dill at serving time.
YIELD: 14 to 16 servings

Mrs. Patrick E. Wilke
(Patricia Settle)

RICE SALAD

My mother has been serving this ever since I can remember —
about 40 years — and I've never had it anywhere else.
It is a nice change from summer potato salad.

1½ cups raw rice
¾ cup mayonnaise
1 teaspoon salt
¾ teaspoon pepper
1/3 cup minced onion
¼ teaspoon rosemary
2 tablespoons lemon
  juice
1 10-ounce package
  frozen small peas,
  cooked slightly, drain-
  ed and chilled
1½ cups chopped celery
¾ cup chopped fresh
  mushrooms

Cook rice according to package directions; drain, and chill. In a small bowl,
combine mayonnaise, salt, pepper,
onion, rosemary, and lemon juice.
Add mayonnaise mixture to rice, peas,
celery, and mushrooms in a salad bowl.
Toss to mix well; cover, and chill for
several hours before serving.
YIELD: 12 servings

Mrs. Walter Cheslock
(Virginia Stout)

B's TACO SALAD

Great for a summer buffet! Serve with Gazpacho Soup (see index).

2 pounds ground round
1 2½-pound can tomatoes, drained
½ of a 1¼-ounce package of taco seasoning mix
1 8-ounce can tomato sauce, with onions
Dash garlic salt
Dash salt
Dash pepper
Dash tabasco sauce
½ head Romaine lettuce, torn
½ head Iceberg lettuce, torn
½ pound longhorn cheddar cheese, grated
½ pound Monterey Jack cheese with peppers, grated
1 4-ounce can green chilies, drained and diced
1 bunch green onions, chopped
2½ ounces green olives, sliced
7 ounces corn chips (we prefer Fritos)
7 ounces taco flavor tortilla chips (we prefer Doritos)
4 fresh tomatoes, quartered

In a large skillet, cook ground beef over medium heat until browned. Stir in drained canned tomatoes, taco seasoning mix, and tomato sauce. Season to taste with garlic salt, salt, pepper, and tabasco sauce. Reduce heat and simmer for about 20 minutes or until mixture cooks down. In a very large salad bowl, combine all remaining ingredients, except fresh tomatoes. Add hot beef mixture, and toss to combine. Garnish with fresh tomatoes. Serve immediately.
YIELD: 8 generous servings

Mrs. Donald May
(Brenda Amburgey)

CHICKEN SALAD

A traditional luncheon party salad. We especially like the water chestnuts, grapes, and salted almonds. At Thanksgiving time, try substituting leftover turkey for the chicken.

2   whole chicken breasts, cooked, skinned, boned, and cubed
½   cup celery, chopped
½   cup water chestnuts, chopped
1   cup green seedless grapes, halved
½   cup red onion, chopped
    Seasoning salt, to taste (we prefer Lawry's)
    Mayonnaise, enough to toss (we prefer Hellman's)
¼   to ½ cup slivered almonds, sauteed in 1 to 2 tablespoons butter and salted to taste
3   tomatoes, cut in quarters

Toss all salad ingredients (except almonds and tomatoes) together with enough mayonnaise to obtain desired consistency. Taste; add more seasoning salt if necessary. Cover and refrigerate. Serve on lettuce; garnish with toasted almonds and tomato wedges.

YIELD: 6 servings

Mrs. David R. Meeker
(Rebecca Bottomley)

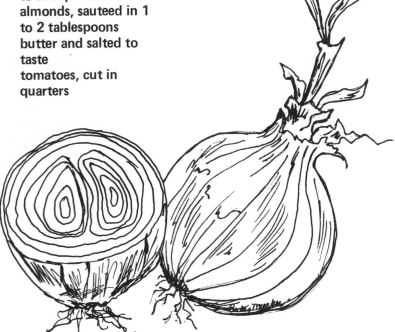

CURRIED CHICKEN SALAD WITH RICE

This recipe came to me from my sister who lived in Madras, India.
A delicious, different chicken salad seasoned with curry,
it must be prepared at least a day ahead.

3 to 4 whole chicken breasts
1 whole onion
Salt and pepper to taste
Celery tops of about 6 ribs; water to cover
1½ cups cooked rice
1 teaspoon curry powder, or to taste
2 tablespoons vegetable oil (we prefer Wesson)
1 tablespoon cider vinegar
½ teaspoon salt or to taste
¼ cup chopped green pepper
1 cup chopped celery
1 cup mayonnaise
Lettuce cups
8 to 10 spiced pears
Fresh parsley sprigs for garnish

At least several days ahead of time in a large saucepan, combine whole chicken breasts, whole onion, salt and pepper, and celery tops. Add water to cover, and cook over medium heat until chicken is tender. Remove chicken from broth, and cool slightly. Skin, bone, and cut chicken into bite-size pieces; cover and refrigerate (If preparing more than several days ahead of time, return chicken to strained broth, and freeze until the day before serving. Then the day before serving, thaw and strain.). The night before serving, combine cooked rice, curry powder, vegetable oil, vinegar, and salt and pepper to taste. Cover and refrigerate. At least 1 hour before serving, add chicken, green pepper, celery and mayonnaise to the rice mixture. Mix well; cover and refrigerate until serving time. Serve in lettuce cups with spiced pears and garnish with parsley.
YIELD: 8 servings

Mrs. William W. Trostel
(Mary Wilson)

DOT'S CHICKEN SALAD

Crunchy pecans and bacon make this chicken salad outstanding.

1	cup sour cream
1	cup mayonnaise (we prefer Hellman's)
1½	teaspoons salt
2	tablespoons lemon juice
4	cups chicken, cooked and cubed (about 7 breast halves)
2	cups diced celery
1	4-ounce jar button mushrooms, drained
¼	cup pecan halves
4	slices bacon, fried crisp, crumbled

In a small bowl, combine sour cream, mayonnaise, salt, and lemon juice. In a large bowl, combine chicken, celery, and mushrooms. Add desired amount of dressing to chicken, and toss gently; chill. Just before serving add pecans and bacon.
YIELD: 8 to 10 servings

Mrs. Richard Karr
(Mary Frances Wheaton)

SPRING CHICKEN SALAD

You'll love the grapes and crispy vegetables.

2	whole chicken breasts, cooked, skinned, boned, and cubed into ¾-inch bites
¾	cup sliced celery
¾	cup pineapple chunks, well drained
¾	cup white seedless grapes
1	8½-ounce can water chestnuts, drained and cut in half
1	cup salad dressing, or more if needed
½	cup pecan halves
4	lettuce cups
	Fresh parsley, for garnish
	Pecan halves, for garnish

In a large bowl, combine chicken, celery, pineapple, grapes, and water chestnuts. Add salad dressing, and toss to coat each piece with dressing. Add additional dressing until salad looks creamy and each morsel is coated with dressing. Fold in pecan halves. Cover and refrigerate at least until thoroughly chilled, or until serving time. Serve in lettuce cups, garnished with parsley and additional pecan halves.
YIELD: 4 servings

Mrs. Gerald Westerbeck
(Judy Richardson)

SUMMER CHICKEN SALAD

**Chicken, fruits, rice and crunchy, toasted almonds
provide a pleasing, refreshing summer treat.**

5 cups cooked and cubed chicken
2 tablespoons vegetable oil
2 tablespoons orange juice
1 teaspoon salt
2 tablespoons cider vinegar
3 cups cooked rice
1½ cups seedless green grapes
1½ cups sliced celery
1 13½-ounce can pineapple chunks, drained
1 11-ounce can mandarin oranges, drained
1 cup toasted sliced almonds
1½ cups mayonnaise

In a large bowl, combine the first 5 ingredients. Cover and refrigerate overnight, or proceed immediately. In another large bowl, combine all remaining ingredients. Add to chicken mixture; toss gently to mix. Cover and refrigerate to chill before serving.
YIELD: 12 servings

Mrs. Alan R. Merrill
(Lynn Wagner)

MOLDED EGG SALAD WITH CRABMEAT SAUCE

Besides tasting delicious, it is so pretty! Perfect for a luncheon; just prepare the day before. The sauce is what makes it!

1   to 2 tablespoons mayonnaise for greasing mold
2   envelopes unflavored gelatin
1/3 cup cool water
2   dozen hard-boiled eggs, chopped
1   cup chopped celery
1   3-ounce package cream cheese
1   cup sour cream dressing (we prefer Sokreem)
1   cup mayonnaise
1   tablespoon Dijon mustard
1   teaspoon salt
½   cup milk
¼   cup chopped green onion
¼   teaspoon white pepper
    Fresh parsley sprigs, for garnish
    Cherry tomatoes, for garnish

Grease a 6-cup mold with 1 to 2 tablespoons mayonnaise; set aside. In the top of a double boiler, soften gelatin in 1/3 cup cool water. Place pan over hot water and stir to dissolve gelatin. Stir in all remaining ingredients, except parsley and tomatoes, until thoroughly mixed. Taste for the possible addition of more salt. Turn mixture into prepared mold. Cover and refrigerate until serving time, or at least until set. Dip mold to the rim in hot water to unmold.

CRABMEAT SAUCE

In a small bowl, combine all ingredients, adding enough dry sherry to make a sauce consistency. Cover and refrigerate until serving time.

YIELD: 12 servings

Mrs. William Kasch
(Sonnie Kern)

CRABMEAT SAUCE

1   cup crabmeat
¾   cup sour cream
¾   cup mayonnaise
1   tablespoon lemon juice
2   to 3 tablespoons dry sherry, or enough to make a sauce consistency

SEAFOOD SALAD

Unique and refreshing.

2　10¾-ounce cans chicken noodle soup, undiluted
2　8-ounce packages cream cheese
1　cup mayonnaise
2　3-ounce packages lemon gelatin
1　cup boiling water
2　to 3 cups chopped vegetables, your choice: celery, onion, green pepper, and/or pimento
3　to 4 cups canned small shrimp, crabmeat, or tuna, well drained

In a large saucepan, heat soup to a boil; add cream cheese, and stir until melted. Stir in mayonnaise. Remove from heat and cool. Dissolve gelatin in boiling water. Refrigerate briefly until slightly thickened, but not set. Add thickened gelatin, vegatables, and seafood to cooled cream cheese mixture. Turn into a 9 x 13-inch pan, cover, and refrigerate until serving time.

YIELD: 12 to 16 servings

Mrs. Alan L. Edmonson
(Patricia Bieser)

HERRING LUNCHEON SALAD

Great salad for herring lovers.

1　16-ounce jar herring in wine
1　large sweet onion, sliced
1　16-ounce can seedless white grapes, well drained
1　3-ounce package sliced blanched almonds
1　tablespoon sugar
2　medium-size apples, sliced
2　tablespoons fresh lemon juice
1　pint sour cream, whipped to soft peaks

Wash herring well in cold water; squeeze, and pat dry. Cut each herring in half. Mix with onion, grapes, almonds, sugar, apples, and lemon juice; then fold in sour cream; refrigerate. Serve on lettuce leaves with rye rounds for luncheon.

YIELD: 4 to 6 servings

Mrs. Stewart A. Levine
(Loraine Kanner)

CHOW CHOW CHOW TUNA SALAD

Great for ladies' luncheons but hearty enough to please a man.

1	10-ounce package frozen Italian green beans
1	7-ounce can tuna, drained and flaked
1	cup diced celery
½	cup salad dressing
1	tablespoon lemon juice
1½	teaspoons soy sauce
	Dash garlic powder
1	cup chow mein noodles
4	lettuce cups

Prepare green beans according to package directions; drain and cool. Toss together with tuna and celery; set aside. Mix together salad dressing, lemon juice, soy sauce and garlic powder. Toss dressing lightly with tuna mixture. Refrigerate until just before serving. Toss chow mein noodles with other ingredients just before serving. Serve in lettuce cups.
YIELD: 4 servings

Mrs. L. Scott Wasmund
(Barbara Berg)

FRUIT SALAD DRESSING

Serve over any type of fruit. It is especially good over melon balls.

3	eggs
1	pound jar honey
	Juice of 3 lemons
1	teaspoon flour
1	teaspoon sugar

Beat eggs; add honey, juice of the three lemons, flour, and sugar. Blend well in a saucepan over low heat, stirring until thickened; cool. Cover and refrigerate.
YIELD: 2 cups

Miss Deborah Ohmer

VINEGAR AND OIL DRESSING

Good on any variety of greens with fresh, sliced mushrooms, artichokes, sliced red or chopped green onions, black olives, chopped eggs, bacon, etc.

¾ cup vegetable oil (we prefer Wesson)
¼ cup olive oil
¾ cup red wine vinegar
3 tablespoons sugar
1 teaspoon salt
1 teaspoon garlic salt
2 garlic buds
1 teaspoon dry mustard or Dijon mustard
½ teaspoon freshly ground pepper
½ teaspoon chopped parsley
½ teaspoon oregano
½ teaspoon basil
1 teaspoon lemon juice

Combine all ingredients in a food processor or blender. Pour into a jar with a tight-fitting lid, cover and refrigerate. Bring dressing to room temperature, and shake well before serving.
YIELD: 1½ cups

Mrs. William Kasch
(Sonnie Kern)

PARMESAN SALAD DRESSING

Good with any combination of greens with the additions of fresh mushrooms, green or red onions, bacon, artichokes, etc.

1/3 cup grated Parmesan cheese
½ cup vegetable oil
¼ cup olive oil
¾ teaspoon salt
¼ teaspoon ground pepper
1 clove of garlic, cut
¼ cup lemon juice
¼ teaspoon paprika
¼ teaspoon oregano

Combine all ingredients in blender or food processor. Pour into a jar with a tight-fitting lid; refrigerate. Let it sit out of refrigerator a while and shake well before using.
YIELD: 1¼ cups

Mrs. William Kasch
(Sonnie Kern)

SWEET SALAD DRESSING

A very sweet dressing which is easy to make.

¾ cup sugar
½ cup vinegar
¼ cup salad oil
½ cup chili sauce
1 teaspoon salt
1 teaspoon paprika
1 teaspoon prepared
   mustard
1 teaspoon dried onion
   (optional)

Put all ingredients in a 24-ounce jar or a shaker cup with tight-fitting lid. Shake to mix; store in the refrigerator. Shake before serving.
YIELD: 1½ cups

Mrs. Thomas B. Talbot, Jr.
(Elma Carey)

GOLDEN BAEHR CELERY SEED DRESSING

Great served on fruit salad.

1 scant cup sugar
½ teaspoon salt
1 teaspoon dry mustard
1 tablespoon celery seed
1 cup salad oil
   Juice and pulp of 2
   lemons

Mix dry ingredients. Add oil and lemon, alternately, beating thoroughly between additions; chill.
YIELD: 1¼ cups

Mrs. Richard S. Sutton
(Janet Robinson)

SPECIAL SWEET FRENCH SALAD DRESSING

Ingredients don't sound special, but wait until you taste . . . special!

½   cup sugar
½   cup cider vinegar
1   cup oil
1½ teaspoons paprika
1½ teaspoons salt
1   teaspoon dry mustard
1   clove garlic
1   onion (size of an egg)
    cut into pieces

Mix all ingredients in blender about one minute; chill.
CHEF'S NOTE: You can vary flavor by using different vinegars — tarragon is especially good.
YIELD: 2 cups

Mrs. Charles R. Cothern
(Peg Fogt)

ANNOR'S DRESSING

A wonderful cooked dressing for potato salad or cole slaw or to combine with ground ham for a delicious, different ham salad. I can still remember seeing small jars of this dressing in my grandmother's refrigerator just waiting to contribute to a luscious summer meal.

1	cup sugar
1	tablespoon flour
1	to 3 teaspoons celery seed
½	teaspoon tumeric
½	teaspoon dry mustard
½	cup water
½	cup cider vinegar
1	egg, slightly beaten
	About ½ cup mayonnaise

Combine dry ingredients in a saucepan, and add water, vinegar, and egg. Cook and stir constantly until thickened; cool. When cold, add about ½ cup mayonnaise or amount required to obtain desired consistency. Cover and refrigerate.

CHEF'S NOTE: If making potato salad, pour the dressing on the potato chunks while they are still hot; the flavor permeates.

YIELD: 2 cups

Mrs. George L. Word
(Paige Early)

INTERN'S SALAD DRESSING

Spicy, tangy dressing which doubles as a fresh vegetable dip.

3	tablespoons diced green onions
½	cup mayonnaise
1	clove garlic, crushed
¼	cup minced parsley
1	tablespoon anchovy paste
1	cup sour cream
¼	cup red wine vinegar
1	tablespoon lemon juice
¼	cup bleu cheese, crumbled
¼	teaspoon salt
	Dash freshly ground pepper

Mix together the chopped onions and the mayonnaise. Stir in the garlic and parsley. Mix anchovy paste with the sour cream, and add to the mayonnaise mixture. Thin with vinegar and lemon juice. Add crumbled bleu cheese; beat thoroughly. Add salt and pepper to taste. Best chilled overnight.

YIELD: About 2½ cups

Mrs. Michael W. Craig
(Susan Hockwalt)

ASPARAGUS CHEESE STRATA

Delicious, great consistency.

1½ pounds fresh asparagus
4   slices bread, crusts removed
2   cups shredded sharp cheddar cheese
3   eggs, slightly beaten
2   cups chicken broth
½   teaspoon salt
½   teaspoon celery salt
1/8 teaspoon pepper
1   teaspoon dry minced onion, reconstituted

Clean asparagus well. Cut off 2-inch length from tip ends. Set tips aside. Cut remaining spears into one-inch pieces. Toast bread; cut into one-inch squares. Place toast squares in the bottom of a 9-inch round casserole. Arrange a layer of 1-inch asparagus pieces on top of toast. Sprinkle with all the cheese. In a small bowl, combine all remaining ingredients. Pour over cheese layer. Salt reserved tips to taste. Wrap in a square of aluminum foil; fold edges to seal. Bake uncovered casserole and foil-wrapped asparagus tips in preheated 325° oven for 60 to 75 minutes (until set and tender). Garnish casserole with baked asparagus tips. Serve hot.

YIELD: 10 servings
          3 to 4 servings as main dish

Mrs. L. Keith Wilson
(Aimee Clunet)

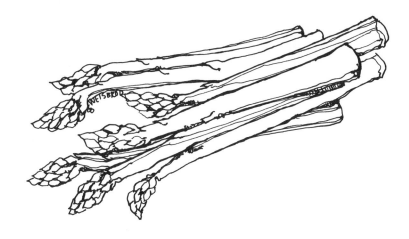

ASPARAGUS PARMESAN

Even non-asparagus lovers often like this!

1½ pounds fresh asparagus, cooked; or canned; or 2, 10-ounce packages frozen asparagus, cooked
1 medium to large onion, chopped
2 cloves garlic, minced
3 tablespoons vegetable oil
1 teaspoon salt
¼ teaspoon tabasco sauce
1 16-ounce can tomatoes
¼ teaspoon thyme
1 8-ounce can tomato sauce
4 ounces mozzarella cheese, thinly sliced
3 tablespoons grated Parmesan cheese

Drain asparagus and arrange in a 7 x 11-inch baking dish. Saute onion and garlic in oil in saucepan until golden. Add salt, tabasco sauce, and tomatoes. Simmer, uncovered, for 10 minutes. Add thyme and tomato sauce, and simmer 20 minutes longer. Pour sauce over asparagus. Place slices of mozzarella cheese over top. Sprinkle with Parmesan cheese. Bake in a preheated 350° oven for 30 minutes.
YIELD: 6 to 8 servings

Mrs. Patrick E. Wilke
(Patricia Settle)

FRESH ASPARAGUS WITH ORANGE HOLLANDAISE SAUCE

This sauce is FANTASTIC!

2 egg yolks
2 tablespoons orange juice
1 teaspoon grated orange peel
Dash of salt and pepper
4 tablespoons butter
¼ cup sour cream
Grated orange peel, for garnish (optional)
1 pound fresh asparagus, steamed and drained

In a saucepan using a wire whisk, combine egg yolks, orange juice, orange peel, salt, and pepper. Cook over low heat. Continue whisking adding one tablespoon of butter at a time until butter is melted and sauce is thickened. Remove from heat; stir in sour cream. Garnish with extra orange peel, if desired. Serve immediately over hot asparagus.
YIELD: 4 servings

Mrs. William Kasch
(Sonnie Kern)

BARBECUED BEANS

This thick sauce is sweet and spicy.

2	pounds bacon, cut strips into thirds
1	large or 2 medium onions, chopped semi-fine
5	pounds canned pork and beans
1	24-ounce bottle ketchup
1	1-pound package brown sugar (2¼ cups), packed
¼	cup prepared mustard
¾	cup worcestershire sauce
2	teaspoons liquid smoke

In a 4 to 6-quart pot, fry bacon until crisp, draining fat when necessary. Add onion, and saute until clear; drain excess fat. Stir in all remaining ingredients. Simmer over low heat for 1 to 2 hours, or until cooked down to consistency desired. Do not cover.
YIELD: 20 to 24 servings

Mrs. Earl F. Pritchard
(Judy Elliott)

ZIPPY BROCCOLI

Dieters delight!
Dill is a pleasant seasoning for this delightfully plain vegetable.

1	pound fresh broccoli
1	tablespoon vegetable oil
¼	teaspoon dry mustard
½	teaspoon salt
1/8	teaspoon pepper
4	tablespoons water
½	teaspoon dill weed

Trim and wash broccoli. Place in a medium-size saucepan. In a small bowl, combine oil, dry mustard, salt, pepper, dill weed, and water. Pour over broccoli. Cover tightly. Cook for 15 minutes over medium heat or until done to taste. Serve hot.

YIELD: 4 servings

Mrs. Lowell Mills
(Susie Taylor)

ELEGANT BROCCOLI CASSEROLE

Water chestnuts make this interesting and tasty.

½	cup chopped onion
½	cup chopped celery
2	tablespoons butter
¾	cup raw rice, cooked and well drained (2 cups cooked rice)
2	10-ounce packages frozen chopped broccoli, thawed and drained
1	6-ounce can water chestnuts, drained and diced
1	10½-ounce can condensed cream of chicken soup, undiluted
½	cup milk
1	cup grated cheddar cheese
	Salt and pepper to taste

Saute onion and celery in 2 tablespoons butter. In a large bowl, mix together onions, celery, and all remaining ingredients. Pour into a buttered 2-quart casserole. Cover and bake in a preheated 350° oven for 35 minutes. Remove cover, and bake for 5 minutes longer.

YIELD: 4 to 6 servings

Mrs. Robert J. Gronek
(Veronica Toth)

BROCCOLI BIANCO

**Especially handy when entertaining.
Prepare ahead and refrigerate until baking time.**

1½ to 2 bunches fresh broccoli, or 3, 10-ounce packages frozen broccoli
1 pint sour cream
1 cup mayonnaise (we prefer Hellman's)
6 tablespoons chopped pimento
3 scallions, chopped (include some green part)
½ cup grated Parmesan cheese

Clean fresh broccoli; cut into thin strips. Steam over medium-high heat about 15 minutes or until tender (or cook frozen broccoli according to package directions). Drain. Place broccoli in single layer in an 8 x 12-inch baking dish. In a small bowl, stir together sour cream and mayonnaise until smooth. Add chopped pimento and scallions; mix well. Spread sour cream mixture over broccoli. Sprinkle Parmesan cheese over top. Refrigerate until baking time. Bake in a preheated 350° oven 20 to 30 minutes or until thoroughly heated. Any leftovers may be reheated.

VARIATION: 1 head fresh cauliflower or 2, 10-ounce packages frozen cauliflower may be substituted for the broccoli.

YIELD: 8 to 10 servings

Mrs. J. Edmund Weinheimer
(Bette Barlett)

BROCCOLI CASSEROLE

Great with a steak and a tossed salad.

3	10-ounce packages broccoli, cooked crisp
8	tablespoons butter, melted
1	cup mayonnaise
1	10¾-ounce can condensed cream of mushroom soup
1¼	cups sharp cheddar cheese, grated
2	tablespoons chopped onion
2	eggs, well beaten
¾	cup cracker crumbs

In a covered pan, cook broccoli in a little boiling water just to thaw; or if fresh, until bright green (still crisp); drain. Place in 1½-quart, buttered casserole; set aside. In a saucepan, melt butter; stir in all remaining ingredients except crumbs. Pour over broccoli. Top with cracker crumbs. Bake uncovered in a preheated 350° oven for 60 minutes. Serve hot.

YIELD: 6 to 8 servings

Mrs. Timothy L. White
(Nancy Wilcox)

DISAPPEARING BRUSSELS SPROUTS

A favorite at parties.

2	10-ounce packages frozen Brussels sprouts
1	cup shredded cheddar cheese
3	hard-boiled eggs, sliced
¼	cup milk
1	10¾-ounce can condensed cream of mushroom soup
½	cup bread crumbs
2	tablespoons butter

Cook Brussels sprouts for 10 minutes; drain. Arrange sprouts in a single layer in the bottom of a 7 x 11-inch casserole. Sprinkle cheese over sprouts. Arrange sliced eggs over cheese. In a small bowl, combine milk and soup; pour over egg slices. Bake in a preheated 350° oven for 15 minutes. In a large skillet, brown bread crumbs in butter. Sprinkle on top of casserole; return to oven, and bake for 10 minutes longer.

YIELD: 6 to 8 servings

Mrs. Ronald Petersen
(Sherry Hess)

CARROT REVEL

Enhanced carrot color and flavor.

1	pound carrots, pared
½	teaspoon salt
1½	tablespoons butter
1½	tablespoons brown sugar
1½	teaspoons grated orange rind
¼	cup slivered almonds, toasted

Cut carrots into 3-inch lengths and cut into fourths lengthwise. Cook in a large, covered pan, using ½ teaspoon salt and a small amount of water, until fork tender. Drain water and remove carrots. Mix butter, brown sugar, and orange rind in the same pan over medium heat until smooth. Add carrots; simmer and stir gently to glaze (about 5 minutes). Garnish with toasted almonds.
YIELD: 4 to 6 servings

Mrs. Robert J. Gronek
(Veronica Toth)

INTENSE CARROTS

**Nothing fancy, but just good, fresh taste.
Paprika intensifies the color.**

1	pound carrots
½	teaspoon salt
1½	tablespoons butter
1	teaspoon paprika
¼	cup water

Pare and slice carrots to please your schedule and eye (I prefer slivered by the food processor.). Combine all ingredients in a saucepan. Cover; steam until carrots are tender, stirring occasionally. Keep heat low so that very little steam escapes. Do not drain when serving.
YIELD: 4 to 6 servings

Mrs. Alan Meckstroth
(Betty Lutz)

"IMAM BAILDI" (BAKED EGGPLANT)

"The Emperor swooned." Ancient tradition in the Middle East holds that when the Imam first tasted this dish, he fainted with ecstasy!

1　medium eggplant
1　teaspoon salt
2　tablespoons olive or corn oil
2　medium onions, very thinly sliced
3　cloves garlic, minced
½　cup finely chopped parsley
1　cup tomato sauce
　　Salt and pepper to taste

Rinse eggplant; cut off stem end. Cut into 8 equal pieces (lengthwise in half, crosswise in half, each piece in half). Sprinkle insides with salt; let stand 2 hours in a colander (This drains excess moisture from eggplant.). Rinse with cold water, and pat dry with paper towels. Brown in oil on all sides in a medium skillet on medium-high heat. Transfer to a 2-quart baking dish; arrange pieces skin side down. In same skillet brown onions in oil on medium heat. Stir in garlic, parsley, tomato sauce, salt and pepper; bring to a boil; remove from heat. Evenly cover eggplant pieces with mixture. Cover and bake in a preheated 350° oven for ½ hour. (May microwave. Time and temperature depend on microwave oven.)

YIELD: 4 to 6 servings

Mrs. P. Stanley Castleman
(Maria Preonas)

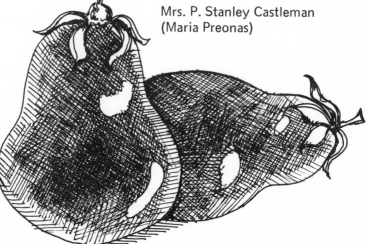

EGGPLANT CASSEROLE

Unusual vegetable dish.

1	eggplant, pared and chopped
1	onion, chopped
1	green pepper, chopped
2	tablespoons butter
1	scant cup bread crumbs (use stale bread rather than canned variety)
½	teaspoon salt
¼	teaspoon black pepper
1	egg, well beaten
3	or 4 tablespoons milk
10	to 12 butter crackers crushed fine (we prefer Ritz)

In a large skillet, combine the eggplant, onion, green pepper, and butter. Cook over a low fire until the vegetables are tender. Remove from heat and stir in the bread crumbs and seasonings. Stir in the egg. Add enough milk to make the mixture moist. Pour into a greased 1-quart casserole. Sprinkle cracker crumbs on top. Bake in a preheated 350° oven for about 20 minutes.

YIELD: 6 to 9 servings

Mrs. David C. Greer
(Barbara Bennett)

GERMAN RED CABBAGE

Best when prepared the day before serving.
This is a family recipe which my husband's mother brought with her when the family came to America from Germany.

1	medium onion, chopped
2	tablespoons bacon grease
1	medium red cabbage, shredded
3	to 4 tart apples, quartered, cored, and peeled
½	cup water
5	whole cloves
5	peppercorns
1	bay leaf
	Salt to taste
	Juice of ½ lemon
2	tablespoons currant or grape jelly

Use a large covered stainless steel or enamel kettle (Do *not* use aluminum.). Saute onion in bacon grease until transparent. Add shredded cabbage (which has been rinsed once), apples, water, cloves, peppercorns, and bay leaf. Salt well. Cover and simmer 1 to 1½ hours, or until apples and cabbage are cooked down. Remove from heat. Add lemon juice and stir in jelly. Refrigerate overnight. About 20 minutes before serving, remove whole cloves, peppercorns, and bay leaf. Heat thoroughly, and serve piping hot.

YIELD: 8 servings

Mrs. Herwig Baumann
(Vickie Overholzer)

GERMAN SAUERKRAUT

This is an old family recipe handed down and added to. Once the sauerkraut is prepared, it may be served with German franks, pork roast, or chops — my husband even puts it on his hamburgers.

1   1-pound pork loin backbone or pork hocks
    Any pork bones left-over (optional)
1   cup water
3   pounds canned or packaged sauerkraut
1   whole onion, peeled
1   13¾-ounce can chicken broth
    White wine — if desired

Brown pork and bones in a small roaster in a preheated 450° oven until dark brown but not burned. Remove bones and pork; place in a 6-quart casserole. Place roaster on top of stove, and add water to soak all the pan drippings off the bottom and sides of roaster (Use wooden spoon to scrape roaster.). Drain sauerkraut, and rinse if necessary under cold water. Pour sauerkraut around pork and bones, and add a peeled onion to the casserole. Pour water with browned bits from roaster over sauerkraut. Add chicken broth, and cover casserole. Bake in a preheated 250° oven all day or for about 6 to 8 hours. Pork may be removed and eaten with the kraut, or it may all be stored together in the refrigerator in a covered container for up to 2 weeks. As liquid disappears and kraut is reheated, water or white wine may be added. Kraut will be dark brown and oh so tasty!
YIELD: 3 pounds

Mrs. J. Edmund Weinheimer
(Bette Barlett)

SWISS CHEESE MUSHROOMS

Dinner party guests always want this recipe!

2	pounds fresh mushrooms
4	tablespoons butter
2	teaspoons lemon juice
2/3	cup sour cream
½	teaspoon salt
¼	teaspoon freshly ground pepper
2	tablespoons flour
¼	cup chopped parsley
1½	cups shredded Swiss cheese

Slice mushrooms through stems into ¼-inch slices. In a large skillet, saute mushrooms in butter. Cover and cook until juices exude and mushrooms are just tender; drain. Sprinkle mushrooms, with lemon juice. In a small bowl, mix together sour cream, salt, pepper, and flour. Stir into mushrooms, and blend well. Place mixture in 9 x 12 x 2-inch casserole. Sprinkle with parsley and shredded Swiss cheese. Cover and refrigerate. When ready to serve, place in preheated 450° oven for 10 minutes or longer at lower temperature to heat thoroughly.
YIELD: 8 to 10 servings

Mrs. Harry G. Ebeling
(Martha Bowman)

KAREN'S "KOOKEY" MUSHROOMS

**Serve as a broth over most any roast or steak.
We like them drained and served as a side dish.**

1	pound mushrooms, sliced and trimmed
1	large cooking onion, diced
2	tablespoons butter or margarine
2	beef bouillon cubes
1	cup boiling water
1	cup dry vermouth

In a large skillet over medium heat, saute mushrooms and onions in butter until onions are transparent. Dissolve 2 bouillon cubes in boiling water. Add bouillon and dry vermouth to mushrooms. Cover and simmer for one hour.
YIELD: 4 to 5 servings

Mrs James F. Crawford
(Karen Folz)

CHAMPION DES CHAMPIGNONS!

This mushroom casserole goes well with all different types of main dishes. Guests will never know the simplicity of the preparation.

1 **pound fresh mushrooms**
½ **cup margarine**
4 **ounces butter crackers, crushed (we prefer Ritz)**
½ **to 1-pint carton half and half or 2% milk**

Clean and stem mushroom caps to fit a 9 x 9-inch baking dish. Chop remaining mushroom caps and stems; set aside. Melt margarine and combine with chopped mushrooms and crushed crackers. Press the mixture into the bottom of the baking dish which has been greased with margarine. Place whole mushroom caps, underside down, on top of the cracker mixture. Refrigerate, covered, until 45 minutes before serving time (This may be made a day ahead.). Forty-five minutes before serving time, pour enough half and half on the casserole so that the liquid just covers the bottom edge of the mushroom caps (about ½ to 1 pint). Cover and bake in a preheated 350° oven for 30 minutes, or until liquid is absorbed. Serve hot!

CHEF'S NOTE: We prefer to use really HUGE mushroom caps.

YIELD: 6 servings

Mrs. Stephen G. England
(Katherine Benham)

PEAS CONTINENTAL

Tasty way to prepare peas.

2 tablespoons margarine
¼ cup minced onion
¼ teaspoon salt
2 10-ounce packages frozen peas, cooked and drained
1 cup sliced canned mushrooms
¼ teaspoon nutmeg
2 tablespoons sherry
1/8 teaspoon dried marjoram
Dash of pepper

Melt margarine in a medium-size skillet. Saute onions until soft and transparent. Stir in all remaining ingredients. Simmer over low heat until thoroughly heated (Do not over cook.). Serve hot.
YIELD: 6 to 8 servings

Mrs. Bruce A. Triplett
(Leslie Conway)

PARTY PEAS

Colorful, tasty, and different.

2 10-ounce packages frozen peas
1 large onion, chopped
8 tablespoons butter or margarine
1 4-ounce jar pimentos, chopped
1 cup water chestnuts, sliced
1 10¾-ounce can condensed cream of mushroom soup
½ to ¾ cup croutons, plain or seasoned

In a saucepan, boil peas just until defrosted (Do not cook.). Drain, and turn into a 1½-quart buttered casserole; set aside. In a large skillet, saute onion in butter until transparent. Add pimento, water chestnuts, and mushroom soup. Mix well; pour over peas. Top with croutons. Bake uncovered in a preheated 350° oven for 30 minutes.
YIELD: 10 servings

Mrs. Bruce A. Triplett
(Leslie Conway)

CRAB-STUFFED POTATOES

Different! Delectable!

4	medium-size Idaho potatoes
1	7-ounce can crabmeat
1/3	cup butter
½	cup milk
1	tablespoon seasoning salt (we prefer Lawry's)
2	tablespoons chopped onion
1	cup grated sharp cheese
1	teaspoon paprika

Bake potatoes in a preheated 400° oven for 1 hour. Cut a slice off the top side of each potato. Scoop out potatoes; save skins. In a mixing bowl, whip potatoes; add crabmeat, butter, milk, seasoning salt, onion, and cheese. Re-stuff potato shells with potato mixture; sprinkle with paprika. Place on a baking pan and return to 400° oven for 15 to 20 minutes, or until hot (These potatoes may also be made ahead and frozen. Thaw and reheat for 20 to 25 minutes.).
YIELD: 4 servings

Mrs. William Kasch
(Sonnie Kern)

GOLDEN POTATO CASSEROLE

Cheese and sour cream combine to make an especially good flavor. Serve with cold ham.

6	medium-size white potatoes
2	cups shredded cheddar cheese (8 ounces)
¼	cup butter
2	cups dairy sour cream (room temperature)
1/3	cup chopped green onions
1	teaspoon salt
¼	teaspoon white pepper
2	tablespoons butter

Cook potatoes in skins; cool, peel, and coarsely shred. In a saucepan, combine cheddar cheese and ¼ cup butter over low heat, stirring occasionally until almost melted. Remove from heat; blend in sour cream, onions, salt, and pepper. Add shredded potatoes; stir gently and turn into a buttered 2-quart casserole. Dot with 2 tablespoons of butter; bake in preheated 350° oven for 25 minutes or until heated through.
YIELD: 8 servings

Mrs. Stephen Cagle
(Pam Shough)

MUSHROOM POTATOES

Easy to prepare; complements many main dishes.

3   cups diced raw white
    potatoes
4   tablespoons butter
    (use this for buttering
    dish — will be quite
    thick with butter)
¾   cup milk
1   10¾-ounce can con-
    densed cream of
    mushroom soup
1   4-ounce can sliced
    mushrooms
1   tablespoon chopped
    chives
1   teaspoon chopped
    parsley
    Salt and pepper, to
    taste

Arrange potatoes in an 8 x 8-inch baking dish which has been greased with 4 tablespoons of butter. In a small bowl, combine all remaining ingredients. Pour mixture over potatoes. Bake in a preheated 250° to 325° oven for about 1 hour, or until potatoes are tender.
YIELD: 6 to 8 servings

Mrs. Patrick E. Wilke
(Patricia Settle)

POTATOES AU GRATIN

**The best potato dish I have ever tasted —
and better yet, the easiest to prepare!
The rich cheesy taste is great for a buffet (may be prepared ahead).**

1½ pounds frozen hash
    brown potatoes
½   pint half and half, or
    milk
¼   pound butter
½   pound American
    processed cheese
    spread (we prefer
    Velveeta)
4   ounces sharp cheddar
    cheese, grated

Arrange frozen hash brown potatoes in a 9 x 9-inch baking dish. Melt all remaining ingredients in a saucepan; pour over potatoes; stir gently to mix. Cover and refrigerate for one hour or longer. Bake uncovered in preheated 350° oven for one hour.
CHEF'S NOTE: May be frozen after baking.
YIELD: 9 to 12 servings

Mrs. James Garrison
(Lesli Janacshek)

DELMONICO POTATOES

A nice potato casserole which is prepared the day before
and cooked the last hour.

8	or 9 red potatoes
8	ounces sharp cheese, grated
1	teaspoon dry mustard
1½	teaspoons salt
½	pint whipping cream, or half and half
1	cup milk
	Paprika

Boil potatoes until cooked but not too tender. Peel when cool enough to handle. Coarsely grate into a buttered 9 x 12-inch casserole. Heat the remaining ingredients over medium heat until the cheese melts; pour over the potatoes. Sprinkle with paprika. Cover and refrigerate for 24 hours. Bake in a preheated 325° oven for 1 hour.
YIELD: 8 to 10 servings

Mrs. Glenn A. Mosier
(Katherine Koenig)

POTATO PUFFS

A good use for left-over mashed potatoes.
Crunchy on the outside, light on the inside.
Use as you would corn fritters — may be served with syrup.

½	cup sifted flour
1½	teaspoons baking powder
¼	teaspoon salt
	Dash of white pepper
1	cup mashed potatoes
2	eggs, well beaten

Sift together flour, baking powder, salt and pepper; set aside. In a small mixing bowl, combine potatoes and eggs; add flour mixture. Drop by teaspoonfuls into hot 375° deep fat and fry for 3 to 4 minutes or until golden brown.
YIELD: 4 servings

Mrs. Harry R. Wise
(Mary Jane Bolender)

SPINACH AND ARTICHOKES

Artichokes and Parmesan cheese give the spinach a different and tasty flavor.

½ cup chopped onion
½ cup butter (not margarine)
2 10-ounce packages frozen chopped spinach, cooked and drained
1 16-ounce can artichoke hearts, drained and diced
1 pint sour cream
½ cup grated Parmesan cheese
Salt to taste
Grated Parmesan cheese for topping

In a small skillet, saute onions in butter. In a 1½-quart casserole, mix together spinach, artichokes, sour cream, ½ cup Parmesan cheese, and salt to taste. Top with additional Parmesan cheese. Bake in a preheated 350° oven for 20 to 30 minutes.
YIELD: 8 servings

Mrs. Herwig Baumann
(Vickie Overholzer)

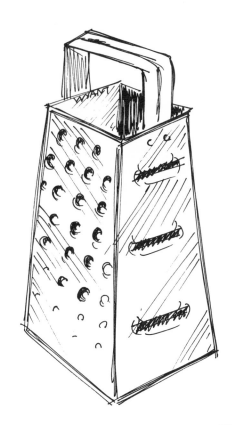

LAYERED SPINACH

Easily assembled; great with ham.

3	tablespoons margarine
2	tablespoons flour
1	teaspoon salt
½	teaspoon paprika
1/8	teaspoon pepper
1	cup milk
2	10-ounce packages frozen chopped spinach, cooked and drained
1	4-ounce package medium noodles, cooked and drained
½	pound Swiss cheese, grated

In a 10-inch skillet, melt margarine over low heat. Stir in flour salt, paprika, and pepper; cook and stir for about 3 minutes. Slowly whisk in milk. Cook and whisk until smooth and thickened; stir in spinach. Layer all noodles in the bottom of a buttered 9 x 13-inch baking dish. Add spinach mixture; top with Swiss cheese. Bake uncovered in a preheated 350° oven for about 20 to 30 minutes. VARIATION: Substitute a 10¾-ounce can cream of celery soup for the first 6 ingredients. Add salt and paprika. YIELD: 6 to 8 servings

Mrs. R. James Heikes
(Bonnie Bright)

YELLOW SQUASH CASSEROLE

Can be made ahead.

2	cups cooked yellow squash
2	large carrots, grated
½	bell pepper, grated (optional)
1	medium onion, chopped
½	cup sour cream
1	10¾-ounce can cream of chicken soup
6	tablespoons butter, melted
1	8-ounce package herb seasoned stuffing
2	tablespoons butter for dotting

In a medium-size bowl, combine the first six ingredients; set aside. Combine melted butter and herb stuffing crumbs. Grease a 2-quart casserole, and dust with crumbs; fill casserole (Alternate layers of squash mixture and crumbs, ending with crumbs.). Dot with 2 tablespoons butter. Bake in preheated 350° oven for 30 to 40 minutes. YIELD: 6 to 8 servings

Mrs. Herwig Baumann
(Vickie Overholzer)

106

SQUASH CASSEROLE

The flavor of the squash comes through!

8	small yellow summer squash (3 cups cooked)
1	medium onion, chopped
½	teaspoon salt
¼	cup sour cream
¼	teaspoon paprika
2	tablespoons butter
1	heaping tablespoon grated cheddar cheese
1/8	teaspoon pepper
1	teaspoon salt
1	teaspoon chives
1	egg yolk, beaten
½	cup herb seasoned stuffing (we prefer Pepperidge Farm)
½	cup grated cheddar cheese
1	tablespoon butter

Remove stem and blossom ends, and slice squash into 1½-inch pieces. Place in large pan. Add onions; add salt and water to cover. Boil until tender (about 15 minutes). Drain well. In a sauce pan combine sour cream, paprika, butter, 1 tablespoon cheese, pepper, salt, and chives. Cook over low heat until cheese melts. Remove from heat; stir in egg yolk. Combine squash and sauce in a 2-quart baking dish. Mix well. Sprinkle the top with seasoned crumbs and cheese. Dot with butter. Bake in preheated 375° oven for 10 minutes or until cheese melts. CHEF'S NOTE: May be frozen before baking.
YIELD: 6 to 8 servings

Mrs. Patrick E. Wilke
(Patricia Settle)

TOMATO PUDDING

Very rich — the best we have ever tasted.

8	ounces tomato sauce
1/3	cup butter
1	cup brown sugar, packed
2	cups cubed bread, (about 4 slices)
	Dash of salt

In a large saucepan, combine tomato sauce, butter, and brown sugar. Bring to a boil; reduce heat, and simmer for 10 minutes, strirring frequently. Add bread and salt; mix well. Turn into a 1-quart greased casserole. Bake uncovered in a preheated 350° oven for 30 minutes.
YIELD: 4 to 6 servings

Mrs. Bruce A. Triplett
(Leslie Conway)

TOMATO SOUFFLE

Very pretty souffle with a mild tomato flavor.

3   large ripe tomatoes
     (1½ pounds)
4   tablespoons butter
1   chicken bouillon cube
½   tablespoon tomato
     paste
     Dash sugar
4   tablespoons flour
1   cup milk
     Salt and cayenne
6   egg yolks
8   egg whites

Peel and seed tomatoes and chop very fine. Melt butter in a skillet and add bouillon cube and tomatoes. Cook over medium-low heat until juices are evaporated. Stir in tomato paste and sugar. Remove from heat. Stir in flour and then milk. Return to heat and cook over medium heat, stirring, until the mixture starts to thicken. Season with salt and cayenne to taste. Remove from heat again and beat in the egg yolks, one at a time. In another bowl, beat the egg whites until they are stiff but not dry. In a separate bowl, carefully fold egg whites into tomato mixture. Pour into a buttered 2-quart souffle dish and bake in a preheated 375° oven for 17 to 20 minutes, or until browned on top and well risen. Serve immediately. YIELD: 8 servings

Mrs. Gene Hughes
(Julie Loeffel)

TOMATO CASSEROLE

Outstanding vegetable dish!

1	medium onion, chopped
2	tablespoons butter
4	medium, ripe tomatoes, sliced
4	ounces sharp processed American cheese, shredded (1 cup)
1	cup soft bread crumbs
1	cup dairy sour cream
2	eggs, well beaten
½	teaspoon salt

Saute onions in butter until soft. Place half of the tomatoes in a 10 x 6 x 1½-inch baking dish. Top with half of each of the onions, cheese, and bread crumbs. Repeat layers. Mix remaining ingredients. Pour over the top of the tomato mixture. Bake, covered, in a preheated 350° oven for 30 minutes. Uncover and bake for 10 additional minutes.
YIELD: 6 servings

Mrs. Lowell Mills
(Susie Taylor)

MICROWAVE TOMATOES

This is an excellent, colorful accompaniment for beef or lamb — especially if the meat has been cooked on a grill.

4	large ripe tomatoes, unpeeled
¾	cup mayonnaise (we prefer Hellman's)
¼	to ½ teaspoon curry powder
½	6-ounce package original ranch salad dressing mix (we prefer Hidden Valley Ranch)

Halve the tomatoes and arrange in a circle, cut-side up, in an 8½ x 11-inch casserole or a 9-inch pie plate. Mix remaining ingredients and spread over the top of the tomatoes. Fast cook for 3 to 5 minutes or according to firmness desired. Turn casserole around after half of the cooking time has elapsed. Do not cover tomatoes. Allow casserole to remain in oven 1 minute after cooking before you serve.
VARIATION: Conventional oven: bake in a preheated 375° oven for 15 minutes. Broil for about 2 minutes before serving.
YIELD: 6 to 8 servings

Mrs. Richard C. Shelton
(Louise Wittenmyer)

VEGETABLES

TORRID TOMATOES

Great with chicken.

1 medium onion, chopped
1 green pepper, chopped
2 tablespoons butter
1 28-ounce can whole tomatoes, undrained
2 teaspoons brown sugar
Few grinds of black pepper
1 cup dry stuffing cubes (we prefer Pepperidge Farm)
About 1 cup grated cheddar cheese

In a large saucepan, saute onion and green pepper in butter. Cut tomatoes into fourths; add to onion mixture. Add all remaining tomato juice, brown sugar, black pepper, and stuffing cubes. Pour into a buttered 1½ to 2-quart casserole, and top lavishly with grated cheese. Bake uncovered in a preheated 350° oven until bubbly (about 30 minutes). Serve hot.
YIELD: 6 servings

Mrs. Alan Meckstroth
(Betty Lutz)

ZUCCHINI-CHEESE BAKE

Flavorful zucchini; good make-ahead recipe.

2 pounds zucchini, diced, not peeled (about 8 small)
½ cup chopped parsley
1 pound Monterey Jack cheese, cubed
1 4-ounce can chopped green chilies, diced
1 teaspoon salt
4 eggs, slightly beaten
2 teaspoons baking powder
½ cup milk
About ½ cup herb-seasoned bread crumbs
2 tablespoons butter

Place cubed squash in a 3-quart saucepan with boiling water to cover. Cook just until tender but crisp; drain. Add parsley, cheese, chilies, and salt; stir to combine. Cover and refrigerate until about ½ hour before serving time, or proceed immediately. In a small bowl, mix together eggs, baking powder, and milk. Stir into squash mixture. Butter bottom of a 10 x 10-inch casserole dish. Sprinkle with ¼ cup bread crumbs. Pour squash mixture into casserole. Sprinkle with remaining ¼ cup bread crumbs. Dot with butter. Bake in a preheated 325° oven for about 30 minutes or until browned and bubbly. Serve hot.
YIELD: 6 to 8 servings

Mrs. Timothy L. White
(Nancy Wilcox)

110

ZUCCHINI ROSSINI

Great for all the garden tomatoes and zucchini.

3	to 4 zucchini
	Garlic salt
	Pepper
	Oregano
2	to 3 large tomatoes, sliced
8	slices American cheese
2	medium onions
4	to 5 strips of bacon

Quarter zucchini lengthwise and line bottom of 9 x 13-inch buttered baking dish. Season with garlic salt, pepper, and oregano. Make a layer of the sliced tomatoes. Again sprinkle generously with garlic salt, pepper, and oregano. Make a layer of the cheese slices. Slice onions thin and separate into rings; place on top of cheese. Top casserole with the bacon strips. Bake in preheated 350° oven for 45 minutes. Cut into squares to serve.
YIELD: 6 to 8 servings

Mrs. Patrick E. Wilke
(Patricia Settle)

SPINACH-STUFFED ZUCCHINI

May be made a day ahead or same day.

3	zucchini (about 1 to 1½-pounds)
1	10-ounce package frozen chopped spinach, cooked and drained
2	tablespoons flour
½	cup milk
	Salt to taste
1/3	cup shredded natural cheddar cheese
4	slices bacon, crisped and crumbled

Trim ends of zucchini; cook whole in boiling water for 10 to 12 minutes. Drain thoroughly; cool. Halve lengthwise; scoop out centers; chop centers. Add chopped zucchini to spinach. In saucepan, blend flour and milk; add spinach mixture; cook, stirring until thickened. Place zucchini halves in lightly-buttered 9 x 12-inch shallow baking dish; sprinkle cavities with salt. Spoon spinach mixture into zucchini shells. Top with cheese and bacon. Bake in a preheated 350° oven for about 15 to 20 minutes.
YIELD: 4 to 6 servings.

Mrs. R. James Heikes
(Bonnie Bright)

STIR-FRY TACO ZUCCHINI

Unusual and good.

¼	cup oil
4	cups thinly sliced zucchini
1	cup shredded carrots
½	cup chopped onion
½	teaspoon garlic salt
¼	teaspoon basil
	Salt and pepper to taste
2	tomatoes, peeled and wedged, or 1-pint tomatoes, drained
1/3	cup mild taco sauce
2	teaspoons prepared mustard

Heat oil in a 10-inch skillet. Add zucchini, carrots, onion, garlic salt, basil, salt, and pepper. Stir-fry over medium-high heat for about 5 minutes, or until vegetables are tender. Add tomatoes, taco sauce, and mustard. Continue cooking until heated through.

YIELD: 4 to 6 servings

Mrs. Alan R. Merrill
(Lynn Wagner)

CORN CHOWDER

Great on a cold winter evening.
A nice change from chili — very filling!

2 cups chopped all-purpose potatoes
½ cup chopped carrots
¼ cup chopped celery
¼ cup chopped onion
Water to cover
2 cups milk
2 tablespoons butter, melted
¼ cup flour
1 17-ounce can of cream style corn
½ cup grated Parmesan cheese
Salt and pepper to taste

In a large saucepan, combine potatoes, carrots, celery, and onion; add water to cover vegetables. Bring to a boil, and cook covered over medium heat until vegetables are tender. Do not over cook. Drain vegetables, and add butter. In a jar with a tight-fitting lid, shake milk and flour to mix well. Stir into vegetables, and cook until the sauce is very thick (You may have to add 1 to 2 tablespoons more flour.). Add corn and Parmesan cheese; mix thoroughly. Serve immediately.
YIELD: 4 to 6 servings

Mrs. James R. O'Donnell
(Marie Stratemeyer)

VEGETABLE-CHEESE CHOWDER

Economical soup with substance.

1 cup chopped potatoes
½ cup chopped carrots
½ cup chopped celery
½ cup chopped onion
½ cup chopped green pepper
4 tablespoons butter
3 cups chicken broth
Salt and pepper to taste
2 cups milk
½ cup flour
3 cups shredded cheddar cheese
1 tablespoon minced parsley

In a large soup kettle, saute potatoes, carrots, celery, onion, and green pepper in butter. Stir in chicken broth; add pepper. Simmer uncovered for about 30 minutes. Blend flour and milk; stir into broth. Stir in cheese and parsley. Cook, stirring frequently, until thick and bubbly. Correct seasoning; serve hot.
VARIATIONS: Try adding left-over chopped ham. Small whole shrimp also make a tasty addition.
YIELD: 8 servings

Mrs. David R. Bart
(Mary Jo Thurman)

BLENDER AVGOLEMONO SOUP

This is the ancient Greek classic chicken and rice soup made easy!

3 to 4 pound stewing hen
1 medium onion, sliced thinly
½ cup chopped celery
½ cup chopped carrot
Salt and pepper to taste
2 quarts water
¾ cup raw rice
4 eggs at room temperature
Juice of 1 to 2 lemons (about 3 tablespoons), or to taste

In a Dutch oven, cover chicken, onion, celery, carrots, salt, and pepper with water. Bring to a boil; cover and simmer for about 1½ hours, or until chicken is tender. Remove the chicken from the broth; cut into serving pieces; set aside. Strain the broth; correct seasoning if necessary. Return to heat; bring to a boil; stir in rice. Cover and simmer for about 30 minutes, or until rice is very tender. In a blender, mix together eggs and lemon juice. Add a stream of hot broth very slowly into the egg mixture with the blender still on. Continue adding more broth into the "on" blender until it is full. Turn off the blender, and pour avgolemono mixture into the rest of the soup (do not let soup separate) stirring constantly. Serve immediately with the chicken. VARIATION: Chicken may be boned and shredded (after cooking), and added to soup along with the rice. YIELD: 6 servings

Mrs. P. Stanley Castleman
(Maria Preonas)

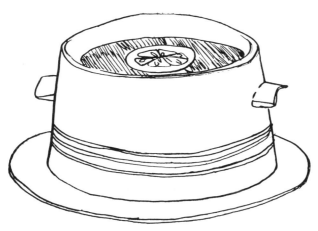

GAZPACHO

Prepare 24 hours ahead. Great for dieters!

6   tomatoes
1   garlic clove
1   4-ounce can pimento
3   envelopes chicken
       broth (we prefer
       Weight Watchers')
¼   cup red wine vinegar
1   tablespoon lemon juice
1   teaspoon lemon
       pepper, or to taste
1   large onion, minced
2   medium cucumbers,
       peeled and minced
1   green pepper, minced
1½   cups croutons (we
       prefer Pepperidge
       Farm, seasoned)
2   tablespoons butter,
       melted
       Dash of garlic

In a blender or food processor, combine tomatoes, garlic, pimento, dry chicken broth, vinegar, lemon juice, and lemon pepper; blend until smooth. Add onion, cucumber, and green pepper. Cover and refrigerate overnight. Combine croutons with butter and garlic salt; spread croutons on a cookie sheet. Dry in a preheated 200° oven for 30 minutes or until crispy. Serve chilled gazpacho in bowls, and pass croutons.
YIELD: 4 servings

Mrs. Allan Johnston, Jr.
(Sandra Wood)

GAZPACHO SOUP

Simple, good, fresh taste.

1 16-ounce can tomatoes diced
Pinch of garlic powder
½ handful chopped parlsey
2½ tablespoons red wine vinegar
3½ tablespoons salad oil
½ teaspoon paprika
1½ cups beef broth
1 large onion, minced
1 46-ounce can tomato juice
2½ ounces sliced green olives
2 green peppers, chopped
2 cucumbers, chopped
1 cup seasoned croutons

In a 1-gallon plastic container, mix all ingredients except green peppers, cucumbers, and croutons. Cover and refrigerate until well chilled. Serve cold; garnish with chopped green peppers, chopped cucumbers, and croutons. Keeps well for 2 weeks.
YIELD: 1 gallon

Mrs. Donald J. May
(Brenda Amburgey)

FRENCH ONION SOUP

This recipe was obtained about 9 years ago from a chef at a French restaurant in Massachusetts. He said the secret was in the choice of Swiss cheese. Select imported Swiss cheese, not our American varieties.

6	slices French bread, diced
6	onions, thinly sliced
6	tablespoons butter
1	teaspoon sugar
1	teaspoon salt
	Dash of nutmeg
7	cups beef bouillon (we prefer College Inn)
¼	cup sherry
½	pound imported Swiss cheese, grated
½	pound grated Parmesan cheese

Place diced French bread on a cookie sheet. Bake in a preheated 250° oven for 25 minutes. Remove, and set aside. In a large skillet, saute onions in butter until limp. Stir in sugar, salt, and nutmeg. Simmer over low heat. Warm the bouillon; add to onions, and bring to a boil. Cook down slightly. Reduce heat, and simmer 10 minutes. Stir in sherry. Ladle soup into 6 to 8 individual size oven-proof casseroles. Top with toasted bread cubes. Sprinkle with Swiss and Parmesan cheeses. Cook in a preheated 300° oven for 10 minutes or until bubbly. YIELD: 6 to 8 servings

Mrs. William R. Thompson
(Sally Decker)

117

BEAN SOUP

The flavor secret is the tomato soup.

1	pound navy beans, dried
1½	quarts water
1	cottage ham, any size (depending on how meaty you like your soup)
3	quarts water
1½	teaspoons salt or seasoned salt
	Pepper to taste
4	to 5 carrots thinly sliced
2	cups dices celery
1	medium onion, chopped
1	10¾-ounce can condensed tomato soup

Wash and sort beans. Add 1½ quarts water and bring to a boil. Simmer 2 minutes. Remove from heat; cover, and let stand 1 hour; drain. Remove covering from ham and cut in half. In a large Dutch oven, combine beans, 3 quarts water, ham, and seasonings. Cover and simmer on stove top for 4 hours. Remove ham; cool, and cut into bite-size pieces. Add vegetables to soup, and continue cooking over medium heat for 30 minutes. Add ham and tomato soup. Cook over medium heat for 30 minutes.
YIELD: About 3 quarts

Mrs. D. Bruce Todd
(Beverly Lynn Wyatt)

CREAMY CHEESE-POTATO SOUP

Outstanding!

4	10¾-ounce cans chicken broth (we prefer College Inn)
1	24-ounce package frozen O'Brien potatoes (we prefer Ore-Ida)
1	cup half and half, or milk
1	cup white wine
2	cups Parmesan cheese
1	teaspoon garlic salt, or to taste
¾	teaspoon pepper, or to taste
1	to 1½ cups grated Swiss chese
	Grated Parmesan cheese for garnish

In a large soup kettle, boil chicken broth and frozen potatoes for 5 minutes. Simmer on medium heat for 25 minutes or until thickened. Remove from heat, and pour into a blender ½ at a time; blend on high speed. Return to cooking pot. Stir in half and half, wine, and 2 cups Parmesan cheese; mix well with spoon. Taste and correct seasoning. At serving time, heat; do not boil. Ladle hot soup over grated Swiss cheese in bottom of cups or bowls. Garnish with more sprinkles of Parmesan cheese.
YIELD: 8 servings

Mrs. David S. McLaughlin
(Barbara Becker)

118

POPCORN POTATO SOUP

**Hearty, inexpensive, and easy. Good Sunday night dinner —
the kids enjoy it.**

6 large white Idaho
   potatoes, peeled and
   diced
1 tablespoon onion
   flakes
1 teaspoon salt
   Dash of white pepper
1/8 teaspoon garlic powder
1/8 teaspoon celery salt
   Water to cover, about
   1 quart
½ cup half-and-half
1 16-ounce can chicken
   broth (we prefer
   College Inn)
¼ to 1 cup diced ham,
   optional
½ cup popcorn kernels
   Salt to taste

Place potatoes, onion flakes, salt, white pepper, garlic powder, and celery salt in 3-quart pan. Add water to cover (about 1 quart). Boil until potatoes are tender (about 20 to 30 minutes); do not drain. Cool slightly. Pour about 3 cups of the potatoes and hot liquid into a blender, and whirl until smooth. Return to pan. Add half and half, chicken broth, and diced ham. Correct seasoning. Pop popcorn; season with salt. Serve soup hot with side bowls of popcorn which is to be sprinkled a few at a time into the soup as it is eaten.

CHEF'S NOTE: Use additional chicken broth if a thinner soup is preferred.

YIELD: 6 servings

Mrs. Robert L. Deddens
(Ruth Carey)

CRAB AND CHEESE SOUP

Sinfully rich!

2	tablespoons butter
2	tablespoons flour
1	cup chicken broth
8	ounces cream cheese, diced
8	ounces American cheese, sliced or diced
¼	cup sherry
1	tablespoon diced onion
1	6-ounce can crabmeat
2	to 3 drops tabasco sauce
3	cups milk

Melt butter over medium heat in soup pot. Blend in flour; cook for one minute. Add broth; cook and stir until thickened. Add cheeses to hot broth, and heat until melted. Stir in milk and heat. Add remaining ingredients, and heat to serving temperature.

CHEF'S NOTE: Crabmeat may be omitted for a delicious cheese soup.

YIELD: 6 to 8 servings

Mrs. James W. Clark
(Patricia Jones)

HARVEST BISQUE

A rich and flavorful soup. Peanut butter is the secret ingredient!

2½	pounds butternut squash (about 4 cups cooked)
1	medium onion, chopped
1	tablespoon butter
½	teaspoon curry powder
¼	teaspoon nutmeg
1	teaspoon worcestershire sauce
1	tablespoon peanut butter (not chunky)
1	quart chicken broth
½	cup cream or undiluted evaporated milk
	Salt to taste
	Red pepper to taste

Prepare squash by washing, cutting in half lengthwise, removing seeds, and placing cut side down in a flat baking dish with about ½-inch salted water. Bake in a preheated 400° oven until soft (about 40 minutes); cool slightly. Saute onion in butter until limp. Spoon cooked squash from skin, and place in blender with all ingredients except cream. Add only enough chicken broth to fill blender. Blend until smooth; turn into soup pot; add remaining ingredients. Taste for possible addition of salt and pepper. Heat to serve.

YIELD: 6 to 8 servings

Mrs. Alan Meckstroth
(Betty Lutz)

CREAM OF ZUCCHINI SOUP

Great way to use bountiful garden zucchini.

1	pound zucchini, sliced (about 4 cups)
½	cup water
½	teaspoon salt
½	teaspoon sugar
3	tablespoons chopped onion
1	cup fresh mushrooms, sliced
2	tablespoons butter or margarine
2	tablespoons flour
½	teaspoon salt
	Dash pepper
2	cups milk
	Grated Parmesan cheese, optional
	Fresh parsley, chopped, optional

In a large saucepan, combine zucchini, water, ½ teaspoon salt, and sugar. Bring to boil; reduce heat and simmer about 15 minutes, or until zucchini is tender. Puree cooked zucchini in food processor or blender; set aside. In a large skillet, saute onion and mushrooms in butter until tender. Blend in flour, ½ teaspoon salt, and pepper. Stir in milk and pureed zucchini. Cook and stir until mixture thickens and boils. Continue to stir and simmer for a few minutes. Ladle soup into oven-proof serving bowls. Top with Parmesan cheese and parsley. Broil briefly.
YIELD: 4 servings

Mrs. William Kasch
(Sonnie Kern)

CHILI

Tasty, rich flavor.

1	large onion, chopped
2	tablespoons vegetable oil
1	pound ground chuck
1	16-ounce can tomatoes
1	6-ounce can tomato paste
2	teaspoons chili powder
1	cup beer
1	teaspoon salt
2	16-ounce cans kidney beans, drained

In a large pot, saute onion in oil until transparent. Stir in ground beef, and brown over medium heat. Add tomatoes, tomato paste, chili powder, beer, and salt. Cook over medium-low heat for 15 minutes, stirring occasionally. Add beans, and cook 20 minutes longer.
VARIATION: Bean and meat amounts may be adjusted to suit your own taste.
YIELD: 4 servings

Mrs. Thomas Shulman
(Ellie Arnovitz)

CHICKEN VEGETABLE SOUP

Hearty and nutritious. Especially good with garden-fresh vegetables.

1	2½ to 3-pound whole chicken
2	carrots
2	stalks celery
1	bay leaf
½	teaspoon sage
1	onion, chopped
	Salt and pepper to taste
2	cups cooked wild rice
½	cup each of four vegetables, your choice: broccoli, zucchini, carrots, cauliflower, celery, lima beans, peas, corn, green beans, or onions

Place chicken in a large soup kettle; cover with cold water. Add carrots, celery, bay leaf, sage, onion, salt, and pepper. Cover and simmer over low heat until chicken is tender (about 1 to 1½ hours). Remove chicken from kettle; cool. Continue simmering broth while cutting chicken meat from bones. Discard skin and other tough meat. Reserve cut-up chicken meat. Return bones to kettle, and continue to simmer for 1½ to 2 hours longer for a total of 3 hours. Remove from heat, strain broth through a wire strainer to remove carrot, celery, bones, bay leaf, etc. Cool broth; cover and refrigerate overnight. Skim fat from top; return to heat. Taste broth; if the broth is not rich enough, add a chicken bouillon cube or continue to simmer uncovered over low heat until broth cooks down. When broth is finished, add cut-up chicken meat, rice, and ½ cup of each of 4 vegetables. Cook until vegetables are tender (about 15 to 30 minutes depending whether you use fresh, canned, or frozen). Taste; correct seasoning. Serve hot.

VARIATION: More vegetables may be added to make the soup really chunky.

YIELD: 4 to 6 servings

Miss Jane Deuser

VEGETABLE-BEEF SOUP

My grandmother's recipe; our family favorite.
Makes lots — and it's even better reheated.

2   to 3-pounds chuck
    roast, well trimmed
3   onions, chopped
4   white potatoes, diced
4   carrots, sliced
½   head cabbage, shredded
1   14 to 16-ounce can of
    peas
1   14 to 16-ounce can
    of green beans
1   14 to 16-ounce can of
    lima beans
1   14 to 16-ounce can of
    navy beans
1   14 to 16-ounce can of
    corn
1   quart tomatoes,
    buzzed in blender
1   6-ounce can tomato
    paste
1   46-ounce can tomato
    juice
2   teaspoons salt
¼   teaspoon pepper
1   tablespoon chili
    powder
¼   pound butter

Place meat in a large kettle. Cover with water, and boil about 2 hours, or until tender. Shred meat; return to broth, and add onions, potatoes, carrots, and cabbage. Cook for 1½ to 2 hours. Add all remaining ingredients (canned liquid too) except butter, and simmer for 2 hours. Float butter on top just before serving.
YIELD: 2 gallons

Mrs. Frank Holloway
(Suzie Headley)

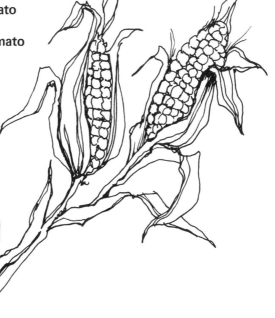

MARGI'S COMPANY STEW

Great aroma; smooth taste.

2   pounds stewing beef, chuck or round steak, cut in bite-size pieces

4   medium onions, cut in chunks

4   to 5 stalks of celery, chopped

5   carrots, cut in chunks

2   8-ounce cans water chestnuts, drained and sliced

1   pound fresh mushrooms, sliced

1   16-ounce can green beans (may substitute fresh)

1   22-ounce can tomatoes

1   cup Burgundy wine

2   teaspoons salt

2   tablespoons brown sugar

5   tablespoons tapioca

Combine all ingredients in a roaster pan with a tight-fitting lid. Bake in a preheated 325° oven for 4 to 5 hours. DO NOT STIR!
YIELD: 6 servings

Mrs. William Kasch
(Sonnie Kern)

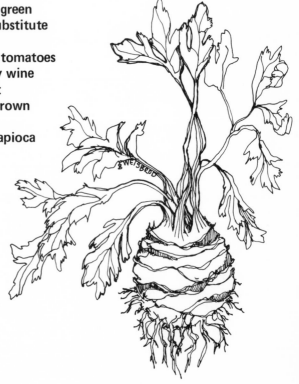

R. BOONE'S STEW

**Good family fare, yet suitable for any occasion.
Sure to be a real man-pleaser!**

2	cloves garlic or equivalent amount of garlic powder (about ¼ teaspoon)
1/3	cup vegetable oil
2	pounds lean beef, cut in 1-inch cubes
½	pound lean lamb, cut in 1-inch cubes
½	pound lean veal, cut in 1-inch cubes
2	large onions, sliced
¼	teaspoon thyme
½	teaspoon oregano
1	tablespoon salt
¼	cup chopped parsley
1	tablespoon butter
¾	cup dry red wine
1½	cups water
4	tomatoes, quartered
8	to 10 small onions, whole
4	to 5 carrots, sliced
¾	pound fresh button mushrooms
1	cup dry red wine Freshly ground pepper, to taste
¾	cup wild rice, uncooked
1	10-ounce package frozen peas

Rub a large soup kettle with 2 cut cloves of garlic. Add oil, and heat until hot. Add all meat cubes and sliced onions. Brown on all sides over medium-high heat. Stir in thyme, oregano, salt, parsley, butter, ¾ cup red wine, and water. Cover and simmer for 1½ hours. Add tomatoes, small whole onions, carrots, mushrooms, 1 cup red wine, and freshly ground pepper. Cover and simmer for 15 minutes. Stir in wild rice. Cover and cook over medium-low heat for 30 minutes. Uncover; add peas, and cook for 10 minutes, or until peas are done. Taste; correct seasoning. Serve hot.

YIELD: 6 to 8 servings

Mrs. Frederick Young
(Joyce Canney)

FRENCH BEEF STEW

**This is one of our family's favorites. Great for a busy day —
no last minute preparation needed.**

3 beef bouillon cubes
2 cups boiling water
2 pounds beef, cut into
   1-inch cubes
2 potatoes, cut into
   1-inch cubes
4 carrots, cut into 4-inch
   strips
1 4-ounce jar sliced
   mushrooms, drained
2 onions, chopped
1 slice bread, crumbled
2 tablespoons tapioca,
   quick-cooking
   Salt and pepper to
   taste

Dissolve bouillon cubes in 2 cups boiling water. Place beef, potatoes, carrots, mushrooms, and onions in a 9 x 13 x 2-inch casserole. Sprinkle with crumbled bread and tapioca; season with salt and pepper to taste. Pour bouillon over all. Cover dish tightly with foil. Bake in a preheated 300° oven for 4 hours. Check several times to be certain liquid has not evaporated; add water if necessary.
YIELD: 5 to 6 servings

Mrs. Roy L. Hohman
(Judy Hoeltke)

126

MA HECK'S LASAGNE

Graciously served by Phyllis Heck at a Junior League December evening membership meeting and greatly enjoyed by all. Accompany with Mrs. Heck's "Hunt Brunch Mixed Green Salad" (see index), French bread, and wine.

2	tablespoons olive oil
1	pound ground chuck
2	cloves garlic, minced
1	envelope dry onion soup mix
1½	cups water
1	12-ounce can tomato paste
1	29-ounce can tomato sauce
½	teaspoon salt
½	teaspoon pepper
½	teaspoon sugar
16	ounces lasagne noodles
15	ounces ricotta cheese, or cottage cheese
8	ounces mozzarella cheese, shredded
1	cup grated Parmesan cheese
½	teaspoon oregano
1	teaspoon paprika

In a large skillet, heat olive oil until hot. Brown ground chuck and cloves. Stir in onion soup mix, water, tomato paste, tomato sauce, salt, pepper, and sugar. Simmer for ½ hour over medium-low heat. Cook lasagne noodles according to package directions. Drain; cover with cold water. In a 9 x 12-inch baking dish, assemble lasagne as follows: layer of ¼ of meat sauce, layer of ½ of noodles to cover meat sauce, layer of ½ of mozzarella cheese and ½ of cottage cheese, layer of ¼ of meat sauce, and layer of ½ of Parmesan cheese. Repeat. Sprinkle top with oregano and paprika. Bake in a preheated 350° oven for 30 minutes. YIELD: 8 to 10 servings

Mrs. Jack Heck
(Phyllis Fraser)

127

LENTEN LASAGNE ROLL-UPS

Well worth the time it takes .

2	10-ounce packages frozen chopped spinach, cooked and drained
15	ounces tomato sauce
6	ounces tomato paste
1/3	cup chopped onion
1	teaspoon sugar
½	teaspoon oregano
½	teaspoon basil
¼	teaspoon garlic salt
2	pounds ricotta or cottage cheese
½	pound mozzarella cheese grated
2	eggs, well beaten
1	cup Parmesan cheese
1	teaspoon salt
2	tablespoons parsley
12	lasagne noodles, cooked, drained
½	to 1 cup Parmesan cheese for topping
¼	teaspoon nutmeg

Cook spinach according to package directions. Drain, reserving ½ cup liquid. In a large saucepan, combine reserved spinach liquid, tomato sauce, tomato paste, onion, sugar, oregano, basil, and garlic salt. Simmer for 20 minutes over medium-low heat; set aside. In a large bowl, combine ricotta or cottage cheese, mozzarella cheese, eggs, Parmesan cheese, salt, spinach, parsley and nutmeg. Mix well; set aside. Spread a thin layer of tomato sauce mixture in a 9 x 12 x 2-inch pan. Divide cheese filling equally among the 12 cooked lasagne noodles. Spread evenly over noodles; roll up and place seam side down in prepared pan. Pour remaining tomato sauce mixture over rolled noodles. Sprinkle with ½ to 1 cup Parmesan cheese. Bake in a preheated 350° oven for about 20 minutes. Remove from oven 5 minutes before serving.

YIELD: 12 servings

Mrs. Alan R. Merrill
(Lynn Wagner)

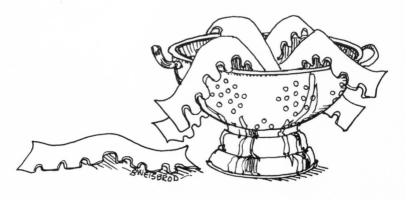

HOMEMADE NOODLES

This recipe was conceived out of love of Grandma's old-fashioned thick, chewy noodles. Use in stew, chicken soup, or serve plain with butter.

2   whole eggs, beaten
1   tablespoon butter, melted
4   tablespoons milk
½   teaspoon salt
1½ cups flour
     Additional flour for kneading and rolling

Mix all the ingredients in a bowl. Knead like bread (the more you knead, the chewier the noodles become). Roll out on a floured board to a scant 1/8-inch thick. Cut into strips ½ x 3-inches long. Let dry at room temperature for 2 to 3 hours. Store in plastic bags in refrigerator until needed, or cook immediately. Boil noodles in chicken broth or stock for about 25 to 30 minutes or until done.
VARIATION: Cut noodles to any size desired; adjust cooking time.
YIELD: 5 to 6 cups

Mrs. Lowell Mills
(Susie Taylor)

NOODLE RING

Excellent with creamed chicken.

2   cups noodles, broken into small pieces
1   quart water
½   teaspoon salt
3   eggs
1/8 teaspoon salt
     A few drops of onion juice
2   tablespoons grated cheddar cheese
½   cup milk

In a 3-quart pan, bring 1 quart water and ½ teaspoon salt to a rapid boil. Add noodles and cook until tender (about 10 minutes). Drain and set aside. In a large mixing bowl, beat 3 eggs until light; add 1/8 teaspoon salt, onion juice, cheese, and milk. Beat until blended; stir in the cooked noodles. Turn into a buttered 10-inch tube pan. Set mold in pan of hot water, and bake in preheated 325° oven for 35 minutes. Unmold on serving platter. Fill center with creamed chicken, crab, or tuna.
YIELD: 6 to 8 servings

Mrs. James Brown
(Ann Nye Guthrie)

PASTA AND GRAINS

NOODLE PUDDING

**Good for brunch or after-dinner dessert.
Try this instead of a sweet roll in the morning.**

½ pound medium or
broad noodles
6 tablespoons butter
½ cup sugar
3 ounce package cream
cheese
3 eggs
1 cup apricot nectar
1 cup milk

Boil noodles in salted water; drain. Add butter to the hot, drained noodles. Put into a well-greased 9 x 12-inch oven dish; set aside. Cream the sugar and cream cheese until very smooth. Add the eggs, beating well. Stir in apricot nectar and milk. Pour the cheese and milk mixture over the noodles.

TOPPING

2 to 3 cups corn flakes,
crumbled (not too
fine)
½ cup sugar
1 teaspoon cinnamon
6 tablespoons butter,
melted

Combine all topping ingredients and sprinkle over the noodle mixture. Bake in a preheated 350° oven for 45 minutes. Remove from the oven, and allow the noodle pudding to rest ½ hour before cutting.
YIELD: 12 servings

Mrs. Richard Prigozen
(Roberta Richmond)

NOODLE CASSEROLE

Good and different side dish.

½ pound fine, flat egg
noodles
1 cup cottage cheese
1 cup sour cream
1 egg, slightly beaten
2 scallions, chopped
½ teaspoon salt
1/8 teaspoon pepper
¼ cup butter, melted
2 tablespoons chopped
parsley

Boil noodles one minute less than package directions state; drain; run under cold water, and drain again. Mix together noodles, cottage cheese, sour cream, egg, scallions, salt, pepper, and butter. Pour into greased 1½-quart casserole, and sprinkle with parsley. Bake in preheated 300° oven for 75 to 90 minutes.
YIELD: 4 to 6 servings

Mrs. Thomas Shulman
(Ellie Arnovitz)

OVEN-BAKED RICE

This is a great way to prepare rice when having company — no stuck pan or overcooked rice. Every grain will be perfect.

1   cup raw rice (not Minute Rice)
2   tablespoons butter or margarine
1   teaspoon salt
2¼ cups water

Measure carefully! Combine all ingredients in a 6-cup buttered baking dish. Cover and bake in a preheated 350° oven for 1 hour, or until tender and all liquid is absorbed.
YIELD: 4 to 6 servings

Mrs. Carl W. Sherman
(Kathryn Hendrickson)

FLO FLO RICE

This is a good accompaniment to most any dinner; it is particularly nice because it can be made ahead of time and refrigerated or frozen.

1   cup chopped onion
¼   cup butter or margarine
4   cups freshly cooked white rice
1   large bay leaf, crumbled
½   teaspoon pepper
1   4-ounce can green chilies, chopped
1   cup cream style cottage cheese
2   cups grated sharp cheddar cheese
2   cups sour cream
2   to 4 tablespoons chopped fresh parsley

In a large skillet, saute onions in butter. Stir in all remaining ingredients, except parsley. Turn into a 2-quart casserole. Bake uncovered in a preheated 375° oven for about 45 minutes, or until bubbly.
YIELD: 6 to 8 servings

Mrs. Richard F. Paolino
(Beth Maloney)

131

CAUCASIAN RICE

**Unusual and appealing. Raisins provide a sweet
flavor which mingles well with the seasonings.**

½ cup chopped onion
1½ tablespoons butter
1 cup raw rice
2 cups chicken broth
1/3 cup golden raisins,
   or currants
½ teaspoon salt
1 8-ounce can
   mushrooms and juice
   (4-ounces drained
   weight)
1/8 teaspoon cinnamon
   Scant ¼ teaspoon
   allspice
1/3 cup roasted pine nuts,
   or roasted slivered
   almonds

In a saucepan, saute onion in butter
over medium heat. Add rice and stir
over low heat until rice is barely
golden. Add remaining ingredients,
except nuts. Bring to a boil. Cover pan
and simmer about 25 to 30 minutes,
or transfer to a buttered 1½ to 2-quart
casserole dish. Cover and bake in a
preheated 325° oven for about 45
minutes. Top with roasted nuts. Serve
hot.
YIELD: 4 to 6 servings

Mrs. Alan Meckstroth
(Betty Lutz)

RICE CASSEROLE

Delicious and fancy rice recipe.

1 large onion, chopped
1 green pepper, chopped
½ cup butter
1 cup raw rice
1 10¾-ounce can
   condensed beef
   bouillon
1 cup water
1 4-ounce can sliced
   mushrooms, drained
1 2-ounce jar pimentos,
   drained and chopped
1 teaspoon salt
1/8 teaspoon pepper
1 8-ounce can water
   chestnuts, drained

In a Dutch oven, saute onion and
green pepper in butter until soft. Stir
in all remaining ingredients. Cover
tightly and bake in a preheated 350°
oven for 45 to 60 minutes, or until
rice has absorbed all liquid.
YIELD: 8 servings

Mrs. William H. Broad, III
(Corinne Crabill)

132

MISSISSIPPI BAKED GRITS

A Castleman family recipe from Mississippi. This is a traditional side dish for brunches, evening buffets, and family meals.

1	cup grits, not quick or instant
4	cups water
½	teaspoon salt
1	egg, beaten
1	teaspoon pepper
½	pound grated sharp cheddar cheese
4	tablespoons butter
1	teaspoon worcestershire sauce
½	cup milk
1/8	teaspoon paprika

Cook grits in water and salt, according to package directions, just until thickened; remove from heat. Add egg, pepper, cheese, butter, worcestershire sauce, and milk. Mix well, and pour into an ungreased 1½-quart baking dish. Sprinkle with paprika. Bake in a preheated 350° oven for 1 hour.

CHEF'S NOTE: Reheat any leftovers, and serve for breakfast with scrambled eggs.

YIELD: 4 to 6 servings

Mrs. P. Stanley Castleman
(Maria Preonas)

GRANOLA

Evolved after a lot of experimenting. Serve dry as a snack, with milk for breakfast, or over yogurt with dried fruits for lunch.

GRANOLA

¾	cup vegetable oil
2/3	cup honey
¼	cup molasses (Blackstrap preferred)
1	cup soy flakes, optional
4	cups regular rolled oats (not instant or quick)
2	teaspoons cinnamon
½	teaspoon nutmeg
1	cup chopped nuts
¾	cup sunflower seeds
1	cup dry-roasted soy beans
1	cup coarse bran
1	cup raw wheat germ
1½	cups dried apple snack

No salt!

To make granola, use a large mixing bowl or stock pot. Combine all but the last 4 ingredients (See chef's note.). Spread mixture in a large shallow pan (broiling pan, perhaps), and place on top rack of oven. Bake in a preheated 250° oven for 45 minutes, stirring every 15 minutes. Add remaining 4 ingredients; stir and bake for an additional 15 minutes. Stir again; turn off heat and allow to remain in oven until cool. Store in sealed container.

CHEF'S NOTE: If chopped nuts or sunflower seeds are already roasted, add with the last 4 ingredients.

DRIED APPLE SNACK

8	ounces dried apple rings (available in natural food stores)

To make dried apple snack use the chopper blade of a food processor and process 2-ounces of apples until very coarse. Empty bowl; repeat. Wipe blade with cold water to prevent apples form sticking. Spread apples in a jelly roll pan and bake in a preheated 200° oven on top rack. Stir every 15 minutes. After 1½ hours turn off oven, and let apples remain until cool — the apples will crisp as they cool.

YIELD: 3 cups dried apple snack
8 cups granola

Mrs. Alan Meckstroth
(Betty Lutz)

Elegant Entrees

Old Courthouse

THE OLD COURTHOUSE

The unconquerable spirit of Dayton is represented by its beautiful Old Courthouse. At the Courthouse Daytonians have rallied together in times of joy and sorrow — from the devastating flood of 1913 to the exultant celebrations of ended wars — and its steps have been the podium for such Presidents as Abraham Lincoln and John F. Kennedy. Constructed of hand-cut limestone blocks from local quarries, the Courthouse was begun in 1847 and completed in 1850 at a cost of $100,000. The massive columned structure, featuring stone floors and six-foot thick walls in the brick-arched basement, has been recognized as one of the most outstanding examples of Greek Revival architecture in the country. The Old Courthouse presently houses the Montgomery County Historical Society, and as the focal point for the beautiful new fountain plaza, the Courthouse once again symbolizes the spirit of Dayton as the city revitalizes its downtown area.

BEEF TENDERLOIN FILET STUFFED WITH CRABMEAT

Delicious, but expensive taste treat. Serve with Bearnaise Sauce.

6	6-ounce beef tenderloin filets with pockets cut
1½	cups fresh crabmeat, or frozen, well drained
6	strips bacon, partially cooked

Fill each filet pocket with crabmeat. Wrap each filet with bacon strip and secure with wooden pick. Grill to desired doneness (Crabmeat absorbs meat juice.). Watch grill carefully; do not overcook. Serve hot with Bearnaise Sauce.

BEARNAISE SAUCE

¼	cup tarragon vinegar
3	tablespoons dry white wine
1	tablespoon finely chopped onion
1	tablespoon lemon juice
2	teaspoons dried tarragon
1	teaspoon chopped parsley
¼	teaspoon white pepper
3	egg yolks
¼	teaspoon salt
½	cup butter

BEARNAISE SAUCE

In a small saucepan, combine vinegar, wine, onions, lemon juice, tarragon, parsley, and pepper. Bring to boil; cook until reduced to about 3 tablespoons. Remove from heat; cool. In food processor, using metal blade, combine egg yolks and salt. Process until thick (about 1 minute). Continue processing; add cooled reduced liquid. Add butter, 2 tablespoons at a time. Serve over beef filets.

CHEF'S NOTE: A blender may be used.

YIELD: 1¼ cups sauce
6 servings

Mrs. William Kasch
(Sonnie Kern)

135

BEEF WITH ARTICHOKES

Excellent served with rice and a tossed salad.

1/3 cup flour
Salt and pepper, to taste
2 pounds beef (stewing beef, chuck, or sirloin tip) cut into bite-size pieces
2 tablespoons oil
2 8-ounce cans tomato sauce
Clove garlic, pressed
1 cup dry red wine
2 beef bouillon cubes
½ teaspoon dill
1 14-ounce can artichoke hearts, drained and halved
1 16-ounce can or jar small white onions, drained
1 4-ounce can whole mushrooms, drained

Put flour, salt, and pepper in a paper bag. Shake meat in bag to coat with flour mixture. In a large skillet, heat oil and brown beef cubes. Stir in tomato sauce, garlic, wine, bouillon cubes, and dill; simmer over low heat for 1½ hours, covered (May be refrigerated or frozen at this point.). Add all remaining ingredients and heat to serving temperature.
YIELD: 6 servings

Mrs. H. Brockman Anderson, Jr.
(Margy Todd)

SAVORY BEEF BRISKET

Tasty tomato sauce surrounds this tender beef.
May also be served as Sloppy Joes.

1 4-pound beef brisket
1 package dry onion soup mix
2 cups ketchup
2 teaspoons horseradish
1 cup water
½ teaspoon garlic salt
1/8 teaspoon pepper
½ teaspoon oregano
½ teaspoon celery salt

Place beef brisket in Dutch oven, and cover with all remaining ingredients. Bake covered in preheated 300° oven for 4 hours. Cool slightly. Cut meat into thin slices, removing excess fat. Refrigerate meat in pan juices overnight. Skim congealed grease. Reheat; serve alone or in sandwich buns.
YIELD: 8 servings

Mrs. William H. Broad III
(Corinne Crabill)

BARBECUE BRISKET

This is a very tasty make-ahead recipe.

1	4 to 5 pound beef brisket
½	teaspoon garlic salt
½	teaspoon coarse pepper
10	to 12 whole cloves
1	cup ketchup
1	cup sherry
	Water
3	bay leaves
1	large clove garlic
	Flour to thicken

Trim all fat from brisket. Season both sides of meat with garlic salt and pepper. Cut 10 to 12 small holes in meat, and insert whole cloves. In a Dutch oven, combine ketchup and sherry. Add beef, turning once, and enough water to cover meat. Add bay leaves and garlic clove to liquid. Cover and bake in preheated 325° oven for 4 to 5 hours or until fork tender. During baking, add more water if necessary. Remove beef to cool. Remove and discard bay leaves and garlic clove. Thicken pan juices, if necessary, with flour. Using an electric knife cut cooled beef into thin slices. Arrange beef in a 9 x 13 x 2-inch baking dish. Pour thickened pan juices over beef. Cover and refrigerate or freeze. Reheat in preheated 350° oven for 45 minutes.
YIELD: 6 to 8 servings

Mrs. William Pees
(Candy Gray)

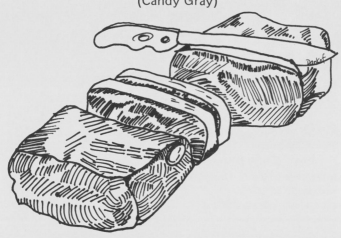

MARINATED CHUCK ROAST

Marinate for three days for a wonderful flavor and tenderness.

1	3 to 4-pound chuck roast
	Meat tenderizer
1	cup vegetable oil
1	teaspoon garlic salt
1	teaspoon onion salt
2	teaspoons lemon juice
2	tablespoons worcestershire sauce
2	teaspoons sugar

In a shaker jar, combine marinade ingredients, and shake well. Place meat in a glass container; add meat tenderizer and tenderize according to package instructions. Pour marinade ingredients over meat. Cover and refrigerate for *3 days*; turn occasionally, being sure to replace cover tightly. Drain well, preserving marinade. Grill for 45 minutes or broil to medium rare. Baste frequently with marinade. Slice thin and serve.
YIELD: 6 servings

Mrs. Stewart A. Levine
(Laraine Kanner)

MARINATED CHUCK ROAST STEAK

Fantastic taste; the marinade tenderizes the meat very well.

3	pounds 2-inch thick chuck roast steak
2	tablespoons steak sauce (we prefer A-1)
2	tablespoons worcestershire sauce
2	tablespoons ketchup
1	teaspoon soy sauce
1	teaspoon tabasco sauce
1	teaspoon garlic powder
1	teaspoon onion salt
1	teaspoon salt
1	teaspoon pepper
2	teaspoons beef bouillon granules
1	teaspoon dry parsley flakes
1	tablespoon wine vinegar
1	cup vegetable oil

Place meat in a large skillet or bowl. In a small bowl, mix together all remaining ingredients, and pour over meat. Cover and refrigerate overnight. Bring to room temperature, and remove from marinade. Charcoal broil over low coals, or low oven broil for 20 to 30 minutes on each side.
YIELD: 4 to 6 servings

Mrs. P. Stanley Castleman
(Maria Preonas)

CAMOUFLAGED CHUCK STEAK

This makes chuck steak so good it could pass for filet mignon — well . . . almost.

1   3 to 4 pound chuck
    steak, 1½-inches thick
    Instant meat tenderizer
    Garlic salt
1   8-ounce bottle French
    dressing

The day before serving, sprinkle meat on all sides with instant meat tenderizer and garlic salt. Poke into meat with a fork. Pour French dressing on both sides, and let stand covered in refrigerator overnight. Turn once or twice in dressing. Use a covered kettle grill with coals at the lowest level. Heat coals for at least 30 minutes, or until they are still hot but past their prime. Put chuck steak on grill; cover, and cook for 15 to 20 minutes on one side. Turn; cover, and cook 15 to 20 minutes for medium. Slice down like chateaubriand to serve.
YIELD: 4 to 6 servings

Mrs. Richard B. Pohl
(Carol Crabill)

GERMAN ROULADEN

This authentic German recipe is great for a buffet.
The beef is very tender; dill pickles and bacon add a delicious,
unusual taste. May be prepared a day ahead or frozen and reheated.

16   slices sirloin tip roast;
      have the butcher slice
      as thinly as possible
      Good German mustard
      (we prefer Plochman's)
      Garlic salt

1   to 2 medium onions,
      sliced in 1/8-inch rings

2   to 3 medium-size dill
      pickles, sliced in
      eighths, lengthwise

½   pound bacon, cut in
      1/8-inch crosswise
      strips

2   tablespoons fat

1   cup water

Spread each slice of beef with mustard; sprinkle with garlic salt. Add 3 onion rings cut in half to make strips, 2 to 3 slices of pickle, and 6 to 9, 1/8-inch slices of bacon. Fold in sides and roll up; secure with a wooden pick or thread. In a heavy or electric skillet brown roulades lightly in hot fat. Add water; cover and simmer 1½ hours. If preparing a day ahead, simmer 1 hour; refrigerate and rewarm ½ hour before serving. Use pan drippings to make delicious gravy to be served over rouladen and German Red Cabbage (see index).

YIELD: 8 servings
          16 rouladen

Mrs. Herwig Baumann
(Vickie Overholzer)

STUFFED FLANK STEAK

My favorite "family" recipe.

Salt or garlic salt
1½ pounds flank steak
(have butcher run
through cuber *twice*)
2/3 cup water
1 tablespoon butter
1½ cups seasoned stuffing
mix
¼ cup minced onion
¼ cup minced celery
1 egg, beaten
1 8-ounce can tomato
sauce
1 cube beef bouillon,
dissolved in ¼ cup hot
water
2 tablespoons chopped
parsley for garnish

Sprinkle one side of steak lightly with salt or garlic salt. In a small saucepan, bring water and butter to a boil. Add stuffing mix, onion, and celery; stir until liquid is absorbed. Cool slightly; stir in egg. Spread all of the dressing across the seasoned side of steak. Roll steak jelly-roll fashion, and tie ends and middle with string. Place in Dutch oven. Pour tomato sauce and bouillon mixture over meat. Cover and simmer on top of stove for 75 minutes or until fork tender. Remove meat to carving board; remove string; slice, and place on warmed serving platter. Garnish meat with parsley. Pass sauce in gravy boat to accompany the meat.
YIELD: 4 servings

Mrs. Thomas Shulman
(Ellie Arnovitz)

FLANK STEAK

Especially good charcoal-broiled.

1 small onion, chopped
1/3 cup olive oil
1/3 cup sherry
1/3 cup soy sauce
½ teaspoon ground
ginger
2 flank steaks,
well-scored on both
sides (about 3 pounds
total weight)

In a skillet, saute onion in olive oil until transparent. Stir in sherry and soy sauce; simmer for 5 minutes. Remove from heat; stir in ginger; cool. Add flank steaks to cooled mixture. Cover and refrigerate for 2 hours to marinate. Broil in preheated oven or over very hot coals for 4 minutes per side for pink center, or 3 minutes per side for rare. To serve, cut thin slices on the diagonal.
YIELD: 4 servings

Mrs. P. Stanley Castleman
(Maria Preonas)

BEEF

KOREAN BEEF

Serve with rice; it's yummy.

1	tablespoon sesame seeds
2	pounds lean steak, sirloin or flank
3	scallions, finely chopped
3	to 4 garlic cloves, minced
5	tablespoons soy sauce
2	tablespoons vegetable oil
¼	cup sugar
2	tablespoons dry sherry
¼	teaspoon M.S.G. (we prefer Accent)
1/8	teaspoon black pepper

Toast sesame seeds lightly in skillet over low heat; set aside. Slice steak on diagonal into very thin slices. In a small bowl, combine remaining ingredients. Mix well. Pour over steak slices. Cover and refrigerate for about 30 minutes. Drain meat; heat marinade in a small saucepan over low heat. Broil steak slices on broiler pan, as near the source of heat as possible, for 1 minute. Turn meat; sprinkle with reserved sesame seeds. Broil 30 seconds. Serve immediately accompanied by rice. Pass reserved heated marinade.
YIELD: 4 to 6 servings

Mrs. Dennis Patterson
(Linda Epstein)

SWEET AND SOUR BEEF WITH PINEAPPLE

Delightful oriental flavor.

1½	pounds sirloin tip, cut in 1" cubes
2	to 4 tablespoons vegetable oil
1	cup water
1	20-ounce can pineapple chunks
¼	cup brown sugar
2	tablespoons cornstarch
¼	cup cider vinegar
1	to 2 tablespoons soy sauce
½	teaspoon salt
1	small green pepper, cut in strips
¼	cup thinly sliced onions

In a large skillet, brown beef in hot oil. Add one cup water; cover, and simmer (do not boil) for about 45 minutes or until tender. Drain pineapple, reserving juice. Combine sugar and cornstarch; add pineapple juice, vinegar, soy sauce, and salt. Add to meat. Cook and stir until sauce thickens. Add pineapple, green pepper, and onion. Heat to serving temperature, and serve over rice.
YIELD: 4 to 6 servings

Mrs. Stewart A. Levine
(Laraine Kanner)

BEEF IN HERB WINE SAUCE

Tender and flavorful.

3 or 4 medium onions, sliced
2 tablespoons bacon drippings
2 pounds lean beef (round steak), cubed
2 tablespoons flour
¾ cup beef bouillon
1 cup red wine (claret or Bordeaux)
¼ teaspoon thyme
¼ teaspoon oregano
1 teaspoon salt
½ teaspoon pepper
½ cup dry red wine
½ pound mushrooms, sliced
¼ cup butter

Saute onions in bacon drippings until transparent; remove from pan; set aside. Add meat cubes; sprinkle with flour and brown thoroughly. Stir in bouillon, 1 cup red wine, herbs, and seasonings. Cover pan and simmer over low heat for about 2 hours (or in 300° oven). Gradually add ½ cup red wine. Saute mushrooms in butter. Add reserved onions and mushrooms. Cook, uncovered, for 30 minutes over low heat, or until meat is tender and liquid thickens. Serve over rice or noodles.
YIELD: 8 servings

Mrs. Benjamin F. Kuhns, Jr.
(Dorothy Elder)

BAKED CORNED BEEF

Very good for dinner or sliced for sandwiches.

3 to 4-pounds corned beef
   Water to cover
¼ cup water
2 tablespoons pickling spice
1 slice lemon
1 slice orange
1 celery stalk with leaves
1 carrot, sliced

Soak meat, if heavily salted, in enough water to cover for about ½ hour. Remove from water and place in a Dutch oven on a large piece of heavy foil. Add all remaining ingredients and seal foil. Bake in a preheated 300° oven for 3½ to 4 hours, or until tender.
YIELD: 8 to 10 servings

Mrs. William R. Thompson
(Sally Decker)

MUSHROOM-FILLED MEATLOAF

Don't skip the sour cream sauce; it is exceptionally good.

1 cup sliced fresh mush-
rooms
1 cup chopped onion
2 tablespoons butter
½ cup sour cream
2 eggs, beaten
½ cup milk
1½ pounds ground beef
¾ cup bread crumbs
2 teaspoons salt
1 tablespoon worcester-
shire sauce
1 cup sliced fresh
mushrooms
2 tablespoons butter

SOUR CREAM SAUCE

1 cup sour cream
1 teaspoon horseradish
1 teaspoon Dijon mustard
½ teaspoon salt
Pinch of pepper
Pinch of nutmeg

Saute 1 cup of mushrooms and 1 cup onion in 2 tablespoons butter. Remove from heat and stir in sour cream; set aside. Combine all remaining meatloaf ingredients except 1 cup mushrooms and 2 tablespoons butter. Put half of the mixture into a 9 x 5-inch loaf pan. Make a shallow trough down the middle of the meat. Spoon reserved sour cream mixture into the trough. Shape the rest of the meat over the filling (Make sure all the filling is covered.). Seal the meatloaf around the edges. Bake in preheated 350° oven for one hour. Let stand 15 minutes before slicing. Saute remaining 1 cup mushrooms in 2 tablespoons butter. Place on top of meatloaf for garnish. Serve with sour cream sauce.

SOUR CREAM SAUCE

Stir all ingredients together in a small saucepan over low heat. Serve hot with meatloaf.
YIELD: 4 to 6 servings

Mrs. David C. Hulme
(Chris Hafstad)

STUFFED MEATLOAF

When you slice this meatloaf, a flow of melted mozzarella cheese comes out. Serve cold as little ham and cheese sandwiches.

2	eggs, beaten
¾	cup soft bread crumbs
½	cup tomato juice
2	tablespoons snipped fresh parsley
½	teaspoon crushed oregano
¼	teaspoon salt
¼	teaspoon pepper
1	clove garlic, minced
2	pounds lean ground beef
8	thin slices boiled ham
6	ounces shredded mozzarella cheese (1½ cups)

In a large bowl, combine eggs, bread crumbs, tomato juice, parsley, oregano, salt, pepper, and garlic. Stir in ground beef, mixing well. Spread ½ of the meat mixture to cover the bottom of a greased 9 x 13 x 2-inch pan. Arrange ham slices on top of meat to cover, leaving an uncovered margin all around edges of pan. Sprinkle cheese over ham. On a large piece of waxed paper, shape remaining meat mixture into a 9 x 13-inch rectangle. Place shaped beef on top of cheese; remove waxed paper. Seal edges of meatloaf. Bake uncovered in a preheated 350° oven for 50 to 60 minutes. Cut into squares and serve. YIELD: 8 to 10 servings

Mrs. Bruce A. Triplett
(Leslie Conway)

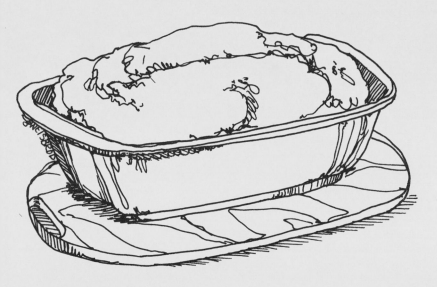

ITALIAN HERO

A one-dish meal — all you need to add is a salad.

1	loaf Italian bread, unsliced
1	8-ounce can spaghetti sauce (we prefer Schiavoni's Marinara Sauce)
½	pound ground beef
½	pound Italian sausage
1	cup large curd cottage cheese
¼	cup grated Parmesan cheese
¼	teaspoon oregano
¼	teaspoon basil
1	4-ounce can sliced mushrooms, drained
12	slices mozzarella cheese
½	green pepper, sliced thin

Slice bread in half lengthwise and hollow out top and bottom; set aside. In a large skillet, brown ground beef and sausage and drain; add marinara sauce; set aside. In a small bowl, combine cottage cheese, Parmesan cheese, oregano, and basil; spread on bottom of bread. Next, add layers (one each) of meat sauce, mushrooms, mozzarella cheese slices, and green pepper. Place sandwiches on a cookie sheet. Bake in a preheated 350° oven for 20 to 25 minutes. Cut into 1 to 1½-inch slices to serve.
YIELD: 6 to 8 servings

Mrs. William Kasch
(Sonnie Kern)

QUICK CHEESE CASSEROLE

A good busy-day recipe. Make ahead and freeze until needed.

1	large onion, chopped
2	tablespoons butter
1½	pounds ground beef
2	15-ounce cans, and 1, 8-ounce can tomato sauce
1	clove garlic, pressed
2	teaspoons salt
1	teaspoon paprika
¾	teaspoon oregano
½	teaspoon basil
½	teaspoon parsley
1	teaspoon worcestershire sauce
4	cups uncooked seashell macaroni
1½	cups grated cheddar cheese

In a large skillet, saute onions in butter. Add ground beef, tomato sauce, garlic, and all seasonings. Simmer about 10 minutes. Meanwhile, cook sea-shells according to package directions; drain, and add to meat mixture. Stir to mix well. Turn into a 9 x 12-inch baking dish. Sprinkle with cheese. Cover and bake in a preheated 375° oven for 30 minutes. Remove cover, and bake 10 to 15 minutes longer. Serve hot with garlic bread and a tossed green salad.
YIELD: 6 servings

Mrs. David C. Hulme
(Chris Hafstad)

MOM'S CABBAGE ROLLS

*Part of remembering youth was smelling these cook.
My family loves them — generally New Year's Day.*

2 small heads of cabbage
½ pound ground pork
2½ pounds ground beef
1 cup rice, uncooked
1 small onion
2 cloves garlic, crushed
2 27-ounce cans sauerkraut
1 28-ounce can tomatoes
1 29-ounce can tomato sauce

Cut core from cabbage; turn upside down in pan of water. Heat until leaves are easy to handle. In a large bowl, mix the next 5 ingredients together. Cut the rib off a leaf of cabbage. Form a ball of hamburger mixture, and place inside leaf. Fold leaf over hamburger. Repeat until all hamburger mixture is used. Spread a layer of sauerkraut on the bottom of a large kettle, then a layer of cabbage rolls. Continue layering, ending with sauerkraut. Top with tomatoes and tomato sauce. Cover and cook slowly over medium low heat for about 4 hours.
YIELD: 16-18 servings

Mrs. William Kendell
(Ponnie Childress)

HAMBURGERS FLORENTINE

This is a dieter's dream: a tasty and hearty main dish, but it only has about 250 calories per patty! Kids like these burgers, too.

1   10-ounce package frozen chopped spinach, cooked, drained well, and chopped again
2   pounds lean ground beef
1   medium onion, finely chopped
1   egg
¼   cup finely crushed crackers (we prefer Ritz or Cheez-its)
2   tablespoons grated Parmesan cheese
½   teaspoon salt
½   to 1 teaspoon crumbled oregano
2   tablespoons vegetable oil
1   8-ounce can tomato sauce
½   cup beef broth

In a large bowl, combine all ingredients except oil, tomato sauce, and beef broth. Shape into 8 to 10 patties using about 2/3 cup mixture for each patty (Patties may be wrapped individually and frozen at this point.). Brown patties in 2 large skillets using 1 tablespoon oil in each pan. When well-browned on each side, remove patties to platter. Pour half of the tomato sauce and half of the broth into each skillet. Stir and scrape bottoms of pans. Add hamburgers and spoon juices over top. Cook over low heat, basting frequently, for 15 minutes. Serve hamburgers on a platter, passing sauce separately.
YIELD: 8 to 10 servings

Mrs. Geoffrey R. Lorenz
(Niel Ruth Phillips)

MACARONI BAKE

**Tastes like lasagne! Children really like this.
Makes 2 loaves; eat one and freeze one.**

1	pound hamburger
1	medium onion, chopped
½	teaspoon garlic salt
1	8-ounce can pizza sauce
1	8-ounce can tomato sauce (we prefer Hunt's)
1	7-ounce package elbow macaroni, cook according to package directions; drain
1	tablespoon oregano
¼	cup Parmesan cheese
½	pound small curd cottage cheese
1	cup sour cream
4	to 6 ounces mozzarella cheese, shredded

In a large skillet, brown hamburger and onion; drain excess fat. Remove from heat, and add all remaining ingredients, except mozzarella cheese; stir to mix well. Turn mixture into 2 greased 9 x 5-inch loaf pans; sprinkle mozzarella cheese over the meat mixture in each pan. Cover and freeze 1 loaf for future use; thaw in refrigerator before baking. Bake in a preheated 350° oven for 45 to 60 minutes.
YIELD: 2 loaves: 5 to 6 servings each loaf

Mrs. William Pees
(Candy Gray)

MIDWEST SCRAPPLE

**Make your own scrapple and be assured of the quality.
Adjust the seasoning to suit your family's taste
and enjoy a real midwestern breakfast!**

¼	cup minced onion
1	pound ground beef
½	pound ground pork
1½	teaspoons ground sage
1/8	teaspoon cayenne
1½	teaspoons salt
½	teaspoon black pepper
3½	cups water
1	cup corn meal

Combine all ingredients except corn meal in a saucepan. Bring to a boil, and boil gently for 20 minutes. Gradually stir in corn meal, and cook, stirring, until thickened. Pour into a 5x9-inch loaf pan and chill. Cut into slices about ½-inch thick. Dust with flour, and fry in oil until lightly browned.
YIELD: 12 servings

Mrs. George L. Word
(Paige Early)

SPAGHETTI-BEEF PIE

Really different spaghetti dish.

6	ounces spaghetti (please use vermicelli)
2	tablespoons butter
1/3	cup grated Parmesan cheese
2	eggs, well beaten
1	pound ground beef
½	cup chopped onion
1	8-ounce can tomatoes, cut up, not drained
1	6-ounce can tomato paste
1	teaspoon sugar
1	teaspoon crushed oregano
½	teaspoon garlic salt
½	to 1 cup shredded mozzarella cheese

Cook spaghetti according to package directions; drain. Stir in butter, Parmesan cheese, and eggs. Form spaghetti mixture into "crust" in buttered 10-inch pie plate. In a large skillet, cook beef and onion over medium heat until beef is browned and onions are tender. Drain off fat. Stir in undrained tomatoes, tomato paste, sugar, oregano, and garlic salt; heat through. Fill spaghetti "crust" with tomato mixture. Bake uncovered in a preheated 350° oven for 20 minutes. Sprinkle with mozzarella cheese, and bake for about 5 more minutes. Serve hot.
YIELD: 6 servings

Mrs. Bruce A. Triplett
(Leslie Conway)

HOMEMADE SALAMI

Great for gift giving — plan ahead!

5	pounds ground beef
5	tablespoons preserving salt (we prefer Morton's Tender Quick Salt)
2½	teaspoons mustard seed
2	teaspoons garlic salt
½	teaspoon garlic powder
2	teaspoons pepper
1	teaspoon hickory-smoked salt
2	to 4 tablespoons whole peppercorns (optional)

In a large bowl mix all ingredients together. Cover and refrigerate for 3 days. Once a day, for 3 days, knead mixture thoroughly (Remove from refrigerator a bit ahead of time so it's not so cold on your hands.). On the 4th day shape the mixture into 4 log rolls; place on oven broiler pan. Bake in preheated 150° oven for 10 hours (Turn logs after 5 hours.). Cool, wrap, and store in refrigerator.
YIELD: 4, 13 ounce logs

Mrs. Richard S. Sutton
(Janet Robinson)

CHINESE PORK ROAST

The international cuisine of Washington, D.C., is reflected in this succulent pork roast. This recipe was given as a going away gift to a noted cook who was leaving the capital city.

1/3 cup soy sauce
2 tablespoons lemon juice
¼ cup sugar
1 small onion, sliced
4 green onions, cut in 1-inch lengths
¼ teaspoon ground ginger
4 cloves garlic, crushed
½ cup water
1 3-pound rib roast of pork
2 tablespoons cornstarch

Combine soy sauce, lemon juice, sugar, onions, ginger, garlic and water in a mixing bowl. Place roast in the marinade; cover and refrigerate for 8 to 10 hours. Remove roast and place on a rack in a roasting pan. Roast in a preheated 325° oven for 1½ hours or until meat thermometer registers 182°. Remove roast to a heated platter and combine pan juices with remaining marinade. Skim off fat. Add water to make 2 cups and thicken with cornstarch. Simmer over medium heat until sauce thickens and boils. Slice roast, serve, and pass sauce in a gravy boat.
YIELD: 4 servings

Mrs. Bruce A. Triplett
(Leslie Conway)

EGG ROLLS

Chinese egg roll is called Spring Roll "Ch'un-chuan" which symbolizes the coming of spring. They are served as an afternoon snack or as part of a dinner during the New Year holidays. Their filling may be made with chicken, pork, ham, beef, shrimp, or barbecue pork. We suggest you prepare fillings (A and B) the day before, and then at serving time make your final preparations while your guests observe.

THE FILLINGS

— A —

1   pound lean pork, ground
1   tablespoon pale dry sherry
1   tablespoon soy sauce
½   teaspoon salt
1   tablespoon cornstarch
1   teaspoon minced ginger root

— B —

1   pound raw bean sprouts, rinsed
2   cups shredded celery, (¼ x 1½ to 2-inch pieces)
1   cup shredded scallions, (¼ x 1½ to 2-inch pieces)
1   cup shredded bamboo shoots, (¼ x 1½ to 2-inch pieces)
½   cup shredded black mushrooms, reconstituted — dried
1   tablespoon soy sauce
2   teaspoons salt
1   teaspoon monosodium glutamate MSG (we prefer Accent)
1   tablespoon sesame seed oil
2   teaspoons dark brown sugar

Mix together all filling A ingredients. In a large skillet, saute with 3 tablespoons hot oil; drain well, and remove to a bowl. Saute all filling B ingredients in 3 tablespoons hot oil for 5 minutes; drain well, and mix with filling A; cool.

In a small saucepan, combine all sauce 1 ingredients. Heat and serve warm. In a small serving bowl, stir together all sauce 2 ingredients. Serve at room temperature.

Place ¼ cup of the filling mixture on the lower half of a wrapper (Prepare no more than 4 egg rolls at a time.). Moisten left and right edges of the wrapper with a mixture of cornstarch and water, or a lightly beaten egg. Fold bottom edge up, left and right edges over, and roll. Moisten top and side edges with cornstarch and water mixture, or egg and seal. Immediately deep fry (no more than 4 at a time) the folded egg rolls in oil preheated to 375° for about 5 minutes, or until golden brown. Serve the egg rolls as soon as possible, arranged attractively on a large, heated platter. If necessary, the egg rolls may be kept warm for an hour or so in a preheated 250° oven, or they may be reheated for about 10 minutes in a preheated 450° oven.

recipe continues . . .

THE SAUCES

– 1 –

½ cup hoisin sauce
1 cup peach or apricot
preserves
Squeeze of lemon
Dash of dried red
pepper

– 2 –

2 parts dried hot
mustard
1 part water

THE WRAPPER

1 pound ready-made egg
roll skin (may be kept
in freezer for days)
2 teaspoons cornstarch
mixed with 2 table-
spoons water, or 1 egg,
slightly beaten
1 to 2 quarts vegetable
oil for deep-frying and
sauteing

CHEF'S NOTE: Specialty items are
available at Chinese grocery stores.
YIELD: 16 to 18 egg rolls

Mrs. Richard Karr
(Mary Frances Wheaton)

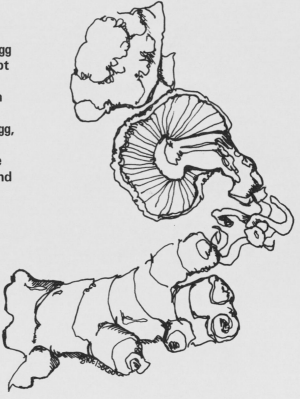

MILD PORK CURRY

Easy family meal.

¼	cup flour
1	tablespoon curry powder
2	teaspoons salt
¼	teaspoon pepper
3	pounds lean pork shoulder, cut into ½-inch cubes
2	tablespoons butter
3	cups chicken broth
1	medium onion, sliced
2	carrots, sliced
1	6-ounce can mushrooms and juice, sliced (we prefer B&B)
1	5-ounce can water chestnuts, drained and sliced
½	cup seedless raisins
1	cup diagonally sliced celery

Combine flour, curry, salt, and pepper. Coat pork cubes with flour mixture. In a Dutch oven, melt butter. Brown pork lightly, and stir in chicken broth and half the onion slices. Bring to a boil. Reduce heat; cover, and simmer for 45 to 60 minutes or until tender, stirring occasionally. Add remaining onion slices to pork, and stir in remaining ingredients. Cover and cook for 15 to 20 minutes, or until carrots are tender. Serve over noodles or rice. YIELD: 8 servings

Mrs. Donald C. Woods
(Peggy White)

PORK CHOPS AND RICE

You'll love the flavor.

6	pork chops
1½	cups Minute Rice, uncooked
1	10¾-ounce can beef consomme
1	tomato, cut into six slices
1	green pepper, cut into six slices

In a small bowl, combine rice and consomme; let stand 2 hours, or until rice is soft. In a large skillet, brown pork chops, and place in a 9 x 12-inch casserole. Top each pork chop with a mound of rice mixture, one tomato slice, and one green pepper slice. Cover and bake in a preheated 350° oven for 1 hour. YIELD: 6 servings

Mrs. William Stephens
(Pam Swartzel)

154

CALIFORNIA CHOPS

My husband and I had these while dining out and really enjoyed the different taste, so I kept experimenting until I came up with this recipe. Especially good with rice.

4 pork chops, any cut, well trimmed
1 tablespoon butter or margarine
1 8-ounce can tomato sauce
1 lemon, sliced thin and seeds removed
1 medium onion, sliced thin
1 green pepper, sliced thin
1 3-ounce can mushrooms, drained
1½ tablespoons cooking sherry
Salt and pepper, to taste

In a large skillet over medium heat, brown pork chops in butter or margarine for 5 to 7 minutes on each side. Drain grease and add remaining ingredients. Cover and simmer over low heat, stirring occasionally, for about 1 hour, or until tender. Garnish each chop with a lemon slice, and pass the tomato sauce separately when serving. YIELD: 4 servings

Mrs. Stephen McClure
(Chris Brewer)

OLDFANGLED PORK CHOPS

'Kraut was never so cunning.

2 cups canned sauerkraut
2 cups pared and chopped apples
1 cup sliced onion
1½ tablespoons brown sugar
1½ tablespoons melted butter
1/3 teaspoon grated nutmeg
4 lean pork chops, well trimmed
1 tablespoon soy sauce
½ cup water

In a colander or strainer, rinse and drain sauerkraut. In a large mixing bowl, combine sauerkraut, apples, onion, brown sugar, melted butter, and nutmeg. Put ½ of this mixture into a buttered 2-quart casserole. Arrange pork chops over mixture. Cover pork chops with soy sauce, then remaining sauerkraut mixture. Add ½ cup water. Cover casserole and bake in a preheated 350° oven for 1½ hours. YIELD: 2 generous servings

Mrs. Alan Meckstroth
(Betty Lutz)

155

BROILED PORK CHOPS STUFFED WITH APRICOTS

Rich, yellow apricots snuggled into glazed pork chops will delight your eye as well as your palate. Try these chops with fresh corn on the cob and a tossed spinach salad for a sensational backyard barbecue.

6	rib pork chops, 1½-inches thick with pockets cut
	Salt and pepper
1	17-ounce can apricot halves
2	tablespoons chopped onion
2	tablespoons cooking oil
1	tablespoon lemon juice
¼	cup ketchup
½	teaspoon dry mustard

Season pockets of chops with salt and pepper. Drain apricots, reserving ½ cup of syrup. Insert two apricot halves in each pocket, and secure with toothpicks. Grill chops over medium coals for 35 minutes, turning once. In the meantime, cut remaining apricots into small pieces. In a saucepan, mix onion, oil, lemon juice, ketchup, dry mustard, ½ cup apricot syrup, and diced apricots. Heat to boiling; reduce heat, and let simmer for 15 minutes. Cook chops 5 minutes more, constantly basting with the sauce. Pass remaining sauce with chops.
YIELD: 6 servings

Mrs. Bruce A. Triplett
(Leslie Conway)

LUAU RIBS

Moist and juicy ribs in full, sweet, flavored sauce.
Everyone raves. Extra easy!

4	pounds spareribs
1	pound canned sliced peaches, drained
½	cup firmly packed brown sugar
1/3	cup ketchup
½	cup vinegar
2	tablespoons soy sauce
2	cloves garlic
2	teaspoons ginger
1	teaspoon salt
	Dash of pepper

Place ribs, meat side up, in a shallow baking pan. Bake in a preheated 450° oven for 45 minutes. Pour off fat. Put remaining ingredients into a blender; cover and whirl at high speed until smooth. Spoon sauce over ribs. Lower oven temperature to 350° and continue baking for 1½ hours or until done. Baste every 15 minutes.
YIELD: 4 to 6 servings

Mrs. Donald May
(Brenda Amburgey)

HAM JAMBALAYA

**Flavor improves if made ahead and reheated.
Excellent use for leftover ham.**

1	cup chopped onion
3	tablespoons butter
1	cup raw rice
1	29-ounce can tomatoes (3½ cups), cut in fourths
¾	cup diced green pepper
½	teaspoon each thyme, allspice, basil, and marjoram
½	cup dry white wine
1	bay leaf
¼	teaspoon black pepper
1	teaspoon paprika
1	tablespoon brown sugar
3	cups firmly packed diced ham
2	tablespoons chopped fresh parsley, or ½ cup grated mild cheese

In large saucepan, saute onion in butter over medium heat until tender. Add raw rice, and stir until rice is barely golden. Add all remaining ingredients except parsley or cheese. Stir until mixture comes to a boil. Cover and simmer for 30 to 35 minutes. Serve, or cover and refrigerate. Serve with top of casserole covered lavishly with minced fresh parsley or grated cheese.
YIELD: 6 servings

Mrs. Alan Meckstroth
(Betty Lutz)

HAM-TOMATO CHEESE PIE

Perfect for a light lunch.

1	9-inch pastry shell, baked and cooled
2	cups ground or chopped, cooked ham
2	medium tomatoes, sliced
1	tablespoon instant minced onion
½	teaspoon oregano
½	teaspoon salt
1/8	teaspoon pepper
¼	cup mayonnaise,
8	ounces cheddar cheese, grated

Line the cooled pastry shell with ham; cover with tomato slices. Sprinkle with onion, oregano, salt, and pepper. Bake in a preheated 300° oven for 20 minutes. Meanwhile in a small bowl, combine mayonnaise with grated cheese. Spread over ham-tomato filling, and continue baking for 5 to 10 minutes, or until cheese melts.
YIELD: 6 to 8 servings

Mrs. William D. Long
(Julie Stayton)

OPEN-FACE BROILED AVOCADO AND HAM SANDWICHES

Tasty new sandwich idea.

1 ripe avocado
1 tablespoon mayonnaise
Juice of ½ lemon
1 green onion, chopped
¼ teaspoon garlic salt
¼ teaspoon fresh ground pepper
Dash of cayenne (red pepper)
4 whole wheat buns, split
8 thin slices ham
1 cup alfalfa sprouts
2 large tomatoes
4 slices mild cheddar cheese
4 slices Monterey Jack cheese

Peel, seed, and mash avocado. Add next six ingredients, and mix thoroughly. Split wheat buns; spread each half with avocado mixture. Layer with a slice of ham, a few tablespoons of alfalfa sprouts, a thick tomato slice, and one slice of either cheese. Place on ungreased cookie sheet 6 inches under broiler, and heat until cheese melts.
YIELD: 4 servings (8 open-face sandwiches)

Mrs. William Miller
(Janet Hadler)

MOM GUNLOCK'S SAUCY HAM LOAF

Moist, flavorful, and easy!

1 pound ground ham (½ fresh, ½ cured)
½ cup dried bread crumbs
1 egg, slightly beaten
½ small onion, grated
1 to 3 tablespoons water

SAUCE
1 cup brown sugar
1 teaspoon prepared mustard
½ cup cider vinegar
½ cup water

Mix all ham loaf ingredients together adding enough water to make a soft loaf. Turn into a 2½-quart loaf pan. In a small saucepan, combine all sauce ingredients. Heat to dissolve sugar. When hot, pour 1/3 of sauce over ham loaf. Bake in preheated 350° oven for about 1 hour. Remove loaf from oven; drain sauce and fat. Add remaining 2/3 sauce mixture to loaf. Return to oven, and bake for 30 minutes longer. Baste occasionally.
YIELD: 4 servings

Mrs. William L. Gunlock
(Sandy Owen)

LAMB SHANKS

Great one-dish meal!

2   lamb shanks
2   cloves garlic, slivered
2   tablespoons flour
2   tablespoons vegetable oil
1   to 2, 10½-ounce cans beef consomme, undiluted
1   cup red wine
2   medium potatoes, diced
2   carrots, diced
1   onion, diced
    Flour or cornstarch, for thickening

Pierce shank skins; place garlic slivers under skin, one clove per shank. Dredge shanks in flour, and brown in a skillet in hot oil. Place shanks in a 9-inch square baking dish and pour over them 1 can consomme and wine. Cover and bake in a preheated 350° oven for 3 to 4 hours or longer. Check occasionally (Add more consomme if liquids cook down too much.), and spoon juices over meat. One hour before serving, add diced vegetables. Return to oven and bake one hour. Remove meat and vegetables; keep warm. Thicken pan juices with flour or corn starch, and correct the seasoning. Pass gravy with the meat and vegetables.
YIELD: 2 servings

Mrs. Alexander B. Hamilton
(Ardith Paul)

LAMB RATATOUILLE

Highly seasoned and very good
served with a basic rice pilaf cooked in chicken broth.

2½ pounds lamb shoulder, cut in cubes and excess fat removed
2 tablespoons vegetable oil
2 medium onions, sliced
2 cloves garlic, crushed
2 teaspoons curry powder
2 chicken bouillon cubes, crushed
½ pound fresh mushrooms, sliced
½ teaspoon thyme
½ teaspoon rosemary
½ teaspoon parsley
1 medium to small size eggplant, chopped into bite-size pieces
½ pound zucchini, sliced
2 1-pound cans tomatoes
2 14-ounce cans artichoke hearts, drained and quartered
4 teaspoons salt
1 teaspoon pepper

In a large skillet, brown lamb cubes in hot oil, one half at a time. Remove lamb as it browns. To drippings add onion, garlic, curry powder, bouillon cubes, mushrooms, thyme, rosemary, and parsley. Saute for about 5 to 10 minutes. Return lamb cubes to skillet and mix well. In a deep 5-quart casserole combine the lamb mixture with all remaining ingredients. Cover and bake in a preheated 350° oven for 1½ hours; remove cover and bake 1 more hour, or until lamb is tender. May be frozen.
YIELD: 8 servings

Mrs. William Kasch
(Sonnie Kern)

QUAIL EXTRAVAGANZA

Not too difficult, but time consuming. Beautiful presentation.

Seedless green grapes, washed and drained for garnish
1 egg white, beaten frothy
Granulated sugar
4 to 6 quail, or 2 pheasants, quartered
4 tablespoons butter
½ cup chopped shallots
½ cup cognac
2 cups chicken broth
2 tablespoons tomato paste
1 small bay leaf
1 teaspoon dry parsley flakes, or 1 tablespoon fresh chopped parsley
¼ teaspoon thyme
¾ pound fresh mushrooms, sliced
2 teaspoons arrowroot
2 tablespoons chicken broth
Salt and pepper to taste

Separate grapes into small bunches and brush with beaten egg white. Shake in a bag with sugar to coat; dry on a rack. Clean quail and brown in butter in a large skillet. Remove quail and add shallots to butter; cook until tender but not brown. In a small saucepan heat cognac. Pour over quail and shallots, in the large skillet, and flame — very carefully! When cognac stops burning, add chicken broth, tomato paste and bouquet garni (To make bouquet garni, place bay leaf, parsley, and thyme together in a cheese-cloth bag.). Bake uncovered in a 350° oven for 1½ hours. Baste every 15 minutes after the first 30 minutes. Add sliced mushrooms and continue baking for 15 minutes. Remove bird to a heated platter and keep warm; discard the bouquet garni. Mix arrowroot and chicken broth together and add to the pan juices. Bring to a boil, stirring constantly. Correct salt and pepper to taste. When mixture is slightly thickened and glossy, pour over birds; garnish with sugar-frosted grapes, and serve immediately.
YIELD: 3 to 4 servings

Mrs. Richard Shelton
(Louise Wittenmyer)

CHICKEN BREASTS DELUXE

**Everyone asks for this recipe! It's so simple;
it's almost embarrassing to tell how easy it really is.**

4   whole chicken breasts,
    split, skinned, and
    boned
1   10¾-ounce can
    condensed cream of
    chicken soup
1   10¾-ounce can
    condensed cream of
    celery soup
½   cup sherry
¾   cup shredded sharp
    cheddar cheese
3   green onion tops,
    finely sliced

Arrange chicken in a 2-quart buttered baking dish. Combine soups and sherry. Stir in cheese and green onion; pour over chicken breasts. Bake uncovered in a preheated 300° oven for 1½ hours. Remove from oven 10 minutes before serving.
YIELD: 6 to 8 servings

Mrs. Richard Karr
(Mary Frances Wheaton)

CHICKEN ARTICHOKE ROLLS

Moist, flavorful combination.

1   8½-ounce can arti-
    choke hearts, drained
1   8-ounce package cream
    cheese
    Lemon juice, about 2
    tablespoons
1   8-ounce package sharp
    cheddar cheese, grated
10 skinned and boned
    chicken breast halves,
    flattened
    Flour
1   10½-ounce can cream
    of chicken soup,
    undiluted

Chop drained artichoke hearts and mix with cream cheese, lemon juice, and grated cheese. Roll mixture into 10 small balls. Place each cheese and artichoke ball in center of each flattened chicken breast. Roll up chicken breasts and secure with wooden picks. Dust each chicken roll with flour and fry until lightly browned. Place in 9 x 12-inch casserole dish. Mix leftover cheese and artichoke mixture with undiluted cream of chicken soup and pour over chicken rolls. Bake in a preheated 350° oven for 1 hour.
CHEF'S NOTE: May be frozen before baking. Thaw and bake at 350° for 1 hour.
YIELD: 8 to 10 servings

Mrs. Frederick C. Setzer, Jr.
(Jane Miller)

162

CHICKEN AND THYME

**The secret of this recipe is cooking it *at least 2 hours* —
it may simmer up to 6 hours, if necessary, and will not be hurt.
Go to the game; come home, and dinner will be ready.**

2 tablespoons olive oil
1 clove garlic
8 large chicken pieces (I use 2 whole chickens cut in quarters)
1 large onion, sliced
3 10½-ounce cans condensed cream of mushroom soup (use 4 cans if cooking over 3 hours)
3 teaspoons thyme

In an extra large electric skillet, heat olive oil and garlic to 280°. When hot, remove garlic, and brown chicken on all sides. You may have to turn the temperature up, but the skin on the chicken should get brown. When browned, turn electric skillet to 200°. Place sliced onion over the top of the chicken. Pour soup over all, and sprinkle with thyme. Cover and let simmer at least 2 hours. Serve with long grain and wild rice or buttered noodles, tossed salad, and a green vegetable.
YIELD: 8 servings

Mrs. J. Edmund Weinheimer
(Bette Barlett)

CHICKEN SUPREME

Easy! Make ahead for dinner!

4 plump chicken breast halves
1 10¾-ounce can condensed cream of chicken soup
¾ cup apple cider
3 teaspoons worcestershire sauce
4 tablespoons dried onion flakes
½ teaspoon garlic salt
1 2½-ounce jar sliced mushrooms, drained

Place chicken in ungreased 9 x 9-inch baking dish. In a small bowl, mix together soup, cider, worcestershire sauce, onion flakes, garlic salt, and mushrooms; pour over chicken. Bake uncovered in a preheated 350° oven for 2 hours. Baste chicken after 1 hour and again after 1½ hours. Chicken sauce makes a delicious gravy. May be ladled over rice.
YIELD: 4 servings

Mrs. Anthony Rocco
(Gerry Anne Cronin)

EASY CHICKEN AND RICE

All you need is a big salad to complete the meal.

1 cup raw long grain rice
2 to 3 whole chicken breasts, boned, skinned, and split
1 teaspoon salt
1/8 teaspoon pepper
Dash of garlic salt
Dash of Accent
Dash of Fines Herbes (we prefer Spice Islands)
2 chicken bouillon cubes
2½ cups boiling water
2 tablespoons butter

Place 1 cup rice in bottom of a 2-quart casserole dish. Season chicken pieces on both sides with salt, pepper, garlic salt, Accent, and Fines Herbes to taste. Place chicken on rice. Dissolve 2 bouillon cubes in 2½ cups boiling water, and pour over rice. Dot chicken pieces with butter. Bake uncovered in a preheated 325° oven for 1 hour.
VARIATION: Substitute other chicken parts for breasts if desired.
YIELD: 4 to 6 servings

Mrs. Michael W. Craig
(Susan Hockwalt)

CHICKEN JUBILEE

Deliciously different!

4 whole chicken breasts, split, skinned, and boned
8 ounces chili sauce
1 whole red onion, thinly sliced
¼ cup raisins
¼ cup water
¼ cup brown sugar, packed tightly
1 tablespoon worcestershire sauce
1 16-ounce can bing cherries, drained and pitted
¾ cup sherry

Place chicken breast halves in a 9 x 12-inch baking pan. In a small bowl, combine chili sauce, onion, raisins, water, brown sugar, and worcestershire sauce. Pour over chicken; cover and bake in a preheated 350° oven for 45 minutes. Meanwhile, in a small bowl, combine bing cherries and sherry. At the end of 45 minutes, pour cherry mixture over chicken. Cover and continue baking for 15 minutes, or until chicken is tender.
YIELD: 6 to 8 servings

Mrs. Paul J. Strom
(Sandra Smith)

APRICOT CHICKEN AND WINE

Perfect dish to take to a new mother who is just home from the hospital. Make ahead to the final baking; then present it to the new father with the apricot sauce and instructions to heat for 45 minutes at 375°.

1   2½ to 3 pound broiler-fryer, cut up
3   tablespoons butter
    Dash of pepper and salt
1   cup chopped celery
1   6-ounce can water chestnuts, drained, sliced
¼   teaspoon garlic salt
¼   teaspoon salt
½   teaspoon dried rosemary, crushed
2   cups (or more) cooked long grain rice
½   cup dry white wine
1   16-ounce can apricot halves
4   teaspoons cornstarch
¼   teaspoon salt
¼   cup dry white wine

Brown chicken in butter; remove from heat and salt and pepper to taste; set aside. In same skillet, add celery, water chestnuts, salts, and rosemary. Cook until celery is tender. Remove from heat and add rice and ½ cup wine. Place in a 9 x 13-inch baking dish, and put chicken on top. Cover with foil and bake in a preheated 375° oven for 45 minutes. While the chicken is baking, drain apricots, reserving syrup. Combine cornstarch, ¼ teaspoon salt and apricot syrup in a small saucepan. Cook until thickened; add ¼ cup wine. Arrange apricots around chicken on top of rice, and pour thickened glaze over all. Bake, uncovered, for another 10 minutes. YIELD: 6 servings

Mrs. Bruce A. Triplett
(Leslie Conway)

SAVORY FILET DE POULET

This is outstanding, truly gourmet, and lovely to serve!

¾	cup flour
¾	teaspoon salt
¾	teaspoon pepper
¾	teaspoon savory
4	whole chicken breasts, split, skinned, and boned
¼	to ½ cup butter
4	thin, deli-style slices of boiled ham
¼	cup butter (if necessary)
1	pound fresh mushrooms, sliced or coarsely chopped
2	small onions, chopped
1	clove garlic, crushed
1	tablespoon minced parsley
¼	teaspoon savory
1	teaspoon salt
	Pinch of pepper
1/8	teaspoon mace
1	cup chicken broth
2	teaspoons light brown sugar
½	cup orange juice

In a small bowl, combine flour, salt, pepper, and ¾ teaspoon savory. Dredge chicken breasts in flour mixture. In a large skillet, heat ¼ cup butter, and fry chicken until golden brown (Add remaining ¼ cup butter as needed.). Drain chicken on paper towels; set aside. Trim ham slices of excess fat; cut in half lengthwise, and roll up. Using the same skillet, brown ham lightly. Drain on paper towels; set aside. In the same skillet, heat additional ¼ cup butter, if needed, and add mushrooms, onions, garlic, parsley, savory, 1 teaspoon salt, pinch of pepper, and mace. Saute over medium heat until mushrooms are tender. Stir in chicken broth, brown sugar, and orange juice. Cook and stir for about 5 minutes. Arrange chicken and ham rolls in a 9 x 13 x 2-inch casserole; pour mushroom-onion mixture over all. Cover tightly with aluminum foil, and refrigerate until baking time, or bake immediately in a preheated 325° oven for 60 minutes.

YIELD: 6 to 8 servings

Mrs. Jerry F. Hawkins
(Donna Odom)

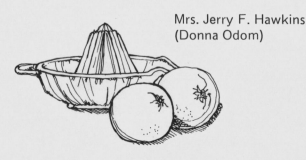

BEER CHICKEN

Very tender and moist chicken breasts
in tomato sauce with carrots and a nice blend of seasonings.

6	chicken breast halves, boned
2	tablespoons butter
1	12-ounce can of beer
1	cup grated carrots
½	cup sliced onions
1	bay leaf
½	teaspoon thyme
1	16-ounce can stewed tomatoes
	Do not add salt or pepper

In an electric skillet or a large skillet, brown chicken breasts in butter. Add beer, carrots, onion, bay leaf, and thyme. Cover and cook slowly for 1 hour (300° electric skillet). Add stewed tomatoes and cook uncovered for 30 minutes more (350° electric skillet). Serve with rice or biscuits.
YIELD: 6 servings

Mrs. Kent H. Collins
(Sallie Morris)

DELUXE CHICKEN HASH

An especially good combination.

¼	cup sauterne
2	cups finely chopped chicken (not ground), cooked
1	10½-ounce can chicken broth
1	garlic clove cut in half
½	teaspoon chervil
1	teaspoon tarragon
1	teaspoon chopped parsley
1	large onion, thinly sliced
2	tablespoons butter or margarine
2	cups fresh bread crumbs, slightly packed
	Salt and pepper to taste

In large flat bowl, pour sauterne over chicken; stir well. Cover and refrigerate for 1 hour. In a small bowl, combine broth, garlic clove, chervil, tarragon, and parsley; cover. Refrigerate until chicken is ready. Remove garlic clove. Saute onion in butter. Add broth and bread crumbs to chicken; then add onion. Let stand until liquid is absorbed by bread crumbs; add seasoning. Spread in a shallow, greased, 10-inch dish. Bake uncovered in a preheated 350° oven for 30 minutes. Brown under broiler if desired.
YIELD: 4 to 5 servings

Mrs. L. Keith Wilson
(Aimee Clunet)

DAYTON CHICKEN

Absolutely delicious! Perfect for company — easy and elegant!

2   cups cooked chicken, shredded

2   10-ounce packages frozen broccoli spears, cooked, drained (do not overcook)

1   envelope onion soup mix

1   pint sour cream

1   cup whipping cream, whipped

1   tablespoon grated Parmesan cheese

In a small bowl, add soup mix to sour cream, and beat with rotary beater until well blended. Arrange broccoli in a 7 x 11-inch shallow casserole in a single layer. Spoon half of the sour cream sauce over broccoli; cover with chicken. Fold the whipped cream into the remaining sauce, and pour over chicken. Bake in a preheated 350° oven for 20 minutes or just until bubbly (Do not overcook.). Sprinkle with Parmesan cheese, and brown under broiler.
YIELD: 4 to 6 servings

Mrs. Earl Pritchard
(Judy Elliott)

RICH CHICKEN AND MUSHROOMS

Delicious when served with wild rice.

4   whole chicken breasts, split

¼   cup vegetable shortening

1   2¾-ounce package cream of leek soup mix

2   cups coffee cream, or half and half

1   4-ounce can button mushrooms with liquid

In a large skillet, brown chicken breasts in hot shortening. Stir soup into coffee cream, and pour over chicken. Cover and simmer for 30 minutes stirring lightly as necessary. Add mushrooms and their juice. Cover and simmer for 15 minutes longer.
YIELD: 4 to 6 servings

Mrs. Stephen Cagle
(Pam Shough)

CHICKEN CONTINENTAL

Unusual and outstanding.

4	chicken breasts, split, skinned, and boned	Pound each chicken breast into a 5-inch square. Place ham and cheese on top of chicken breast, cutting to
8	thin slices ham, preferably Proscuitto	fit. Top with tomato pieces, sage, and oregano. Tuck sides in, and roll
8	thin slices mozzarella cheese	jelly-roll style. Combine bread crumbs, Parmesan cheese, and parsley.
½	cup seeded and finely chopped tomatoes	Roll chicken first in melted butter and then in the crumb mixture. Place seam
¾	teaspoon sage	side down in a buttered 9 x 12-inch
¾	teaspoon oregano	pan. Bake uncovered in a preheated
½	cup dry fine bread crumbs	350° oven for 45 to 55 minutes, or until chicken is tender.
3	tablespoons grated Parmesan cheese	CHEF'S NOTE: Place chicken breast half in a plastic bag to make the
2	tablespoons chopped parsley	pounding procedure more convenient. YIELD: 4 servings
6	tablespoons butter, melted	

Mrs. George L. Word
(Paige Early)

SUPER SIMPLE CHICKEN BREASTS WITH CHIPPED BEEF

Tastes like wild pheasant!
The sauce is good on wild rice as an accompaniment.

5	whole chicken breasts, split, skinned, and boned	Wrap each boned chicken breast diagonally with bacon. Grease a 9 x 13 x 2-inch baking dish. Line dish
½	pound bacon	with chipped beef; place chicken
6	to 8 ounces dried chipped beef (if beef is very salty, rinse and drain)	breasts on chipped beef. Mix together mushroom soup and sour cream; pour over chicken. Bake uncovered in a preheated 275° oven for 3½ to 4
3	10½-ounce cans condensed cream of mushroom soup	hours, or until chicken is tender. YIELD: 8 to 10 servings
3	8-ounce cartons sour cream	Mrs. Robert M. O'Hara (Barbara Nichols)

CHICKEN-ASPARAGUS AU GRATIN

Easy; nice for brunch.

2   10-ounce packages frozen asparagus or broccoli spears

1   10½-ounce can condensed cream of chicken soup

1   8-ounce jar American processed cheese spread (we prefer Cheez-Whiz)

½   cup milk

3   cups cooked, shredded chicken

Butter, for dotting

¾   cup cheese crackers, crushed (we prefer Cheez-its)

½   cup slivered almonds

Cook asparagus or broccoli according to package directions; drain. In a small saucepan, combine soup, cheese spread, and milk. Cook over low heat until hot. Layer a 2½-quart casserole with half of the asparagus or broccoli, half of the chicken, and half of the sauce. Dot with butter; sprinkle with slivered almonds, and arrange ½ of the cheese crackers on top. Repeat layers, ending with cheese crackers. Bake covered in a preheated 350° oven for 25 to 30 minutes.
YIELD: 6 to 8 servings

Mrs. Walter Scott Mills
(Sherry Smith)

CHICKEN A L'ORANGE AMANDINE

Easy, but elegant company dish.
Less than 30 minutes preparation time.

2   large whole chicken breasts, split

½   teaspoon salt

½   teaspoon black pepper

¼   cup butter

1   6-ounce can frozen orange juice concentrate, thawed

1   orange juice can water

1/3   cup slivered almonds

1/3   cup dry sherry, optional

Season chicken with salt and pepper. In a large pan over medium heat, brown chicken breast halves in butter on both sides. Add orange juice concentrate and water. Reduce heat to low. Cover and simmer for 45 minutes or until tender. Remove chicken to a warm serving dish. Sprinkle with almonds; cover, and keep warm until serving time. Stir sherry into pan juices; heat to serving temperature. Pour over chicken. Serve hot.
YIELD: 4 servings

Mrs. William vonReichbauer
(Virginia Dilts)

DICED CHICKEN WITH HOISIN SAUCE

Spicy, oriental flavor.

6   to 7 small, dried black
    mushrooms
    Boiling water to cover
    mushrooms
1   large whole chicken
    breast (about 1 pound)
2   teaspoons cornstarch
1   egg white
1   tablespoon pale dry
    sherry
½   teaspoon salt
¾   cup vegetable oil
1   tablespoon vegetable
    oil
½   teaspoon salt
1   medium green pepper,
    cut in ½-inch squares
6   water chestnuts, cut in
    ¼-inch cubes
2   tablespoons hoisin
    sauce
¼   cup roasted cashews or
    almonds

Place mushrooms in a small bowl; add boiling water to cover, and let stand for about 1½ hours. Squeeze out excess water by hand, and slice; set aside. Place the whole chicken breast on a chopping board; carefully remove all the meat from both sides of the breastbone with a sharp knife. Pull out the skin and white membranes, and discard them. Cut the breast meat and filets into ½-inch cubes. In a large mixing bowl, coat the diced chicken meat with cornstarch. Add the egg white, sherry, and ½ teaspoon salt, and mix them thoroughly. Heat ¾ cup vegetable oil in a large skillet over high heat for 30 seconds; stir-fry chicken cubes for 20 seconds until the chicken cubes turn white; then drain, and remove to a plate. Set aside. Heat 1 tablespoon oil. Add ½ teaspoon salt, green peppers, water chestnuts, and mushrooms; stir-fry briskly for 2 minutes. Add the fried chicken cubes and the hoisin sauce; stir well, and cook for 2 more minutes. Drop in the cashews or almonds, and stir to heat them through. Transfer to a heated platter, and serve at once with white boiled and steamed rice.

VARIATION: If you enjoy spicy food, add one crushed chili pepper to the above dish while cooking.

YIELD: 4 main course servings
       6 servings if part of a Chinese
       meal

Mrs. Richard Karr
(Mary Frances Wheaton)

RIPE OLIVE-STUFFED CHICKEN BREASTS

Yummy dressing.

1½ tablespoons dry minced onion
1 cup canned pitted ripe olives, chopped — reserve 1/3 cup liquid
6 tablespoons butter or margarine, melted
1 teaspoon marjoram
¼ teaspoon salt
1/8 teaspoon pepper
6 cups coarse day-old bread crumbs
1 6-ounce can water chestnuts, drained and chopped
¼ cup chopped parsley
4 small whole chicken breasts, boned but *not* skinned
2 tablespoons butter
1 tablespoon vegetable oil

Mix instant onion with 1/3 cup liquid from ripe olives. In a small saucepan, melt 6 tablespoons butter with marjoram, salt, pepper, and olive-onion liquid. Pour over bread crumbs, tossing to mix evenly. Add ripe olives, water chestnuts, and parsley. Mix gently. Place chicken breasts skin side down. Spoon one cup of stuffing in center of each. Fold chicken over stuffing and fasten with small skewers. Spoon remaining stuffing into 4 well-greased custard cups, pressing stuffing down gently. In a large skillet, heat remaining 2 tablespoons of butter with oil. Add chicken breasts, and brown on all sides. Arrange chicken in shallow 8 x 12-inch baking dish. Bake chicken and cups of stuffing in a preheated 350° oven for 40 to 45 minutes, or until chicken is tender. Arrange chicken and stuffing cups on serving platter.
YIELD: 4 servings

Mrs. Stephen Cagle
(Pam Shough)

CHICKEN AND MARINADE

Make ahead — great for guests.

6	whole chicken breasts, split, skinned, and boned
¼	cup lemon juice
4	teaspoons celery salt
¼	teaspoon garlic juice
½	teaspoon pepper
2	cups sour cream
4	teaspoons worcestershire sauce
2	teaspoons paprika
1	8-ounce package herb seasoned stuffing mix, crushed (we prefer Pepperidge Farm)
½	cup butter, melted
¼	cup butter, melted

In a shallow bowl, mix lemon juice, celery salt, garlic juice, pepper, sour cream, worcestershire sauce, and paprika until well blended. Place chicken in marinade. Cover and refrigerate at least 3 hours or overnight. Drain and discard marinade. Roll chicken in crushed stuffing, and place in 2, 9 x 13 x 2-inch baking dishes. Drizzle about ½ cup butter over the chicken. Bake uncovered in preheated 350° oven for 30 minutes. Add remaining ¼ cup butter, and bake for 15 minutes more.
YIELD: 10 to 12 servings

Mrs. David H. Kennett
(Susy Lamar)

CHEESY BAKED CHICKEN

One of my favorite chicken recipes.

5	slices slightly dry bread
4	ounces sharp cheddar cheese, cubed
2	teaspoons salt
1/8	teaspoon pepper
1	teaspoon monosodium glutamate (we prefer Accent)
½	teaspoon garlic salt
¾	cup butter, melted
2½	to 3 pounds frying chicken, or pieces you prefer (I use breasts)

Break 1 slice of bread into 4 pieces, and drop into a blender or food processor; add ¼ of the cubed cheese. Blend on low speed until it is a fine texture; turn into a bowl; repeat for all remaining bread and cheese. Stir in all seasonings. Dip chicken into melted butter and then into cheese mixture. Arrange in a 9 x 12-inch baking dish, and drizzle with remaining butter. Bake in a preheated 350° oven for 1 hour.
YIELD: 6 servings

Mrs. Charles Sutherland
(Joyce Jehl)

MARSALA CHICKEN

Gives chicken a distinctive pheasant-like flavor,
and it is excellent with rice.

3   whole chicken breasts,
    split, skinned, and
    boned
    Flour for coating
    chicken
3   tablespoons butter
    Salt and pepper
1   cup Marsala wine
2   tablespoons butter
2   tablespoons flour
1   cup milk, boiling hot
½   cup heavy cream
    Salt and pepper, to
    taste

In a skillet, over medium-high heat, brown both sides of flour-dusted chicken in 3 tablespoons butter. Add salt, pepper, and wine; simmer until chicken is cooked. Remove meat to a heated platter (Reserve all pan juices.). In a saucepan, melt 2 tablespoons butter over low heat. Blend in 2 tablespoons flour, stirring, to make a smooth paste. Cook over low heat for 1 minute, stirring constantly. Add boiling milk and blend well. Gradually add cream and reserved pan juices. Season with salt and pepper. Cook over low heat, stirring until thickened. Pour sauce over chicken.
YIELD: 6 servings

Mrs. J. T. Patterson, Jr.
(Sharon Rafferty)

CHICKEN PARMESAN

Delicious, moist chicken. Crispy crust with no frying mess.

2   fryers, cut into serving
    pieces
    Salt
1   cup bread crumbs
1   cup grated Parmesan
    cheese
½   teaspoon garlic powder
½   teaspoon paprika
1   teaspoon salt
    Vegetable oil

Clean and salt chicken pieces 1 to 2 hours ahead of time; cover and refrigerate. In a small bowl, combine bread crumbs, Parmesan cheese, garlic powder, paprika, and salt; set aside. Remove chicken from refrigerator. Roll in vegetable oil, then in the crumb mixture. Put on a cookie sheet. Bake in a preheated 350° oven for one hour.
YIELD: 8 servings

Mrs. Ben N. Miller
(Ruth Gambill)

TENDER CRISP CHICKEN BREASTS

The secret is soaking the chicken breasts in broth with bay leaves.
Very moist and tender chicken
with a hint of garlic on the crispy outside.

2	16-ounce cans chicken broth
2	bay leaves
4	whole chicken breasts, split (leave skin on)
½	cup butter
½	cup flour
2	tablespoons garlic powder
	Salt and pepper to taste
	Paprika to taste

In a large saucepan, bring chicken broth and bay leaves to a boil. Turn off heat; add chicken breasts to hot broth, and soak until broth cools; drain. Arrange breasts in a 9 x 13 x 2-inch baking pan. Place bits of butter under skin of each breast. Dot remaining butter around chicken. Sprinkle each breast with about 1 tablespoon flour and ¾ teaspoon garlic powder. Season to taste with salt, pepper, and paprika. Bake in a preheated oven at 375° for 50 to 60 minutes, or until chicken is tender.
YIELD: 6 to 8 servings

Mrs. Charles Castle
(Susan Ohmer)

HAWAIIAN CHICKEN

Tangy and flavorful, quick chicken dish.

3	large chicken breasts, split, skinned, and boned (if desired)
1	8-ounce bottle Russian dressing
1	envelope dry onion soup mix (we prefer Lipton)
1	8-ounce jar apricot-pineapple jam (or ½ jar of each)

Place chicken in a greased 9 x 12 x 2-inch baking dish. In a small bowl, mix together all remaining ingredients; pour over chicken. Bake uncovered in a preheated 350° oven for about 1½ hours, or until chicken is tender.
VARIATION: Substitute any other chicken parts for breasts, if desired.
YIELD: 4 to 6 servings

Mrs. Timothy White
(Nancy Wilcox)

JERRY'S SHERRY CHICKEN

Jerry devised this recipe as a result of an acquaintance with the Peruvian Ambassador to the Vatican. We had the privilege of attending a Peruvian New Year's Eve party, and the Ambassador was the chef. The turkey was cooked on the rotisserie, injected with sherry, and was delightful. We had always prepared chickens on the rotisserie with a garlic-butter sauce, and we thought the addition of black pepper on the skin and sherry injections into the meat would be delicious. We recommend the results!

2   small young fryers
    Seasoned pepper

BASTING SAUCE

½   cup butter or margarine
½   teaspoon garlic powder
    Juice of ½ lime (lemon may be substituted)
2   tablespoons olive oil
    Baster with a deep-injection attachment
1/8 cup sherry, warmed (for basting syringe)
½   cup smoky barbecue sauce (warmed)

Preheat grill to 250 to 275°. Sprinkle birds liberally with seasoned pepper, inside and out. Attach birds to skewers, and roast with lid down. Combine basting sauce ingredients. Baste birds when golden brown, and sprinkle again with pepper (Reduce cooking temperature if chickens flame.). Fill a baster with deep-injection attachment with heated sherry, and inject into chicken at multiple points; wait five minutes. Baste and pepper again; wait five minutes; inject sherry again; wait five minutes. Baste with smoky barbecue sauce; wait five minutes. Remove from grill; wait five minutes. Remove from skewers, and serve.

CHEF'S NOTES: Best when grilled, especially with dampened hickory chips on the hot coals! However, you may use your oven with good results. This recipe makes a 20-pound turkey melt in your mouth! 20-pounds of meat takes about 6 hours to cook. We would triple the sherry and the sauce amounts.

Mr. and Mrs. Gerald Gibson
(Manja Moore)

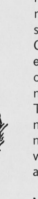

CHICKEN TETRAZZINI

This is so flavorful that it can be "dressed up"
with a spinach salad (see index) and wine for company.

4	whole chicken breasts
1	onion, chopped
¾	pound very thin spaghetti, broken into thirds (4 cups cooked)
1	cup sliced mushrooms (fresh or canned)
2	tablespoons butter
2	tablespoons sherry
2	cups veloute sauce

VELOUTE SAUCE

4	tablespoons melted butter
6	tablespoons flour
½	teaspoon salt
½	teaspoon paprika
2	cups canned chicken broth
½	cup heavy cream
1	cup grated Romano or Parmesan cheese Paprika

Put chicken in foil with chopped onion, and bake at 350° until chicken is tender (about 30 minutes). Cook spaghetti according to package directions. If using fresh mushrooms, saute in butter. Season with sherry, and set aside. If using canned mushrooms, drain liquid and add sherry to can to marinate until needed.

In a medium-size saucepan, melt butter over low heat for veloute sauce. Stir in flour, salt, paprika. Cook, stirring until it makes a smooth paste. Slowly add broth, stirring to mix very well. Cook over medium heat until sauce thickens to very heavy cream consistency. Remove from heat, and add cream a little at a time, stopping before sauce becomes too "soupy" or thin. Put all the spaghetti in a shallow 3-quart baking dish; spoon ½ sauce on top; arrange chicken, torn into pieces, mushrooms, sherry, and onions. Top with remaining sauce. Sprinkle with Romano or Parmesan cheese; add 4 dashes of paprika for color. Bake in a preheated 400° oven for 20 minutes. May be frozen before baking. Thaw and heat to serving temperature.
YIELD: 8 servings

Mrs. Geoffrey R. Lorenz
(Niel Ruth Phillips)

CHICKEN ENCHILADAS SUPREME

A true Mexican delight. Hot!

1 clove garlic, crushed
1 medium onion, chopped
1 tablespoon vegetable oil
1 4-ounce can whole green chilies, seeded and chopped
1 16-ounce can tomato sauce
½ teaspoon salt
Fresh ground pepper to taste
1 teaspoon oregano
4 to 6 chicken breast halves, skinned
1¼ cups sour cream
1¼ cups shredded mild cheddar cheese
12 corn tortillas
Vegetable oil
½ cup shredded mild cheddar cheese
Sour cream for garnish
Green olives, chopped, for garnish, optional
Black olives, chopped, for garnish, optional

In a medium-size saucepan, add garlic and onions to hot oil. Cook until onions are tender, not browned. Add green chilies to cooking onions along with tomato sauce, salt, pepper, and oregano. Simmer 20 minutes (Sauce may be pureed in blender if desired.). Meanwhile, place chicken breasts in medium-size saucepan. Add enough water to cover. Poach over medium-high heat 20 minutes or until tender. Remove chicken to cool slightly on a plate; shred meat into large mixing bowl. Add 1¼ cups sour cream and 1¼ cups shredded cheese; mix well. In a medium-size skillet, heat enough vegetable oil to cover the bottom. Heat tortillas, one at a time, in hot oil just until limp. Place 1 tablespoon tomato sauce mixture on each tortilla; spread over surface. Place about 1/3 cup of chicken filling mixture on each tortilla; roll up tightly; place seam side down in a 7½ x 11¼-inch baking dish. Continue rolling enchiladas until all filling is used. Pour remaining sauce evenly over top of enchiladas. Sprinkle with ½ cup shredded cheese. Bake in a preheated 350° oven for 20 minutes or until thoroughly heated. Garnish enchiladas on plate with a dollop of sour cream. Sprinkle with chopped green and black olives. May be frozen just before baking. Bake for about 1 hour at 350° or until heated through.
YIELD: 8 to 12 enchiladas

Mrs. William Miller
(Janet Hadler)

PARTY SANDWICHES

This is my mother's version of her favorite sandwich
at the old St. Louis Statler Hotel.

6	large slices of rye bread
6	slices of white turkey meat, same size as bread slice
6	medium-size tomatoes, sliced
6	hard boiled eggs, sliced
6	tablespoons caviar

Place slice of rye bread on each of six serving plates. Lay turkey on rye bread; lap tomato slices across the turkey, and lap egg slices across the tomatoes. In a small bowl, mix together the three dressing ingredients. Cover each sandwich generously with dressing. Garnish each sandwich with about 1 tablespoon of caviar if desired.

YIELD: 6 servings

DRESSING

1	cup sour cream
1	cup mayonnaise
6	ounces chili sauce

Mrs. Thomas Shulman
(Ellie Arnovitz)

SEAFOOD PLAKI

Outstanding flavor. Especially good way to prepare
frozen fish, yet fresh fish makes it even better.

2	pounds turbot, red snapper, or white fish
2	medium onions, diced
3	carrots, diced
4	stalks celery, diced Sliced potatoes (optional)
2	tablespoons butter or margarine
1	cup tomato sauce, or 1 pound freshly sliced tomatoes
¼	cup dry white wine (optional)
¼	cup vegetable oil
3	tablespoons chopped parsley
¼	cup raisins (optional) Salt and pepper to taste

Cut fish into serving-size pieces and place in an ungreased 9 x 13-inch baking dish. In a large skillet saute onions, carrots, celery, and potatoes in butter until tender. Drain and arrange over fish. In a small bowl, stir together tomato sauce (or sliced fresh tomatoes), wine, oil, parsley, raisins, salt, and pepper. Pour over fish and vegetables. Cover and bake in a preheated 350° oven for 25 minutes. Uncover and bake an additional 20 minutes. Serve immediately.

YIELD: 6 servings

Mrs. C. H. Houpis
(Mary Stephens)

SEAFOOD

EASY CRABMEAT FONDUE

Men just love this one!

½ pound butter
½ pound American
processed cheese
spread (we prefer
Velveeta)
1 6½-ounce can crab
meat, drained and
rinsed

In a large saucepan over low heat,
melt together all ingredients very carefully and slowly. Stir constantly until
smooth and hot. Pour into a fondue
pot over very low heat. Serve with
bite-size chunks of French bread —
fondue forks work well!
YIELD: 8 servings

Mrs. George E. Phillips
(Diane Kitzerow)

CRAB BRUNCH SANDWICHES

Filling and tasty. Great with a salad.

1½ cups crabmeat, rinsed
¼ cup chopped onion
¼ cup chopped green
pepper
3 tablespoons butter
3 tablespoons flour
1 cup milk
½ teaspoon seasoned salt
1/8 teaspoon pepper
¼ teaspoon dry mustard
2 tablespoons mayonnaise
1 cup shredded sharp
cheddar cheese
1 teaspoon lemon juice
1 tablespoon dry sherry
4 English muffins, split,
toasted, and buttered
8 thick tomato slices

Reserve some of crab pieces for
garnish. In a large skillet over medium
heat, saute onion and green pepper in
butter until soft and golden; stir in
flour. Remove from heat, and add
milk, salt, pepper, dry mustard, and
mayonnaise. Stir in cheese, crab,
lemon juice, and dry sherry. Heat and
stir until thickened and all the cheese
is melted. Top each toasted muffin
half with a tomato slice and 1/8 of the
crab mixture. Garnish with reserved
pieces of crab. Place on a cookie sheet,
and bake in a preheated 350° oven
for 10 to 12 minutes.
YIELD: 8 servings

Mrs. William Kasch
(Sonnie Kern)

180

CRAB FLORENTINE

Elegant and expensive — perfect for a ladies' luncheon.

1   10¾-ounce can condensed cream of mushroom soup, undiluted
2   10-ounce packages frozen chopped spinach, thawed and very well drained
1   8-ounce can small mushrooms, drained
4   tablespoons butter or margarine
4   tablespoons flour
2   tablespoons dry sherry
1½ cups milk
2   tablespoons mayonnaise
1   teaspoon onion salt
½   teaspoon white pepper
1   teaspoon nutmeg
1½ cups shredded Swiss cheese
1½ pounds crabmeat, frozen or canned, rinsed
1   8-ounce can water chestnuts, drained and sliced
4   tablespoons grated Parmesan cheese

In a large bowl, combine soup, spinach, and mushrooms; set aside. In a large skillet, make a roux of butter and flour. Add sherry, milk, mayonnaise, onion salt, white pepper, and nutmeg stirring until thickened over medium heat. Add Swiss cheese, crab, and water chestnuts to sauce. Layer in a 9 x 12 x 2-inch casserole: ½ of the spinach mixture; ½ of the crabmeat sauce. Repeat layers. Sprinkle with grated Parmesan cheese. Bake uncovered in a preheated 300° oven for 1 hour.

VARIATION: Poultry may be used as a substitute for crabmeat.

YIELD: 8 to 10 servings

Mrs. William Kasch
(Sonnie Kern)

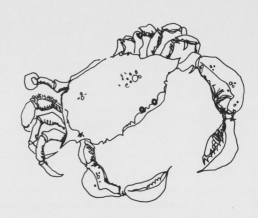

CRAB CASSEROLE

Easy and elegant. Every time I serve it I'm asked for the recipe.

6 ounces crabmeat, frozen or canned, rinsed
2 hard boiled eggs, chopped
4 ounces water chestnuts, sliced
4 slices bread, broken
1 cup coffee cream, or half and half
1 cup mayonnaise
Salt and pepper to taste
Worcestershire sauce to taste
1 3-ounce can French-fried onions (we prefer Durkee)

In a large bowl, mix together all ingredients except onion rings. Place in 9 x 11-inch casserole. Bake in a preheated 325° oven for 25 minutes or until hot and bubbly. Add onion rings, and bake another 5 minutes, or until onion rings are golden brown.
YIELD: 4 to 6 servings

Mrs. Charles Sutherland
(Joyce Jehl)

TURBOT SUPREME

Easy and delicious. Great family meal.

2 pounds turbot
2 10½-ounce cans condensed cream of shrimp soup
2 tablespoons sherry
1 tablespoon flour
1 to 2 tablespoons Parmesan cheese
1 to 2 tablespoons butter

Cut turbot into serving-size pieces. Place in a buttered 9 x 13-inch baking dish. Mix together soup, sherry, and flour; pour over fish. Sprinkle top with Parmesan cheese. Dot with butter. Bake uncovered in a preheated 375° oven for 30 minutes.
VARIATION: One 6-ounce package of frozen, cooked, or fresh-cooked shrimp, well-drained, may be added before baking.
YIELD: 4 to 6 servings

Mrs. L. Scott Wasmund
(Barbara Berg)

SALMON MELANGE

Good family dish.

1 cup medium white
sauce, or 1, 10¾-ounce
can cream of celery
soup diluted with
1/8 can water
¾ cup salad dressing
¼ teaspoon dill weed
¼ teaspoon salt
Dash pepper
1 8-ounce can salmon,
drained well and
flaked
1 cup cooked rice
1½ cups sliced zucchini
1/3 cup chopped green
onion
½ cup sliced green
pepper
¼ cup pimento strips
Grated sharp cheddar
cheese to top

In a large bowl, stir first five ingredients together. Add all remaining ingredients except cheese. Mix gently. Turn into greased 2-quart baking dish. Top with grated sharp cheddar cheese. Bake in a preheated 350° oven for 35 to 40 minutes.
YIELD: 4 to 6 servings

Mrs. Harry R. Wise
(Mary Jane Bolender)

SALMON PATTIES

Quick and easy; tastes great!

1 15-ounce can pink
salmon
1 egg
1/3 cup minced onion
½ cup flour
1½ teaspoon baking
powder
1½ cups vegetable shortening (we prefer Crisco)

Drain salmon, reserving 2 tablespoons of the juice. In a medium-size mixing bowl, combine salmon, egg and onion until sticky; stir in flour. Add baking powder to reserved salmon juice, and stir into salmon mixture. Form mixture into small patties. In a large skillet, heat shortening, and fry patties until golden brown (about 5 minutes per side or until done). Serve with tartar sauce.
YIELD: 4 to 6 servings

Mrs. Jonathan Wyant
(Barbara Jones)

SALMON TURBOT

Family recipe for 75 years.

2 tablespoons butter
2 heaping tablespoons flour
Salt and pepper to taste
2 cups milk
2 eggs, well beaten
1 15-ounce can Alaskan red salmon
2 pieces white bread, trimmed and cubed
Additional butter for dotting

Melt 2 tablespoons butter, and blend in flour, salt, and pepper. Stir in milk, and cook, stirring until thickened. Remove from heat, and stir in the eggs. In a buttered baking dish, place a layer of salmon, then a layer of sauce, alternately. Cover with bread cubes, and dot with butter. Bake in a preheated 350° oven for 45 minutes. Serve immediately.
CHEF'S NOTE: This is excellent served with broccoli, whole brown potatoes, and a slaw salad.
YIELD: Serves 6

Mrs. Alan A. Biegel
(Kathy Tehan)

FISH MOUSSE

This recipe is an old one used by my parents who were ardent fishermen for years. They created this recipe to use the quantities of rainbow and brown trout that filled their freezer every spring and summer.

2 pounds raw fish, skinned, boned (may use frozen)
2 cups dry white bread crumbs
1 cup whipping cream
1 teaspoon salt
¼ teaspoon white pepper
½ teaspoon onion juice
¼ teaspoon paprika
1 teaspoon lemon juice
4 egg whites, stiffly beaten

Put fish through food processor or mince into very fine pieces. Soak crumbs in cream; stir to make a smooth paste. Add all remaining ingredients except egg whites, and mix well. Fold in egg whites. Turn mixture into an ice-cold, well-greased, 5-cup mold. Place mold in a pan. Fill pan with hot water. Bake in a preheated 350° oven for 45 minutes.
CHEF'S NOTE: My family serves this with Hollandaise sauce, but a cucumber sauce or any sauce that goes nicely with fish would do.
YIELD: 6 servings

Mrs. Nelson Mead
(Ruth Cummings)

SHRIMP RICE CASSEROLE

Prepare ahead or same day. Easy.

1   6-ounce package long grain, wild rice (we prefer Uncle Ben's)
¼   cup butter or margarine
1   small onion, chopped
½   green pepper, chopped
¼   pound sliced almonds
2   pounds cooked shrimp
2   10½-ounce cans condensed cream of mushroom soup
½   cup white wine, or water

Cook rice according to package directions; set aside. In a large skillet, melt butter, and saute onion, green pepper, and almonds until soft. Add rice and all remaining ingredients. Heat thoroughly; turn into a buttered 9 x 13 x 2-inch casserole. Bake in a preheated 350° oven for 45 minutes.
YIELD: 8 to 10 servings

Mrs. William Bell
(Kathy Smith)

SHRIMP-SCALLOP CREOLE

Received about 25 years ago.

3   large onions, sliced
½   cup chopped celery
½   pound margarine or butter
2   28-ounce cans whole tomatoes, quartered
2   whole cloves
2   bay leaves
   Salt and pepper to taste
1   teaspoon sugar
1   12-ounce can tomato paste
1½ pounds cooked shrimp
1   pound raw scallops, sliced

In a Dutch oven, saute onions and celery in butter or margarine until onions are golden in color. Add canned tomatoes, and bring to a boil. Add cloves, bay leaves, salt, pepper, sugar, and tomato paste. Cook for about 45 minutes on medium heat, or until mixture thickens. Remove all cloves and bay leaves. Add shrimp and scallops, and simmer for another 6 to 10 minutes. Cool; cover, and refrigerate. Reheat to serving temperature. Serve hot over rice.
VARIATION: This may be made without shrimp; increase scallops. Remaining sauce may be frozen for future use.
YIELD: 8 servings

Mrs. Samuel G. Sava
(Elizabeth Tsourounis)

SEAFOOD

SHRIMP CREOLE

Delightful!

½ cup chopped onion
½ cup chopped celery
Garlic clove, minced
3 tablespoons vegetable oil
1 16-ounce can whole tomatoes
1 8-ounce can seasoned tomato sauce
1½ teaspoons salt
1 teaspoon sugar
½ teaspoon chili powder
Dash tabasco sauce
1 tablespoon worcester-shire sauce
1 teaspoon cornstarch, dissolved in 2 tea-spoons water
12 ounces raw shrimp, cleaned
½ cup bite-size pieces green pepper

In a Dutch oven, combine all ingredients except shrimp and green pepper. Cover and simmer for 45 minutes. Add shrimp and green pepper; cover and simmer for 5 minutes. Serve over rice.
YIELD: 6 servings

Mrs. James C. Medford
(Carolyn Lowe)

SHRIMP MOUSSE

Make ahead. Delicious party appetizer!

1 10¾-ounce can condensed tomato soup, undiluted
8 ounces cream cheese
1 tablespoon unflavored gelatin (1 envelope)
½ cup cold water
1 cup mayonnaise
1 cup chopped celery
½ cup chopped onion
18 ounces frozen tiny Alaskan shrimp, thawed
Fresh parsley

In a medium-size saucepan, heat soup. Add cream cheese and gelatin which has been softened in ½ cup cold water. Beat until smooth. Remove from heat. Add remaining ingredients; mix well. Pour into oiled mold; chill until set. Unmold 1 hour before serving; garnish with fresh parsley. Serve with melba toast or sesame seed wafers.
YIELD: 1, 5-cup mold

Mrs. Donald J. May
(Brenda Amburgey)

SHRIMP CASSEROLE

Easy, delicious dinner for guests.

2   10-ounce packages frozen chopped broccoli
      Boiling water
2   10¾-ounce cans condensed cream of celery soup
1½   teaspoons curry powder
1   cup mayonnaise (we prefer Hellman's)
      Juice of 1 lemon
4   cups frozen whole shrimp, cooked and well drained
½   cup slivered almonds
¼   cup chopped fresh parsley for garnish (optional)

Place frozen broccoli in a large strainer; pour boiling water over broccoli to separate. Do not cook; drain. Arrange broccoli in a buttered 7 x 11-inch casserole dish; set aside. In a small bowl, combine all remaining ingredients except shrimp, almonds, and parsley. Pour ½ of the sauce mixture over broccoli. Arrange cooked shrimp over broccoli. Add remaining sauce. Sprinkle with slivered almonds. Top with chopped parsley if desired. Cover and bake in a preheated 350° oven for 25 minutes.
YIELD: 6 to 8 servings

Mrs. Walter Scott Mills
(Sherry Smith)

PARTY SHRIMP CASSEROLE

Absolutely delicious. Great party recipe for a large crowd.

3	4-ounce cans mushrooms, drained
5	onions, chopped
½	cup margarine
3	10½-ounce cans condensed cream of mushroom soup
2	10½-ounce cans condensed cheddar cheese soup
3	10½-ounce cans condensed cream of chicken soup
2	envelopes dry onion soup mix
	Seasoned salt, to taste
1	teaspoon pepper
4	tablespoons dry parsley flakes
½	teaspoon crushed garlic
3	cups sour cream
1	cup cooking sherry
2½	cups raw rice (we prefer Uncle Ben's)
2	6-ounce packages wild rice (we prefer Uncle Ben's)
1	pound colby cheese, grated
1	pound Swiss cheese, grated
4½	pounds frozen cooked shrimp
	Croutons

Saute mushrooms and onions in margarine. In a large bowl, mix together all ingredients. Turn mixture into 3 greased 3-quart casserole dishes (Do not fill too full.). Layer croutons on top. Bake covered in a preheated 350° oven for 1 hour or until done.
YIELD: 20 to 24 servings

Mrs. Alan A. Biegel
(Kathleen Tehan)

SEAFOOD-ARTICHOKE CASSEROLE

Rich and highly seasoned; doubles as an appetizer or a main dish.

1	20-ounce can artichoke hearts, drained
¾	pound medium-size shrimp, cleaned and cooked
	OR
1	pound fresh shrimp, cleaned and cooked
	OR
1	pound scallops, sauteed in 2 tablespoons butter
¼	pound fresh mushrooms, sliced
2	tablespoons butter
2	tablespoons flour
2	tablespoons butter
1	cup milk
½	tablespoon worcestershire sauce
¼	cup dry sherry
	Salt, (we prefer Aunt Jane's Crazy Salt)
	Pepper, to taste
¼	teaspoon thyme
½	teaspoon oregano
¼	cup grated Parmesan cheese
	Dash paprika
	Fresh chopped parsley

Arrange artichokes in a buttered 7 x 11-inch baking dish. Spread cooked shrimp or scallops over artichokes. Saute sliced mushrooms in 2 tablespoons butter for 5 to 6 minutes. Add to artichoke mixture. In a small saucepan, make a cream sauce of 2 tablespoons flour, butter, and milk, stirring over medium heat until thickened. Add worcestershire sauce, sherry, salt and pepper to taste, thyme, and oregano. Pour over mushrooms. Sprinkle the top with Parmesan cheese; dust with paprika. Bake in a preheated 375° oven for 20 minutes. Garnish with chopped parsley; serve. VARIATION: Substitute small shrimp and bake in shells to serve as an appetizer.
YIELD: 4 to 5 servings

Mrs. Kieran Devery
(Carol Stefan)

SEAFOOD SAINT "JACKS"

May be prepared ahead and reheated in microwave oven.

1 cup fresh mushrooms, sliced
2 tablespoons butter or margarine
1½ cups dry white wine
1 medium onion, sliced thin
1 tablespoon minced parsley
1¼ teaspoons salt
1 pound fresh scallops, with liquid
2 tablespoons butter or margarine
1 tablespoon lemon juice
2 tablespoons butter
6 tablespoons flour
1½ cups half and half or coffee cream
½ cup grated Gruyere cheese
Pinch of pepper
1 6-ounce package cooked frozen shrimp, thawed
1 7-ounce can Alaskan King crabmeat, flaked
1½ cups soft bread crumbs, buttered

In a large skillet, saute mushrooms in 2 tablespoons butter; set aside. In a saucepan, combine wine, onion, parsley, and salt. Bring to a boil; add scallops; simmer 5 minutes. Add mushrooms and their liquid, 2 tablespoons butter and lemon juice. Simmer until butter is melted. Remove scallops and mushrooms; measure liquid adding enough water to make 3 cups; set aside. In a large skillet, melt remaining 2 tablespoons butter; blend in flour; add scallop liquid (3 cups) and cream. Cook and stir over low heat until thickened and smooth. Add cheese and pepper; stir until cheese melts. Add scallops, mushrooms, shrimp, and crabmeat. Heat to serving temperature. Turn into a shallow 3-quart casserole; sprinkle with buttered bread crumbs. Brown under broiler. Serve with rice.
YIELD: 8 to 10 servings

Mrs. Peter J. Kaufman
(Cindy MacFadden)

MICROWAVE SCALLOPS

A last-minute meal that tastes like you worked for hours.

1½   pints scallops, drained, rinsed, and dried
6   tablespoons butter
½   cup chopped green onions
1/8 teaspoon garlic powder, or to taste
¾   cup soft bread crumbs
2   tablespoons dry white wine (Chablis)
     Parsley for garnish (optional)

Drain scallops; rinse and dry. Place butter in an 8½ x 11-inch baking dish and melt (See directions in your microwave cookbook.). Add chopped green onion to melted butter; cover with wax paper, and microwave for 45 seconds. Stir in garlic powder, wine, and chopped parsley (optional). Add scallops, and stir to coat with butter. Sprinkle bread crumbs over all, and cover with wax paper. Microwave for 4 minutes on high. Stir lightly; turn casserole around, and microwave 2 minutes more. Correct seasoning. Broil casserole in conventional oven until bread crumbs brown. Serve immediately.
YIELD: 4 to 6 servings

Mrs. Richard C. Shelton
(Louise Wittenmyer)

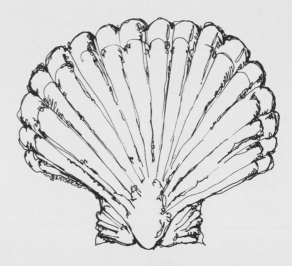

QUICHE FLORENTINE

Perfect for luncheons with a green salad and a slice of melon for dessert. Superb for simple supper or the perfect dish for a picnic; don't forget the wine!

2	unbaked 9-inch pastry shells
1	pound fresh spinach
16	slices bacon crisply fried and crumbled
12	ounces Swiss cheese, shredded
6	eggs
3	cups minus 3 table-spoons half and half
1	teaspoon dry mustard
¼	teaspoon salt, or to taste
1/8	teaspoon red pepper, or to taste
3	tablespoons dry white wine

Line two pie plates with pastry and flute edge. Wash spinach and cut off stems. Without drying spinach, put it in a large pot over medium heat and cook 5 to 10 minutes, or until tender (do not add more water), stirring and turning leaves often. Drain well; use paper towels to squeeze out as much moisture as possible. Chop spinach into very small pieces and set aside. Toss together bacon and cheese, and sprinkle them into the pastry-lined pans. Spread spinach on top. Beat together all remaining ingredients, and pour over the cheese, bacon, and spinach to just below the rim of each pie shell. Bake in a preheated 450° oven for 10 minutes. Reduce temperature to 300° and bake for 45 to 50 minutes, or until the custard is set and the top is light brown.
YIELD: 2, 9-inch pies

Mrs. Frederick Schantz
(Susan West)

CRAB QUICHE

Very light!

2	tablespoons minced shallots
2	tablespoons butter
6	to 8-ounces canned or frozen crab, well drained
¼	teaspoon salt
	Pinch of pepper
2	tablespoons dry white vermouth
3	eggs
1	cup whipping cream
1	tablespoon tomato paste
¼	teaspoon salt
	Pinch of pepper
1½	cups grated sharp cheddar cheese
1	9-inch deep dish frozen pastry shell, partially baked (10 minutes at 375°)

Saute shallots in butter about 1 to 2 minutes — do not brown. Add crab, and stir gently. Simmer 2 minutes. Add salt, pepper, and vermouth. Bring to a boil, and remove from heat. Set aside to cool. In a medium-size bowl, beat eggs with cream. Add tomato paste, salt, and pepper. Gradually add cooled crab mixture. Pour into partially baked pie shell. Sprinkle grated cheese on top. Bake in upper 1/3 of preheated 375° oven for 30 to 45 minutes or until puffy and golden brown.
YIELD: 6 to 8 servings

Mrs. Frank Babel
(Linda Klein)

GREEN CHILI QUICHE

Super quick! Serve as main dish or appetizer.

2	4-ounce cans of *whole*, peeled green chilies, seeded (NOT HOT CHILIES)
8	ounces Monterey Jack cheese, grated
4	eggs, well beaten
3	teaspoons worcestershire sauce

Butter a 9-inch pie pan. Line pan with chilies, opened out flat (This will be the "crust."). Fill pie pan with the grated cheese. Add worcestershire sauce to beaten eggs, and pour evenly over cheese. Bake in a preheated 275° oven for about 45 minutes, or until knife inserted near center comes out clean. Cool about 15 minutes before slicing.
YIELD: 4 to 6 servings as main dish
　　　　12 servings as appetizer

Mrs. Patrick E. Wilke
(Patricia Settle)

CHILI CHEESE CASSEROLE

Spicy, Mexican taste, makes this an unusual brunch or late night supper dish.

8	slices white bread, crusts trimmed and buttered on one side
4	cups shredded sharp cheddar cheese (16 ounces)
4	cups shredded Monterey Jack cheese (16 ounces)
2	4-ounce cans California green chilies, minced and seeds removed
12	eggs, beaten
3½	cups milk
1	tablespoon salt
1	tablespoon paprika
2	teaspoons oregano
1	teaspoon pepper
½	teaspoon garlic powder
½	teaspoon dry mustard

Arrange bread slices, buttered side down, in a greased 8 x 13-inch baking dish. Sprinkle cheddar cheese evenly over bread, then sprinkle Monterey Jack cheese evenly over the cheddar cheese. Arrange the chilies on the cheeses. In a large bowl beat eggs; add milk and all remaining ingredients; beat until blended. Pour over chilies. Cover and refrigerate overnight. Bake uncovered in a preheated 325° oven for 1½ hours, or until top is golden brown.
YIELD: 12 to 14 servings

Mrs. Harry R. Wise
(Mary Jane Bolender)

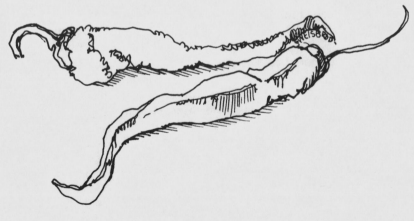

194

CHEESE SOUFFLE SANDWICHES

Very versatile recipe. Various meats or seafood may be added to sandwiches if desired. The sandwiches must be prepared ahead. Excellent for a winter brunch served with "Hot Curried Fruit" (see index).

12	slices of bread, crusts removed
12	slices of sharp cheddar or American cheese
1	to 2 cups shredded meat or seafood: chicken, ham, crab, or your choice (optional)
6	eggs
1	teaspoon dry mustard
3	cups milk
½	teaspoon salt
	White pepper, to taste
½	cup butter
2	cups corn or wheat flakes, crushed
1	10¾-ounce can condensed cream of mushroom soup, undiluted (optional)

Make 6 sandwiches, each with 1 slice bread, 1 slice cheese, meat and 1 slice of bread. Place sandwiches in a greased 9 x 13-inch baking dish. In a bowl, beat eggs; add dry mustard, milk, salt, and pepper. Pour over sandwiches. Add 1 slice of cheese on top of each sandwich. Cover and refrigerate for at least 6 hours, or overnight. In a large skillet, melt butter and add corn or wheat flakes; toss to mix. Add to top of baking dish. Bake, uncovered, in a preheated 325° oven for 1 hour. If desired, serve with heated, undiluted cream of mushroom soup. YIELD: 6 to 8 servings

Mrs. Alexander B. Hamilton
(Ardith Paul)

QUICHE DE CREME

Reigns supreme!

1	8-ounce package cream cheese
1	9-inch pastry shell, unbaked
2	tablespoons chives
3	small eggs
	Dash nutmeg
	Salt and pepper to taste
8	ounces coffee cream
6	to 8 strips bacon, fried and crumbled

Bring all ingredients to room temperature. Cut up cream cheese in small chunks, and cover the bottom of a 9-inch pie shell. Sprinkle chives over cream cheese. Whirl all other ingredients (except bacon) in blender. Pour mixture over cream cheese and chives. Place pie pan on cookie sheet, and bake in a preheated 350° oven for about 30-45 minutes, or until crust is golden and filling firm. Sprinkle with bacon if desired.
YIELD: 6 to 8 servings

Mrs. Dennis Patterson
(Linda Epstein)

CRUSTY CHEESE CASSEROLE

This is perfect for a luncheon or Sunday night supper.
Prepare this cheesy casserole in the morning and refrigerate
until guests arrive; then, just pop it in the oven for 30 minutes.

12	to 16 white bread slices, (we prefer Pepperidge Farm)
6	to 8 tablespoons margarine or butter
10	to 16 ounces freshly grated cheddar cheese
6	eggs, beaten
1	cup half and half
2	cups milk
1	teaspoon salt
¼	teaspoon paprika
½	teaspoon dry mustard
1	teaspoon worcestershire sauce

Trim crusts off bread slices. Butter both sides of slices and fit flat on bottom and sides of 9 x 12-inch buttered baking dish (Side slices should extend about 1-inch above dish.).Cover bread slices with grated cheese. Combine eggs and remaining ingredients. Mix thoroughly. Pour mixture gently over cheese. Bake in a preheated 350° oven for 30 to 40 minutes or until puffed and done!
YIELD: 12 servings

Mrs. Nelson Mead
(Ruth Cummings)

BROCCOLI OR SPINACH MOCK SOUFFLE

It is originally called Pirosnac — I changed the name.
People always ask for this recipe.
So simple and the flavors blend together beautifully.

6	tablespoons butter or margarine
2	pounds large curd cottage cheese
½	pound cheddar cheese, grated
6	eggs, beaten
6	tablespoons flour
2	10-ounce packages frozen chopped broccoli or frozen chopped spinach, partially thawed, drained.

Melt butter in a 3-quart casserole; tilt dish to grease on sides. Stir in remaining ingredients. Bake uncovered in a preheated 350° oven for 60 minutes (shallow casserole), or 75 minutes (deep casserole). Eat and enjoy.
YIELD: about 12 servings

Mrs. Jeffrey B. Shulman
(Celia Spiegelman)

BAKED EGGS MORNAY

Good for brunch or Sunday night suppers.

3	tablespoons butter
3	tablespoons flour
¾	teaspoon salt
1	teaspoon Dijon mustard
	Dash of pepper
1½	cups milk
¼	pound cheddar cheese, grated (1 cup)
6	eggs
3	English muffins, split, toasted, and buttered
	Bacon, fried crisp, for garnish

In the top of a double boiler, melt butter; stir in flour, salt, mustard, pepper, and milk. Cook, stirring until thickened. Add cheese and stir until melted. Pour half of the sauce into a greased 6 x 10 x 2-inch baking dish. Carefully break 6 eggs, one by one, into a cup. Slide each egg into sauce, side by side. Cover with remaining sauce. Bake, uncovered, in a preheated 325° oven until eggs are set (about 20 minutes). Serve immediately on English muffins. Garnish with crisp bacon.
YIELD: 4 to 6 servings

Mrs. Donald May
(Brenda Amburgey)

EGG AND SAUSAGE CASSEROLE

Our family enjoys this recipe for Christmas brunch.
I am able to prepare it the day before;
therefore, I can enjoy Christmas morning under the tree.

8   slices bread, without crusts and cubed, (we prefer Pepperidge Farm)

1   pound pork sausage, cooked, crumbled, drained

1½   cups fresh mushrooms, sauteed and drained

2   cups cheddar cheese, grated

4   eggs

2½   cups milk

¼   teaspoon dry mustard

1   10¾-ounce can condensed cream of mushroom soup

½   soup can of milk
Buttered bread crumbs (we use ½ cup Pepperidge Farm Herb Stuffing mix heated with 2 tablespoons melted margarine)

Place bread cubes in bottom of an 8 x 12-inch dish. Add sausage, mushrooms, and cheese to the bread cubes. In a separate bowl, mix together eggs, milk, and dry mustard. Pour liquid ingredients over ingredients in casserole. Cover and refrigerate overnight. The next day, bring casserole to room temperature. Mix mushroom soup with ½ can of milk. Pour over casserole. Cover with buttered seasoned bread crumbs. Bake in a preheated 325° oven for 75 minutes.
YIELD: 10 to 12 servings

Mrs. H. Brockman Anderson, Jr. (Margy Todd)

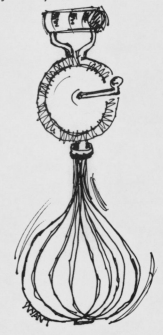

SWISS SANDWICH LOAF

Great new sandwich idea.

3	cups shredded Swiss cheese
1	6-ounce package chopped dried beef, OR
1	cup chopped ham
2/3	cup chopped tomato
½	cup chopped green onion
2/3	cup mayonnaise
1	round loaf pumpernickel bread, unsliced

In a small bowl, mix together all ingredients except bread. Slice bread almost completely through 11 times. Fill every other slit with cheese mixture. Wrap loaf in foil. Bake in a preheated 325° oven for about 30 minutes, or until cheese melts. Separate into 6 sandwiches.
YIELD: 6 servings

Mrs. William Kasch
(Sonnie Kern)

BRUNCH BAKE

Make-ahead for a cold weather brunch. Serve with "Hot Sherried Fruit Compote" (see index), sweet rolls, and coffee.

¼	cup margarine
¼	cup flour
1	teaspoon salt
½	teaspoon pepper
2	cups milk
1	tablespoon grated onion
½	teaspoon dry mustard
1/8	teaspoon soy sauce
½	pound sharp cheddar cheese, grated
1½	dozen eggs, hard boiled, sliced
¼	pound bacon, fried crisp, crumbled

Melt margarine in top of double boiler over medium-high heat. Add flour, salt, and pepper. Stir until smooth. Add milk gradually; stir until thickened. Add onion, dry mustard, soy sauce, and cheese. Cook over medium heat, stirring constantly, for 5 minutes. Remove from heat; set aside. Layer all sliced eggs in a buttered 9 x 13-inch baking dish. Pour sauce over eggs and sprinkle with all the crumbled bacon. Cover and refrigerate until ready to bake, or proceed immediately. Bake uncovered in a preheated 350° oven for about 30 minutes, or until mixture bubbles.
YIELD: 12 to 14 servings

Mrs. Lawrence Kramer
(Edla Armstrong)

GREAT BRUNCH SCRAMBLE

**Great for company brunch or as a quick family dinner.
Filling and delicious!**

3	cups soft bread cubes, no crust
2½	cups milk
12	eggs, beaten
½	teaspoon salt
1	teaspoon seasoned salt
¾	pound Swiss cheese, grated
12	slices bacon, fried and crumbled

Soak bread cubes in milk for 5 minutes. Drain unabsorbed milk into beaten eggs. Set bread cubes aside. Add salt and seasoned salt to egg mixture and scramble over medium heat until half cooked. Stir in bread cubes. Place mixture in a 9 x 13 x 2-inch pan. Sprinkle with Swiss cheese. Top with crumbled bacon. Bake in a preheated 400° oven for 20 minutes. YIELD: 12 servings

Mrs. Alan R. Merrill
(Lynn Wagner)

LEMON BARBECUE MARINADE FOR CHICKEN

Great flavor.

½	cup lemon juice
¼	cup vegetable oil
1	tablespoon minced onion
	Dash of salt
	Dash of pepper
½	teaspoon thyme
	Dash of garlic salt
3	whole chicken breasts, split and skinned
	Fresh lemon slices for garnish, optional

In a 9 x 13-inch baking dish, combine all ingredients except lemon slices. Cover and refrigerate for 24 hours. Turn chicken occasionally. Bake chicken in marinade, covered, in a preheated 350° oven for about 75 minutes or until tender; baste occasionally. Remove cover to brown during the last 15 minutes. Garnish with fresh lemon slices if desired. YIELD: 4 to 6 servings

Mrs. James Garrison
(Lesli Janacshek)

SUPERB KABOB MARINADE

An Egyptian specialty for an unusual treat. Excellent and easy
cooked on an outdoor grill with lamb, beef, or ham.

½ cup red wine
½ cup salad oil
1 clove garlic, mashed
½ cup finely chopped
   onion
1 teaspoon salt
1 teaspoon celery seed
1 teaspoon marjoram
1 teaspoon thyme
1 teaspoon sugar
1 tablespoon lemon juice
3 pounds meat (lamb,
   beef, or ham), cut into
   chunks

Blend all ingredients and pour over
meat chunks. Refrigerate overnight
(The kebobs may also be prepared,
marinated, and served the same day.).
Grill.
YIELD: 1½ cups, marinade enough
for 3 pounds of meat. Serves 12.

Mrs. James N. Nesmith
(Edythe Engel)

BROWN SAUCE

Tasty sauce to accompany beef, poultry, or pork chops.

½ cup butter
1 onion, chopped
¼ cup diced celery
1 large carrot, chopped
1 clove garlic, pressed
3 tablespoons corn-
   starch
3 cups beef broth
2 to 3 tablespoons
   Madeira wine
½ teaspoon thyme
½ teaspoon salt
1 large bay leaf
5 peppercorns

Melt butter in saucepan; saute onion,
celery, carrot, and garlic until limp.
Mix together cornstarch and beef
broth, and stir into vegetable mixture.
Add all remaining ingredients. Cook,
stirring constantly, until mixture
comes to a boil. Cover pan and
simmer for 30 minutes. Strain the
sauce, and serve hot. May be prepared
early in the day and reheated at serving time (Store at room temperature.).
YIELD: about 2 cups

Mrs. Lowell Mills
(Susan Taylor)

SAUCES

PEPPERONI SPAGHETTI SAUCE

This rich and thick, chili-like sauce has been our family's favorite for 30 years. It is very different from any spaghetti sauce you have ever tasted. Make ahead; it improves with age!

3	pounds ground chuck
1	pound ground pork or lean sausage
1	pound ground pepperoni
3	6-ounce cans tomato paste
1	quart tomato puree
6	to 8 garlic cloves, minced
1	large green pepper, diced
4	large onions, diced
8	to 9 bay leaves (4 to 5 if Spice Islands)
1	quart water
¼	teaspoon cloves
¼	teaspoon allspice
¼	teaspoon cinnamon
2	tablespoons worcestershire sauce

Over medium heat, brown beef, pork, and pepperoni, combined (It's easier if you use two large skillets.). Place browned meats in a very large kettle. Add all remaining ingredients; bring to a boil. Turn heat very low — just so sauce continues to boil; cover. Cook for 4 to 5 hours, stirring often (Watch carefully until heat is properly adjusted to prevent sticking.). Add a little sugar to taste, if desired. Cool; cover, and refrigerate. Heat to serving temperature. Serve over spaghetti. YIELD: 16 to 18 servings

Mrs. William R. Shelton (Ruth Shannon)

GREAT GRANDMOTHER'S CHILI SAUCE

This sweet relish is a great way to use bountiful garden produce.

24	large tomatoes, chopped
8	large onions, diced
6	green peppers, diced
2	cups vinegar
1	tablespoon salt
1	tablespoon celery seed
1	teaspoon cinnamon
1	teaspoon red pepper
1	teaspoon cloves
1	teaspoon dry mustard
1	teaspoon ginger
3	cups sugar

Combine all ingredients in large pot. Bake in a preheated 350° oven for 4 hours or until thickened. Stir occasionally. Freeze for future use. YIELD: 6½ pints

Miss Deborah Ohmer

202

MUSTARD BARBECUE SAUCE FOR CHICKEN

For mustard lovers only!
Use mustard sauce to baste chicken being cooked on outside grill.
Delightful change from traditional tomato-base barbecue sauce.

½ cup margarine
¾ cup prepared mustard
½ cup cider vinegar
1½ teaspoons black pepper
1½ teaspoons ketchup
Dash of tabasco sauce

Combine all ingredients in medium saucepan. Cook over low to medium heat for ½ hour, stirring occasionally. Use to baste chicken when grilling on outdoor grill.

YIELD: 1¾ cups

Mrs. Bruce A. Triplett
(Leslie Conway)

CREAMY MUSTARD SAUCE

This recipe came from the American Embassy in India some years ago and was used by our Ambassador during his tour there. This sweet and sour mild mustard sauce is especially delicious served with a ham dinner.

4 tablespoons butter or margarine
¾ cup sugar
2 tablespoons flour
½ cup white (distilled) vinegar
1 egg, slightly beaten
2 tablespoons prepared mustard
1/8 teaspoon salt

Melt butter. Blend in a mixture of the sugar and flour, stirring until smooth. Gradually stir in vinegar, mixing thoroughly. Remove from heat, and, stirring constantly, slowly add egg, mustard, and salt. Cook until smooth and thickened. Cool and refrigerate. Serve with baked ham, ham loaf, hamburgers, or try as a vegetable garnish.
VARIATIONS: ¼ cup raisins may be added. Try substituting a hot mustard.
YIELD: 1½ cups

Mrs. Robert Coyne
(Bobbe Dailey)

STRAWBERRY SAUCE FOR HAM

A good Easter recipe. Children love it! When we have leftovers, we especially like to serve this sauce over ice cream.

2	**10-ounce packages frozen strawberries, thawed**
2	**tablespoons cornstarch**
¼	**teaspoon cinnamon**
¼	**teaspoon ground cloves**

Put all ingredients in a 2-quart saucepan. Cook over medium heat, stirring constantly, until mixture is thickened (maximum of 10 minutes). During last 20 minutes of roasting time for ham, you may baste ham with sauce. Serve remainder in sauce boat, warm.
YIELD: 2 cups

Mrs. Charles Sutherland
(Joyce Jehl)

SWISS CHOCOLATE SAUCE

Very creamy and rich — great for ice cream or fondue.

4	**tablespoons butter**
½	**pound unsweetened chocolate (we prefer Baker's)**
1¾	**cups sugar**
2	**tablespoons cornstarch**
	Pinch of salt
¼	**cup light corn syrup (we prefer Karo)**
1	**13-ounce can evaporated milk (we prefer Pet)**
1	**teaspoon vanilla**

In the top of a double boiler, combine butter and chocolate. Heat over boiling water to scald. Stir in all remaining ingredients. Cook, stirring until smooth and thickened.

Mrs. Bruce A. Triplett
(Leslie Conway)

Sweet Endings

Deeds Carillon

DEEDS CARILLON

A desire to share music's beauty with others and to give tribute to Colonel Deeds, one of Dayton's greatest benefactors, resulted in the gift of the Carillon to Dayton on Easter Sunday in 1942. Donated by Mrs. E. A. Deeds, the Carillon graces the northeast corner of the beautiful sixty-one acre Carillon Park on South Patterson Boulevard. The 151-foot tower, containing thirty-two bells, is believed to be the first carillon in the world built with exposed bells. As a result, the Carillon's clear tones can be heard throughout south Dayton when concerts are played every Sunday during the summer months. Operation of the admission-free park and the Carillon was insured through a foundation established by Colonel Deeds while he was chairman of the board of the National Cash Register Company. Deeds Carillon is visible from I-75, reminding motorists of Dayton's cultural spirit.

HUNT CLUB PIE

Lightly flavored with almond and chocolate, this easy pie
may be served creamy cold or as a frozen dessert.

1 8-ounce almond
   chocolate bar (we
   prefer Hershey)
5 to 6 tablespoons water
½ pint whipping cream,
   whipped
1 baked 9-inch graham
   cracker crust

Break chocolate bar into top of
double boiler. Over low heat, melt
chocolate. Add 5 to 6 tablespoons
water and stir until smooth. Remove
from heat. Cool. Fold cooled mixture
into whipped cream. Fill crust and
refrigerate or freeze.
VARIATION: If desired, almonds
may be chopped.
YIELD: 8 servings

Mrs. Kent H. Collins
(Sallie Morris)

HOMESTEAD RHUBARB PIE

An old-fashioned rhubarb treat.

1 cup sifted flour
5 tablespoons
   confectioners sugar
½ cup margarine
¼ cup sifted flour
1 cup granulated sugar
1 egg, slightly beaten
4 cups sliced (½-inch)
   rhubarb, fresh or
   frozen (thawed)

Sift together 1 cup flour and confectioners sugar. In a small bowl, cut
margarine into the flour and confectioners sugar until a cornmeal
consistency; reserve ½ cup of crust
mixture for topping. Pack remaining crust mixture into an 8-inch glass
pie plate; set aside. Sift together ¼
cup flour and granulated sugar. In a
large bowl, add egg to the flour and
granulated sugar; mix well. Add rhubarb, and stir to coat rhubarb with
mixture. Turn into the prepared
crust, and sprinkle reserved crust mixture over top. Bake in a preheated
325° oven for 40 to 50 minutes until
crust is browned. Serve warm or cold.
YIELD: 6 servings

Mrs. William L. Augustine
(Katherine Carey)

GRANDMOTHER'S FRESH STRAWBERRY PIE

Like eating fresh strawberries, but even better.

1   9-inch pie shell, baked
2   quarts strawberries,
    washed, drained,
    hulled and halved if
    large
½   cup cool water
1   cup sugar
2½ tablespoons cornstarch
1   tablespoon butter
½   pint whipping cream,
    whipped

Crush 2 cups berries, and combine with water, sugar, and cornstarch in the top of a double boiler. Cook over hot water, stirring until thickened and clear. Stir in butter; remove from heat and cool slightly. Arrange remaining whole and half berries one by one in the cooled pie shell, spooning a little glaze over each layer. Build a pyramid with the berries, and spoon any remaining glaze over top and into holes. Chill well before serving. Garnish with whipped cream.
YIELD: 6 to 8 servings

Mrs. Geoffrey Lorenz
(Niel Ruth Phillips)

BROWN BAG APPLE PIE

This makes a very pretty pie; easy too!

½   cup granulated sugar
2   tablespoons flour
¾   teaspoon cinnamon
6   to 7 medium baking
    apples, pared and
    sliced
1   9-inch pie shell,
    unbaked
½   cup butter, melted
½   cup granulated sugar
½   cup flour

Mix ½ cup sugar, 2 tablespoons flour, and the cinnamon together and toss with the apples. Heap into the pie shell. Combine butter, ½ cup sugar, and ½ cup flour to make a thin paste. Spread paste over apples, coating evenly. Place pie in a brown paper bag and close securely with paper clips or staples. Place pie in center of the oven rack, taking care that the paper bag does not come in contact with any interior oven surface. Bake in pre-heated 400° oven for 1 hour. When pie is done, cut away the bag.
YIELD: 8 servings

Mrs. Lowell Mills
(Susie Taylor)

PEACH BLUEBERRY PIE

Delicious deep-dish pie.

4	cups peeled and sliced fresh, firm peaches
2	cups fresh blueberries
¾	cup sugar
1/3	to ½ cup flour
½	teaspoon cinnamon
1/8	teaspoon salt
2	teaspoons lemon juice
2	tablespoons butter
1	9 or 10-inch deep dish 2 crust pastry shell, unbaked

In a large bowl, combine peaches and blueberries. In a small bowl, mix together sugar, flour, cinnamon, salt, and lemon juice. Toss sugar-flour mixture with fruit. Pour into unbaked pastry shells, heaping fruit in center. Dot with butter. Put on full or lattice-style top crust; trim and flute edges. Cover edge with 1½-inch strip of aluminum foil to prevent excessive browning. Bake in a preheated 425° oven for 45 minutes (lattice) or 60 minutes (full crust).
YIELD: 8 servings

Mrs. James E. Swaim
(Pamela Dunlop)

LEMON DIVINITY PIE

Unusually light pie; very pretty!

4	egg yolks
3	tablespoons hot water
½	cup sugar
¼	cup fresh lemon juice
4	egg whites
½	cup sugar
1	8-inch pie shell, pastry or graham cracker, prebaked

Beat egg yolks slightly, and combine with water, ½ cup of the sugar and lemon juice in saucepan. Cook over medium heat, stirring constantly, until thickened. Remove from heat; cool slightly. Beat egg whites until very stiff. Gradually add remaining ½ cup sugar to egg whites, beating constantly. Slowly fold egg yolk mixture into stiffly beaten egg whites. Turn into a prebaked pie shell. Bake in a preheated 350° oven for about 10 minutes or until slightly browned on top.
YIELD: 6 servings

Mrs. John D. Shafer, Jr.
(Carol Hardey)

LUSCIOUS LEMON MERINGUE PIE

Not too sweet and not too tart
with a generous cloud of meringue on top.

1½ cups sugar
Dash of salt
5 tablespoons corn starch
1½ cups cold water
3 egg yolks, slightly beaten
Juice of 3 lemons (½ cup)
4 tablespoons butter, no substitutes
1 8 or 9-inch pie crust, baked
3 egg whites
3 tablespoons sugar
6 tablespoons sugar
1 teaspoon sugar

In a medium-size heavy saucepan, mix together 1½ cups sugar, salt, and cornstarch. Add the cold water, and cook over medium heat, stirring constantly until the custard clears (will still be somewhat cloudy — about 5 minutes). Stir in 3 slightly beaten egg yolks in a steady stream, and cook stirring occasionally for 5 minutes longer (The custard should be thick.). Add the juice of 3 lemons and 4 tablespoons butter. Pour into the baked pie shell immediately, or the custard will discolor. In a mixing bowl, beat the 3 egg whites until they hold a stiff peak. Beat in 3 tablespoons of sugar until the mixture is glossy. Gently fold in 6 tablespoons sugar — this helps the meringue to retain the air beaten into it (Overbeating causes the sugar to liquify resulting in a flat meringue.). Carefully spread the meringue on the pie. Make sure that the meringue touches the pastry all the way around. Sprinkle 1 teaspoon sugar on the top of the meringue. Bake in a preheated 275° oven for 15 minutes, or until the meringue is lightly browned.
YIELD: 8 servings

Mrs. Stephen G. England
(Katherine Benham)

LEMON CHESS PIE

Fresh lemon flavor — delicious!

4   eggs, well beaten
1¼ cups white Karo syrup
1¼ cups sugar
3   heaping tablespoons flour
    Juice of 3 lemons
    Rind of 1 lemon
¼   cup butter (or margarine)
1   9-inch, unbaked pie shell

Combine sugar and flour; add to eggs. Blend in syrup, lemon juice, and rind. Add softened butter, and beat together until well mixed. Pour into a 9-inch, unbaked pie shell. Bake in a preheated 350° oven for 45 to 50 minutes or until pie tests done. Cool until set before serving.

YIELD: 8 to 9 servings

Mrs. Patrick E. Wilke
(Patricia Settle)

CHOCOLATE CHESS PIE

Easy! Tastes like a rich brownie . . . . yummy!

1½ cups sugar
3½ tablespoons powdered bitter chocolate
2   eggs
1   5.33 ounce can evaporated milk
4   tablespoons melted butter
1   8-inch unbaked pie shell — plain or graham cracker

Beat eggs. Add other ingredients; beat until smooth and well mixed. Pour into pie shell. Bake in a preheated 350° oven for 45 to 55 minutes or until set like a custard. Test with silver knife until it comes out clean. Serve warm or cold with ice cream or whipped cream.

YIELD: 6 to 8 servings

Mrs. David N. Meeker
(Rebecca Bottomley)

GRAHAM CRACKER PIE

My family's favorite dessert.
Must be made ahead and refrigerated before serving.

PIE CRUST

18	double graham crackers, finely crushed
½	cup sugar
1	teaspoon cinnamon
1	teaspoon flour
½	cup butter, melted

FILLING

3	tablespoons flour
½	cup sugar
3	egg yolks, beaten
1	teaspoon vanilla
2	cups milk

MERINGUE

3	egg whites
½	cup sugar

In a medium-size bowl, combine all of the crust ingredients. Use ½ of the crust mixture to line the bottom and sides of a 10-inch pie pan. Note: mixture does not mold together. Set reserved crust mixture aside.

FILLING

In a medium-size saucepan, combine flour and sugar. Stir in egg yolks, vanilla, and milk. Cook over medium-low heat, stirring until thickened. Pour filling into prepared crust.

MERINGUE

In a medium-size mixing bowl, beat egg whites until foamy; gradually add sugar, and beat until stiff. Spread over filling. Sprinkle reserved crust mixture over meringue. Bake in a preheated 375° oven for 15 minutes. Cool. Refrigerate at least 4 hours (imperative) to allow pudding to set.
YIELD: 8 servings

Mrs. Frank Holloway
(Suzie Headley)

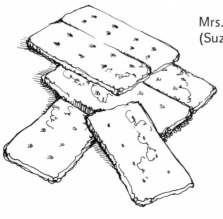

COCONUT CUSTARD PIE

Quick and easy with a delicious flavor.

1¼ cups sugar
4 tablespoons butter, softened
3 eggs, beaten
¼ cup buttermilk
1 teaspoon vanilla
1 cup shredded coconut
1 8-inch pastry shell, unbaked
½ pint whipping cream, whipped
¼ cup shredded coconut, toasted (optional)

Cream sugar and butter until light and fluffy. Mix in eggs and buttermilk. Stir in vanilla and coconut. Pour into an unbaked 8-inch pie shell. Bake in a preheated 350° oven for 30 to 40 minutes or until set. Cool.
VARIATION: Garnish with whipped cream and toasted coconut.
YIELD: 6 servings

Mrs. Lowell Mills
(Susie Taylor)

TOFFEE-COFFEE PIE

Different taste with a light and subtly sweet flavor.

1 egg white
¼ cup water
2/3 cup brown sugar
1½ teaspoons vanilla
1 teaspoon lemon juice
2 teaspoons instant coffee
1 cup whipping cream, whipped
2 1-1/8-ounce Heath bars, crushed
1 8 or 9-inch graham cracker crust

In a medium-size mixing bowl combine egg white, water, brown sugar, vanilla, lemon juice, and instant coffee. Beat at high speed for 8 to 10 minutes. Fold in whipped cream and crushed Heath bars. Spoon mixture into graham cracker crust. Freeze. Remove from freezer about 20 minutes before serving.
YIELD: 8 servings

Mrs. Denis Thomas
(Barbara Butt)

CHOCOLATE VELVET PIE

Light, fluffy and melts in your mouth. Easy, make ahead!

2 squares unsweetened baking chocolate
8 tablespoons butter, softened
¾ cup sugar
1 teaspoon vanilla
2 eggs
1 8-inch graham cracker crust
½ pint whipping cream, whipped
2 teaspoons powdered sugar, optional
2 teaspoons creme de menthe, optional

Melt chocolate. Let it cool. In a medium-size mixing bowl, cream together butter and sugar. Add vanilla and chocolate; mix well. Add eggs, one at a time, beating well after each addition (Do not underbeat.). Turn into 8-inch graham cracker crust. Chill overnight. At serving time, top with whipped cream which may be flavored with 2 teaspoons powdered sugar and 2 teaspoons creme de menthe.
YIELD: 6 servings

Mrs. Stewart A. Levine
(Laraine Kanner)

CHOCOLATE WAFER PIE

Very unusual, no-crust pie!

3 egg whites
Dash salt
¾ cup sugar
¾ cup chocolate wafer crumbs
½ cup chopped walnuts
½ teaspoon vanilla
½ pint whipping cream
Sugar to taste
Unsweetened chocolate, or milk chocolate bar, shaved, for garnish

In a medium-size mixing bowl, beat egg whites with salt and sugar until soft peaks form. In a small bowl, mix crumbs, nuts, and vanilla. Add to meringue, folding carefully to mix. Pour into greased 9-inch pie pan. Bake in a preheated 325° oven for 35 minutes; cool. Cover and refrigerate for 3 hours. Adding sugar to taste, spread whipped cream over pie. Garnish with chocolate.
YIELD: 6 servings

Mrs. Kieran Devery
(Carol Stefan)

DERBY PIE

This recipe, given to me by a Louisville friend, is a Kentucky favorite
at Kentucky Derby time, or anytime!
Very rich . . . serve small portions.

1   cup semi-sweet
    chocolate chips
½   cup English walnuts,
    chopped
½   cup pecans, chopped
2   eggs, beaten
1   cup sugar
½   cup butter or
    margarine, melted
½   cup flour
1   teaspoon vanilla
1   9-inch pie shell,
    unbaked
½   pint whipping cream,
    whipped

In a large bowl, combine chocolate chips and nuts. Stir in eggs, sugar, butter, flour and vanilla; mix well by hand. Pour into unbaked 9-inch pie shell. Bake in a preheated 350° oven for 30 minutes, or until knife inserted near center comes out clean. Garnish with whipped cream.
VARIATION: Use 1 cup pecans, omitting English walnuts.
YIELD: 8 to 10 servings

Mrs. Robert L. Walker
(Susan Katterjohn)

DATE AND NUT TARTS

Made by my grandmother for Christmas.
The dates are a tasty addition.

PASTRY

Use your favorite pastry
recipe — enough for a
double-crusted pie.

FILLING

2   eggs
1   cup sugar
1   cup butter, melted
1   cup chopped dates
1   cup chopped pecans
    or walnuts
1   teaspoon vanilla

Combine all filling ingredients. Mix
well. Spoon into pastry-lined tart
pans, filling ¾ full (about 1 teaspoon).
Bake in a preheated 350° oven for 10
minutes. Reduce temperature to 250°;
bake 10 minutes, or until crust is
golden brown. Remove from pans as
soon as tarts are cool enough to
handle. Place on rack until completely
cooled. Can be stored in a tin for a
week or more.
CHEF'S NOTE: Leftover filling may
be frozen. Tarts may also be frozen.
YIELD: 3 to 4 dozen tarts, depending
upon size

Mrs. Charles J. Roedersheimer
(Alice Murray)

GRASSHOPPER PIE

A very rich and elegant dessert.
Best when prepared 24 hours before serving.

16   Oreo cookies
5   tablespoons butter,
     melted
¾   cup milk
16   to 20 large marsh-
     mallows
2   tablespoons creme de
     menthe
2   tablespoons creme de
     cacao
1   cup whipping cream,
     whipped
½   teaspoon vanilla

Crush cookies and blend in melted
butter. Spread evenly in a 9-inch pan,
reserving a few crumbs for the top.
Heat milk and marshmallows in a
saucepan until the marshmallows are
melted. Cool. Add creme de menthe
and creme de cacao; fold in whipped
cream and vanilla. Pour into crust
and sprinkle with remaining cookie
crumbs. Refrigerate 24 hours.
YIELD: 6 to 8 servings

Mrs. Karl A. Stein
(Diana Headley)

AUNT ES'S ANGEL PIE

Meringue crust filled with a rich chocolate mixture.
Time-consuming, but worth the extra effort for a special dessert.

4   egg whites
½   teaspoon salt
1   teaspoon vinegar
1   cup granulated
    sugar
1   teaspoon vanilla
2   cups chocolate bits
    (12-ounce package)
½   cup sugar
¼   cup water
4   egg yolks, lightly
    beaten
1   pint whipping cream
¼   cup sugar
¼   to ½ cup chopped
    pecans (pecan halves
    may be used)

In a large mixing bowl, beat egg whites, salt, and vinegar until almost stiff. Add 1 cup sugar, one tablespoon at a time; beat until smooth; add vanilla. Line a cookie sheet with aluminum foil; grease well. Spread meringue on prepared cookie sheet in a 12-inch circle, making the bottom ½-inch thick and building up the edges. Bake in a preheated 275° oven for 60 minutes. Turn off heat, and allow meringue to cool in oven for 2 hours. In a double boiler, melt chocolate bits over hot water; remove from heat and cool slightly. Spread 4 tablespoons of the melted chocolate over the cooled meringue. Add ½ cup sugar, water, and egg yolks to remaining chocolate. Return to heat, and cook over hot water until thickened; cool, and set aside. In a large mixing bowl, whip cream until stiff; add ¼ cup sugar. Spread ½ the whipped cream over chocolate in the shell. Fold the remaining chocolate mixture into the reserved whipped cream; spread over the whipped cream in the meringue shell. Sprinkle pecans over the top, and refrigerate until serving time. May be prepared a day ahead.
YIELD: 10 to 12 servings

Mrs. H. Brockman Anderson, Jr.
(Margy Todd)

215

CHOCOLATE ANGEL PIE

It looks elegant!

2	egg whites
1/8	teaspoon salt
1/8	teaspoon cream of tartar
½	cup sugar
½	teaspoon vanilla
¾	cup finely chopped pecans
1	4-ounce bar German sweet chocolate (we prefer Baker's)
3	tablespoons water
1	teaspoon vanilla
½	pint whipping cream, whipped

In a glass or metal mixing bowl, beat egg whites with salt and cream of tartar until foamy. Add sugar, 2 tablespoons at a time, beating well after each addition. Continue beating until stiff and mixture holds peaks. Fold in vanilla and nuts. Spoon carefully into a greased 8-inch or 9-inch pie pan. To form shell, build up sides to ½ inch above edge of pan. Bake in a preheated 300° oven for 50 to 55 minutes. Set aside to cool completely. In a large saucepan, stir chocolate and water over low heat until melted. Remove from heat, and cool until thickened. Stir in vanilla; fold whipped cream into chocolate mixture. Pile into meringue shell, and chill for at least two hours before serving.
YIELD: 6 to 8 servings

Mrs. Richard Cammerer
(Molly Wall)

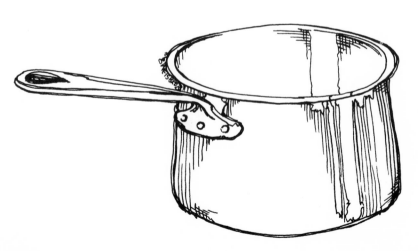

BECKY'S BOURBON PIE

Rich, smooth, and delicious!

¼ cup butter, melted
1-1/3 cups crushed ginger snaps
1½ cups granulated sugar
1 tablespoon cornstarch
3 egg yolks, lightly beaten
1½ cups milk
1 tablespoon gelatin
3 tablespoons cold water
1½ squares bitter chocolate
½ teaspoon vanilla
3 tablespoons bourbon
Dash of nutmeg
3 egg whites, whipped stiff
1 cup whipping cream, whipped and sweetened to taste
Chocolate curls or grated bitter chocolate for garnish

In a small saucepan, melt butter; remove from heat, and stir in crushed ginger snaps. Pat crust mixture into an 8 or 9-inch pie pan; set aside. In a small saucepan, lightly beat egg yolks. Combine sugar and cornstarch, and stir into egg yolks. Gradually stir in milk. Cook and stir over low heat until mixture thickly coats spoon. Remove from heat. In a cup, soften gelatin in 3 tablespoons cold water. Stir gelatin and water into the hot egg yolk mixture. In the top of a double boiler, melt chocolate. Remove from heat; stir in 1/3 of the custard mixture and ½ teaspoon vanilla. Spread on the prepared crust; cover and refrigerate. Cool remaining 2/3 of the custard mixture. Stir in bourbon and nutmeg. Carefully fold in whipped egg whites. Spread mixture over chocolate layer. Refrigerate until cool. Top with sweetened whipped cream. Garnish with chocolate curls or grated bitter chocolate. Refrigerate until serving time.
YIELD: 6 to 8 servings

Mrs. Donald C. Woods
(Peggy A. White)

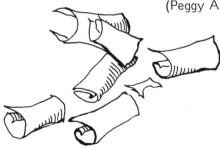

AMARETTO PIE

Must be prepared ahead. Very rich and tasty — serve sparingly.

1½ cups chocolate wafer crumbs
¼ cup melted butter
1 egg
1 egg yolk
¾ cup sugar
½ cup sifted all-purpose flour
1 cup boiling milk
3 tablespoons butter
2 teaspoons vanilla extract
¼ teaspoon almond extract
½ cup pulverized almonds
3 tablespoons Amaretto liqueur
2 egg whites
½ cup heavy cream, whipped
½ cup heavy cream
Unsweetened chocolate, shaved
4 tablespoons sugar
1 tablespoon Amaretto

Prepare crust by mixing cookie crumbs and butter. Press firmly and evenly into a 9-inch pie pan. Bake in a preheated 350° oven for 10 minutes; cool. For filling, with an electric mixer at medium speed, beat 1 egg and 1 egg yolk in a large mixing bowl. Add ¾ cup sugar very, very gradually until mixture is pale yellow and thick. Beat in the flour. Beat in the boiling milk in a thin stream of droplets. Turn mixture into a saucepan, and set over medium heat, stirring constantly with a large wire whisk. When mixture begins to coagulate into lumps, beat it vigorously until it smooths and thickens into a stiff paste. Reduce heat to medium low, and beat mixture with a wooden spoon for 2 to 3 minutes (Be careful not to scorch the custard.). Remove from heat. Beat in butter, flavorings, almonds, and 3 tablespoons Amaretto. Remove from heat, and set aside to cool. Beat egg whites with mixer until stiff but not dry. Fold ¼ custard mixture into egg whites; then fold the egg-custard mixture into the remaining custard. Fold whipped cream into the custard mixture. Pour into baked pie shell, and refrigerate for at least 10 hours before serving. Just before serving, whip ½ cup cream; add 4 tablespoons sugar and 1 tablespoon Amaretto. Spread on the pie and garnish with shaved chocolate.
YIELD: 8 servings

Mrs. Arnold I. Schwartzman
(Judith Bassman)

MARGARITA PIE

Unusual and delicious.

¾ cup crushed pretzels
1/3 cup butter or margarine
3 tablespoons sugar
½ cup lemon juice
1 envelope unflavored gelatin
4 egg yolks
½ cup sugar
¼ teaspoon salt
1 teaspoon grated lemon peel
1/3 cup tequila
3 tablespoons triple sec
4 egg whites
½ cup sugar

Combine pretzel crumbs, butter, and sugar; mix well. Press against the bottom and sides of a greased 9-inch pie pan. Sprinkle lemon juice with unflavored gelatin; let stand until softened; beat egg yolks in top half of double boiler; blend in ½ cup sugar, salt, and grated lemon peel. Add softened gelatin; cook over boiling water, stirring constantly until slightly thickened and gelatin is completely dissolved. Transfer to a bowl; blend in tequila and triple sec. Chill until mixture is cold but not further thickened. Beat egg whites until foamy; gradually beat until egg whites hold soft peaks. Poor cooled gelatin mixture slowly on egg whites about 1/3 at a time, folding very carefully after each addition. Let stand until mixture mounds in spoon. Swirl into prepared crust; chill until set. Decorate top of pie with pretzel twists if desired.
YIELD: 6 to 8 servings

Miss Jane Deuser

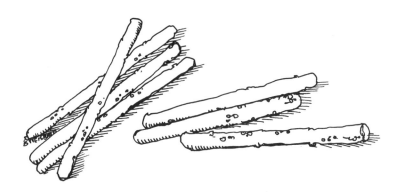

219

KAHLUA PIE

Outstanding — very rich.

1	cup butter, softened
1½	cups granulated sugar
2	squares unsweetened chocolate, melted
4	eggs
¼	cup Kahlua
1	9-inch deep-dish pie crust, baked and cooled
½	pint whipping cream
2	tablespoons granulated sugar
¼	cup sliced or slivered almonds, toasted in skillet in 1 teaspoon butter and drained

In a large mixing bowl, beat together butter, sugar, and melted chocolate. Add one egg and beat on high speed for 5 minutes. Repeat until all 4 eggs have been added. Stir in Kahlua. Pour into baked pie crust. In a small mixing bowl, whip cream until stiff; add sugar gradually. Spread on top of pie. Sprinkle with toasted almonds. Chill until serving time.

VARIATION: Recipe may be halved if using small crust.

YIELD: 8 to 10 servings

Mrs. Richard S. Sutton
(Janet Robinson)

PATTI'S PASTRIES

Truly scrumptious!

1	pound butter (no substitutes)
1	pound cream cheese, softened
4½	cups flour, unsifted

In a mixing bowl combine all pastry ingredients; blend thoroughly. Cover and refrigerate until well chilled. On a floured board, roll pastry to ¼-inch thickness.

FILLING

2	teaspoons cinnamon
1	cup sugar
½	cup raisins
	Adjust the filling ingredients to your family's taste

FILLING

Mix cinnamon and sugar together. Sprinkle liberally over dough. Sprinkle with raisins. Roll up like a jelly roll. Cut diagonally so slices are one inch thick. Place on ungreased cookie sheet and bake in a preheated 350° oven for 15 minutes.

YIELD: 4 dozen

Mrs. Charles Ballard
(Patti Davis)

CREAM CHEESE COFFEE CAKE

Easy to make because three coffee cakes are mixed and baked,
and the kitchen is cleaned up in only one hour!

½	cup butter, softened
8	ounces cream cheese, softened
1½	cups sugar
2	eggs
2	cups flour
2	teaspoons baking powder
½	teaspoon salt
1	teaspoon baking soda
½	cup milk
1	teaspoon vanilla
¼	cup butter, softened
¼	cup flour
1	cup brown sugar

Cream together butter, cream cheese, and sugar. Add eggs; beat well. Sift together flour, baking powder, salt, and baking soda. Add dry ingredients alternately with milk and vanilla. Divide dough evenly among three 8 or 9-inch greased and floured cake pans. In a small bowl, mix ¼ cup butter, ¼ cup flour, and 1 cup brown sugar. Sprinkle brown sugar mixture on top of cakes. Bake in a preheated 350° oven for 20 minutes, or until cakes test done.
YIELD: 18 to 24 servings

Mrs. William Henry Macbeth
(Helen Daley)

RICH BUTTER PECAN COFFEE CAKE

This cake freezes well! I serve one to my family
and keep the other in the freezer for unexpected guests.

1	cup granulated sugar
1	cup dark brown sugar
1	cup butter or margarine
2	cups flour
8	ounces sour cream
2	eggs, beaten
1	teaspoon baking soda
½	teaspoon salt
1	teaspoon vanilla
4	ounces chopped pecans

Mix granulated sugar, brown sugar, butter, and flour with pastry blender until fine crumbs are formed. Reserve 1 cup of this mixture for topping. To the remaining crumb mixture, stir in remaining ingredients, except pecans. Spread into two greased and floured 8-inch round pans. Sprinkle with reserved topping mixture and pecan pieces. Bake in a preheated 350° oven for 35 to 40 minutes. Do not overbake.
YIELD: Two 8-inch round cakes

Mrs. Roy L. Hohman
(Judy Hoeltke)

BONNY BLUE BERRY BREAD

Great as a cake for coffee time; the kids love it, too.

½ cup butter, softened
¾ cup sugar
1 egg
1/3 cup milk
2 cups sifted flour
2 teaspoons baking powder
½ teaspoon salt
1 21-ounce can blueberry pie filling
½ cup sugar
½ cup unsifted all-purpose flour
½ teaspoon cinnamon
2 tablespoons butter

In a medium-size mixing bowl, cream ½ cup butter and ¾ cup sugar; beat in egg; blend in milk. Sift together 2 cups flour, baking powder, and salt. Add to creamed mixture; mix well. Spread half of the batter in a greased 8-inch square pan; cover with ¾ can blueberry pie filling. Spread remaining batter over pie filling; top with remaining ¼ can pie filling. In a small bowl, mix ½ cup sugar, ½ cup flour, and cinnamon; cut in 2 tablespoons butter; sprinkle over batter. Bake in a preheated 375° oven for about 1 hour, or until wooden pick comes out clean.
YIELD: 9 servings

Mrs. Earl F. Pritchard
(Judy Elliott)

AUNT IDA'S CHOCOLATE CAKE

Yummy — four layers!

1¾ cups flour
1¾ cups granulated sugar
1¼ teaspoons baking soda
1¼ teaspoons salt
¼ teaspoon baking powder
2/3 cup butter or margarine, softened
1¼ cups water
1 teaspoon vanilla
4 squares unsweetened chocolate, melted
3 eggs

Sift dry ingredients together. In a large mixing bowl, add flour mixture to creamed margarine, water, and vanilla. Mix well. Add melted chocolate and beat on low speed until well blended. Beat two minutes on medium speed. Add eggs, one at a time, beating well after each addition. Pour into four greased 9-inch cake pans. Bake in a preheated 350° oven for 20 minutes, or until cake tests done with a wooden pick. Frost cooled cakes with "Fluffy Flour Frosting" (see index) or your favorite 7-minute frosting.
YIELD: 10 servings

Mrs. Thomas Shulman
(Ellie Arnovitz)

VANILLA WAFER CAKE

This is my Grandmother's recipe, a family favorite.
Very moist and flavorful!

1 cup margarine, softened
2 cups sugar
6 eggs
14½ ounces vanilla wafers, finely crushed
½ cup milk
1 3½-ounce can flaked coconut
1 cup chopped pecans

Cream margarine and sugar. Add eggs, one at a time, beating after each addition. Blend in wafers gradually. Mix in milk, coconut, and pecans. Pour into a well-greased 10-inch tube pan. Bake in a preheated 325° oven for 75 minutes or until done. Allow cake to cook, right side up in pan, for 30 minutes before turning out.
YIELD: 1, 10-inch cake
            24 servings

Mrs. Robert L. Walker
(Susan Katterjohn)

CHRISTMAS CAKE

**Prepare Thanksgiving week to serve Christmas Day.
Like fruit cake, but we rate it better!**

2	cups white sugar
½	pound butter
6	egg yolks
1	pound cake flour
	(½ of a 2-pound box)
½	teaspoon salt
1	teaspoon baking
	powder
½	cup whiskey or
	brandy
1	pound white raisins
1	pound pecans, chopped
6	egg whites, stiffly
	beaten
	Whiskey or brandy

In a mixing bowl, cream sugar and butter; beat in egg yolks. Sift together flour, salt, and baking powder. Add dry ingredients alternately with ½ cup whiskey. Stir in raisins and nuts. Fold in stiffly beaten egg whites. Turn into a well-greased and floured bundt or angel food cake pan. Bake in a pre-heated 300° oven for 2 hours; cool. Wrap cake in cheese cloth wet with additional whiskey or brandy. Wrap in foil, and store in can or cake tin with a tight-fitting lid. Store in refrigerator. The longer it ages, the better it is!

YIELD: 1, 10-inch cake
        32 servings

Mrs. James C. Medford
(Carolyn Lowe)

PLAIN JANE CAKE

Crispy outside. Great as a base for berries or sauces.

2	cups sugar
4	eggs
1½	cups flour
1	cup milk
¼	cup butter
2	teaspoons baking
	powder
¼	teaspoon salt
½	cup flour
1	teaspoon vanilla

In a large mixing bowl, cream sugar and eggs well. Slowly beat in 1½ cups flour. Scald milk; melt butter in the milk; add slowly to creamed mixture. Sift together baking powder, salt, and remaining ½ cup flour. Mix into creamed mixture. Add vanilla. Pour into greased and floured 10-inch tube pan. Bake in a preheated 400° oven for 35 minutes. or until done.

YIELD: 1 cake

Mrs. David W. Thompson
(Phyllis Kane)

BANANA CAKE

The really delicious taste of this rich cake
makes the extra time spent worthwhile!

CAKE

2/3	cup butter
1-2/3	cups granulated sugar
2	eggs
3	medium-size ripe bananas, mashed
2/3	cup pecan pieces
2½	cups cake flour
1½	teaspoons baking soda
1	teaspoon salt
1¼	teaspoons baking powder
2/3	cup buttermilk

ICING

½	cup vegetable shortening
4	tablespoons butter
1	teaspoon vanilla
½	teaspoon banana extract
1	cup granulated sugar
1	cup whipping cream
2½	tablespoons flour

Cream butter and sugar until fluffy. Add eggs, one at a time, beating well after each addition. Add mashed bananas and pecans to creamed mixture, beating well. Sift together dry ingredients. Add alternately with buttermilk, just to blend (Do not beat.). Pour into two 9-inch cake pans which have been greased and lightly floured. Bake in a preheated 350° oven for 25 to 35 minutes, or until cake tests done. Cool and frost between layers and on top.

ICING

Cream together first 5 ingredients until light and fluffy. In a shaker jar, combine whipping cream and flour. Shake to mix; then pour into a saucepan, and cook over medium heat, stirring until thickened. Refrigerate to cool. Add to creamed mixture and beat until you cannot taste the sugar (about 20 minutes). Frost cooled banana cake generously, between layers and on top.

YIELD: 14 to 16 servings

Mrs. Charles Ballard
(Patti Davis)

FRESH APPLE TORTE

Moist and tasty, but not too sweet.

1	egg, beaten
¼	cup butter, melted
¾	cup sugar
1	cup sifted flour
¾	teaspoon baking soda
1/8	teaspoon salt
½	teaspoon cinnamon
2	cups tart apples (about 4) peeled, cored, and chopped
½	cup chopped dates
½	cup chopped nuts

In a large bowl beat egg. Gradually beat in butter and sugar. Sift together dry ingredients; stir into creamed mixture until well mixed. Stir in remaining ingredients (Dough will be stiff.). Spread the dough into a well-buttered 8-inch square cake pan. Bake in a preheated 325° oven for about 50 minutes. Serve warm with ice cream or whipped cream.

CHEF'S NOTE: Jonathan, early green Transparents, or Staman Winesap varieties are our favorite apple choices.

YIELD: 1, 8-inch cake, 9 servings

Mrs. Alan Meckstroth
(Betty Lutz)

CUNNINGHAM'S APPLE DUFF CAKE

Just sweet enough.

¼	cup butter, softened
1	cup sugar
1	egg
1	cup flour
1	teaspoon baking soda
1	teaspoon cinnamon
½	teaspoon nutmeg
½	teaspoon cloves
¼	teaspoon salt
2	cups diced apples (about 2 apples)
½	cup chopped walnuts

In a medium-size mixing bowl, cream butter and sugar. Beat in egg. Sift together dry ingredients; stir into egg mixture. Stir in apples and walnuts. Turn batter into a greased 9-inch square pan. Bake in a preheated 350° oven for 30 minutes, or until cake tests done. Meanwhile prepare sauce.

recipe continues...

226

SAUCE

1   cup sugar
½   cup butter
½   cup evaporated milk (*not* **sweetened condensed**)
½   teaspoon vanilla

SAUCE

In a small saucepan, combine all sauce ingredients over low heat. Stir until sugar is dissolved. To serve, pass warm sauce with warm cake.
YIELD: 9 to 12 servings

Mrs. James A. Deddens
(Marcia Kramer)

KATY'S APPLE CAKE

**Very moist cake with a not-too-sweet flavor.
Doubles as a breakfast or dessert cake.**

1   cup margarine
2   cups granulated sugar
3   eggs
3   cups flour
3   teaspoons baking powder
1   teaspoon salt
½   cup orange juice
2½   teaspoons vanilla
4   large apples, peeled, cored, and sliced
    Cinnamon
    Sugar

In a large mixing bowl, cream margarine and sugar. Add eggs, one at a time, beating well after each addition. Sift together flour, baking powder, and salt; add alternately with orange juice. Beat well. Stir in vanilla. Pour ½ batter into a greased and floured 10-inch bundt or tube pan. Sink ½ of the apple slices into the batter. Sprinkle generously with cinnamon and sugar. Pour remaining batter into the pan. Top with remaining apple slices. Sprinkle with sugar and cinnamon. Bake in preheated 375° oven for one hour, or until cake tests done. Serve warm or cold.
VARIATIONS: Drizzle with confectioners sugar icing. Stir in ½ to 1 cup chopped pecans for a yummy addition.
YIELD: 12 to 16 servings

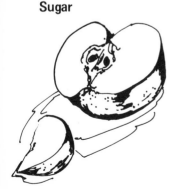

Mrs. William Augustine
(Katherine Carey)

KEY LIME CAKE

Very unusual and refreshing! Especially nice in summer.

1-1/3 cups sugar
1 3-ounce package lime gelatin
2 cups all purpose flour
2/3 teasopoon salt
1 teaspoon baking powder
½ teaspoon baking soda
5 eggs
1-1/3 cups cooking oil
¾ cup orange juice
½ teaspoon vanilla
1 teaspoon lemon extract
Whipped cream

TOPPING

1/3 cup lime juice
1/3 cup powdered sugar

Preheat oven to 350º. In a large mixing bowl, combine all dry ingredients. Add eggs, oil, orange juice, vanilla, and lemon extract. Beat until well blended. Pour batter into a greased and lightly floured 9 x 13 x 2-inch pan. Bake for 25 to 30 minutes, or until a wooden pick comes out clean. Remove from oven. Let stand for 15 minutes.

Prick cake all over with a fork. Mix together topping ingredients. Drizzle over entire top of cake. Cover and refrigerate. Garnish with whipped cream when serving.
YIELD: 12 to 15 servings

Mrs. David C. Hulme
(Chris Hafstad)

THREE-TIER BLACKBERRY JAM CAKE

Very moist, spicy cake.

1 cup butter
2 cups sugar
6 eggs
1 cup buttermilk
1 teaspoon baking soda
3 cups sifted cake flour
2 teaspoons cinnamon
2 teaspoons allspice
2 teaspoons ground cloves
2 cups seedless blackberry jam

In a large mixing bowl, cream butter and sugar. Add eggs, one at a time, beating well after each addition. Add soda dissolved in buttermilk. Sift together dry ingredients. Stir into batter. Add jam. Mix well. Pour batter into three greased and floured 9-inch cake pans. Bake in a preheated 325º oven for 35 minutes, or until cake tests done with a wooden pick. Cool slightly. Remove from pans and ice in three tiers.

recipe continues ...

BUTTER ICING

BUTTER ICING

2 pounds powdered sugar
½ cup butter
1 egg
1 tablespoon vanilla

Cream butter. Add remaining ingredients, continuing to cream until light and fluffy. Beat in enough hot milk to make a good spreading consistency.
VARIATION: Nuts and/or raisins may be added.
YIELD: 12 to 16 servings

Mrs. James C. Medford
(Carolyn Lowe)

ORANGE-APRICOT SPONGE CAKE

Extremely moist cake which retains the distinct fruit flavors. Very rich!

1 18½-ounce box cake mix, deluxe yellow or orange supreme (do not use butter yellow)
¾ cup vegetable oil
2 tablespoons lemon extract
¾ cup apricot nectar
5 eggs
Juice and grated rind of one orange
Juice and grated rind of one lemon
¾ cup honey
Confectioners sugar

In a large mixing bowl, combine cake mix, oil, lemon extract, and apricot nectar. Add eggs, one at time; beat 10 minutes. Pour into an ungreased 10-inch tube pan. Bake in a preheated 325° oven for 1 hour. While cake bakes, combine juice and rind of one orange, juice and rind of one lemon, and honey. At the end of one hour, remove cake from oven. Punch deep holes at close intervals with an ice pick. Pour fruit mixture over cake. Bake for 10 more minutes. Cool cake right side up. Remove from pan only after cake is completely cold. May be wrapped and frozen at this point. Just before serving, sprinkle cake with powdered sugar or drizzle with your favorite white frosting glaze.
YIELD: 10 to 12 servings

Mrs. Russell J. Hohman
(Barbara Hosic)

CHERRY COCONUT CAKE

Easy, rich, and gooey! Almost like an upside-down cake.

1   **21-ounce can cherry pie filling**
1   **20-ounce can crushed pineapple (do not drain)**
1   **18½-ounce box yellow cake mix, (we prefer Duncan Hines)**
1   **cup butter, melted**
1   **3½-ounce can shredded coconut**
½   **cup pecan halves, lightly salted**
    Whipped cream for garnish, optional

Mix cherry pie filling and crushed pineapple together. Pour into a buttered 9 x 13-inch pan. Sprinkle cake mix over the cherry mixture. Drizzle melted butter over the cake mix. Sprinkle coconut over butter; top with pecans. Bake in a preheated 350° oven for 1 hour (Cover loosely with foil for the first ½ hour; remove foil for the last ½ hour to permit browning.). Serve warm or cold; garnish with whipped cream.
YIELD: 15 to 18 servings

Mrs. Earl F. Pritchard
(Judy Elliott)

CARROT CAKE

Best carrot cake ever!
Walnuts, raisins, and icing are delicious additions.

CAKE

2   **cups sugar**
2   **cups cooked, mashed carrots, cooled**
1½   **cups corn oil (we prefer Mazola)**
3   **cups flour**
2   **teaspoons baking soda**
2   **teaspoons baking powder**
2   **teaspoons cinnamon**
4   **eggs**
¾   **cup chopped walnuts**
¾   **cup raisins**

In a large mixing bowl, combine sugar, carrots, and oil. Sift together flour, baking soda, baking powder, and cinnamon. Beat into carrot mixture. Add eggs, one at a time, beating well after each addition. Stir in walnuts and raisins. Pour batter into 10-inch tube pan which has been greased and floured. Bake in a preheated 350° oven for 45 minutes, or until a wooden pick inserted in middle comes out clean. Cool right side up for 15 minutes. Remove from pan, and cool completely before icing.

recipe continues . . .

ICING

½ cup milk
2½ tablespoons flour
½ cup butter, softened
½ cup sugar
1 teaspoon vanilla

ICING

In a small saucepan, combine milk and flour. Bring to a boil, stirring constantly until a thick paste consistency. Cool. In a medium-size mixing bowl, cream butter well. Add sugar; beat until light and fluffy. Add cooled paste; beat well for about four minutes. Mix in vanilla. Spread icing on cooled carrot cake.
YIELD: 12 servings

Mrs. Peter J. Kaufmann
(Cynthia MacFadden)

PUMPKIN CAKE

Very moist dessert cake.

4 eggs
2 cups flour
2 cups sugar
2 teaspoons baking soda
1 teaspoon baking powder
1 teaspoon salt
1 heaping teaspoon cinnamon
Dash of nutmeg
1 cup vegetable oil
2 cups solid pack pumpkin

In a large mixing bowl, beat eggs until light. Sift together flour, sugar, baking soda, baking powder, salt, cinnamon, and nutmeg; add alternately with oil to eggs. Mix well. Stir in pumpkin. Pour into 2, 9-inch or 3, 8-inch greased and floured cake pans. Bake in a preheated 350° oven for 35 minutes, or until wooden pick comes out clean. Cool and frost layers with cream cheese frosting.

CREAM CHEESE FROSTING

½ cup margarine, softened
1 8-ounce package cream cheese, softened
1 1-pound box confectioners sugar
1 teaspoon vanilla

CREAM CHEESE FROSTING

In a small mixing bowl, beat together margarine and cream cheese until smooth and creamy. Gradually beat in confectioners sugar until well mixed; stir in vanilla. Frost cooled cakes. Store in refrigerator.
YIELD: 8 to 10 servings

Mrs. William H. Otte
(Linda Bruggeman)

231

ZUCCHINI CAKE

Summers always bring an abundance of zucchini to our garden. This rich, moist cake is so good; the kids love it.

1½	cups vegetable oil
2	cups sugar
4	eggs, well beaten
2	cups flour
2	teaspoons baking soda
2	teaspoons cinnamon
2	teaspoons baking powder
1	cup chopped pecans
3	cups grated, peeled, zucchini (wring out extra juice)
1	cup raisins (dark or white)
1	cup coconut

BUTTERCREAM FROSTING

5-1/3	tablespoons butter
1	pound confectioners sugar
¼	teaspoon salt
1	teaspoon vanilla
5	to 6 tablespoons milk

Mix together oil and sugar; add eggs, beating well. Sift together dry ingredients. Add slowly to eggs and mix until well blended. Fold in remaining ingredients. Divide batter evenly between three 8-inch round cake pans that have been generously greased and dusted with flour. Bake in a preheated 325° oven for 60 minutes or until done.

Beat together frosting ingredients until smooth and creamy. Frost between layers and on top only. Unique looking and delicious!
YIELD: 16 servings

Mrs. Richard B. Pohl
(Carol Crabill)

MARY POPPINS CAKE

Lots of crunchy little poppy seeds make this cake a delightful addition to coffee or dessert time. Must make ahead. Rave reviews!

¼	cup poppy seeds
1	cup buttermilk
1	cup margarine
1½	cups granulated sugar
4	eggs
1	teaspoon vanilla
2½	cups flour
½	teaspoon salt
1	teaspoon baking soda
½	cup granulated sugar
1½	teaspoons ground cinnamon

In a small covered container, soak poppy seeds in buttermilk for eight hours or overnight in refrigerator. Cream margarine. Add 1½ cups sugar, gradually, and beat until fluffy. Add eggs, one at a time, beating well after each addition. Add vanilla. Sift flour, salt, and baking soda together. Add to creamed mixture alternately with buttermilk-poppy seed mixture. Blend well. In a small bowl mix together ½ cup sugar and cinnamon. Grease a 10-inch bundt cake pan. Sprinkle enough of the cinnamon-sugar mixture over pan to coat lightly, but evenly. Put batter in pan in three layers, sprinkling cinnamon-sugar mixture evenly between layers. Bake in a preheated 350° oven for 50 minutes, or until cake tests done. Cool 45 minutes before inverting and unmolding cake on serving plate (Do not leave cake in pan longer than an hour as it will become impossible to remove.). Cool completely, and keep tightly covered for storage.
YIELD: 16 servings

Mrs. Gerald Westerbeck
(Judy Richardson)

CAKES

HEATH BAR CAKE

Great for company.

2 cups brown sugar (1-pound)
2 cups flour
½ teaspoon salt
1 teaspoon baking soda
8 tablespoons butter
1 egg
1 cup milk
1 teaspoon vanilla
1 cup chopped pecans or walnuts
1 cup milk chocolate chips
4½ ounces Heath candy bars, crushed

In a large mixing bowl, combine brown sugar, flour, salt, and baking soda. Cut in butter, until the mixture is the consistency of coarse cornmeal. Reserve 1 cup brown sugar mixture; set aside. To the remaining brown sugar mixture add egg, milk, and vanilla; mix well. Pour into greased and floured 9 x 13-inch pan. To the reserved brown sugar mixture add nuts, chocolate chips, and crushed Heath candy bars. Stir to mix well. Sprinkle brown sugar and nut mixture evenly over cake batter. Bake in a preheated 350° oven for 30 to 40 minutes, or until cake tests done with a wooden pick. Do not overbake!
YIELD: 12 to 15 servings

Mrs. G. F. Miller, Jr.
(Barbara Wallace)

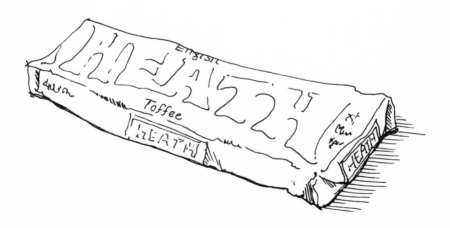

234

BUTTER SPONGE CAKE

This cake uses the egg yolks that are always left over from baking an angel food cake. With fudge frosting, it is terrific! Egg whites can be used in "Chocolate Angel Food Cake" (see index).

CAKE

11	egg yolks
2	cups granulated sugar, sifted
1	cup milk, scalded
1	teaspoon vanilla
2¼	cups sifted cake flour
2	teaspoons baking powder
½	cup butter, melted

FROSTING

½	cup milk
6	tablespoons butter
1½	cups semi-sweet chocolate bits
1½	teaspoons vanilla
3	cups sifted confectioners sugar

Beat egg yolks and sugar about 10 minutes or until light and fluffy. Sift together cake flour and baking powder. Add to egg yolks, alternately with milk. Add vanilla. Mix well. Fold in cooled melted butter. Butter two, 10-inch (not 9-inch) cake pans. Line the bottom with waxed paper. Again butter waxed paper. Lightly flour the bottom and sides. Pour batter into prepared pans. Bake in a preheated 350° oven for 30 to 40 minutes, or until cake tests done. Cool 10 minutes, and turn out to cool completely before frosting.

FROSTING

In a small saucepan combine milk and butter. Over medium heat, bring just to a boil, stirring constantly. Remove from heat. Add chocolate bits and vanilla. Stir until smooth. Cool to room temperature. Pour frosting into large mixing bowl. Blend in confectioners sugar very gradually (about ¼ cup at a time). Beat frosting hard until it thickens. When it reaches spreading consistency, promptly ice the cooled cakes. This frosting becomes firm and fudge-like when it sets.
YIELD: 16 servings

Mrs. Gerald Westerbeck
(Judy Richardson)

YELLOW ANGEL FOOD CAKE

May be frozen. This is a companion cake to "Chocolate Angel Food Cake" (see index).

10   egg yolks
½   cup water
    Pinch of salt
1   cup sugar
1½   cups sifted cake flour (measure after sifted)
½   teaspoon cream of tartar
½   teaspoon baking powder
½   teaspoon vanilla
½   teaspoon lemon flavoring

In a large mixing bowl, beat egg yolks, water, and salt for 15 minutes or longer at high speed (until you can make a line that stays); fold in sugar. Sift together 1½ cups sifted cake flour, cream of tartar, and baking powder; sift 5 times. Gently and thoroughly fold into egg and sugar mixture. Add vanilla and lemon flavoring. Turn mixture into an ungreased 10-inch tube pan. Bake in a preheated 350° oven for 45 to 50 minutes, or until cake is done. Turn upside down until cool. No frosting needed. Good with lemon ice cream or sherbet.

CHEF'S NOTE: CAUTION Do not bang oven door . . . it makes this cake fall!

YIELD: 10-12 servings

Mrs. Stephen Elling
(Sue Struble)

CHOCOLATE ANGEL FOOD CAKE

This recipe has been handed down in my husband's family for several generations. The original recipe calls for using a wire whisk to beat the egg whites; that is the best way, but I always use a mixer! Try the "Yellow Angel Food Cake" or the "Butter Sponge Cake" to use the egg yolks from this recipe (see index).

¾ cup plus 2 tablespoons cake flour
¾ cup sugar
¼ cup cocoa (We prefer Hershey's)
1 cup sugar
1½ cups egg white (about 1 dozen large eggs)
1½ teaspoons cream of tartar
1/3 teaspoon salt
1¼ teaspoons vanilla

CHOCOLATE BUTTER ICING

¼ pound butter, softened
1 egg yolk
1 pound powdered sugar (or more), sifted
¼ cup cocoa, adjusted to obtain desired color — preferably light brown (we prefer Hershey's)
Milk, enough to make spreading consistency
1½ teaspoons vanilla

Sift flour with ¾ cup sugar 3 times; set aside. Sift cocoa with 1 cup sugar; set aside. In a large grease-free bowl, beat egg whites until frothy. Beat in cream of tartar and salt. Continue beating until egg whites are glossy and form stiff peaks (If you can turn bowl nearly upside down and egg whites do not slide, they are ready.). Being careful not to break down egg whites, gradually fold in sugar and cocoa; fold in vanilla. Fold in flour and sugar mixture. Pour batter into an ungreased 10-inch angel food cake pan, and cut through with a knife a few times to break any large air bubbles. Bake in a preheated 325° oven for 60 to 65 minutes. Turn pan upside down. Let cake hang until cold. Remove from pan and frost with "Chocolate Butter Icing."

CHOCOLATE BUTTER ICING

In a large mixing bowl, cream butter; beat in egg yolk. Add sugar and cocoa gradually. Gradually add milk as needed (Be careful — a little goes a long way.). Spread on a completely cooled cake.
YIELD: 10-12 servings

Mrs. Stephen Elling
(Sue Struble)

BROWN SUGAR POUND CAKE

. . . the stuff dreams are made of. Unbelievable!

1   cup butter
½   cup shortening
1   pound light brown sugar
1   cup granulated sugar
5   eggs
3   cups sifted flour
½   teaspoon baking powder
1   cup milk
1   teaspoon vanilla
1   cup coarsely broken walnuts (preferably black, but English will do)

WALNUT GLAZE

1   cup sifted confectioners sugar
2   tablespoons butter
6   tablespoons cream
½   teaspoon vanilla
½   cup coarsley broken black walnuts

Cream butter and shortening together; gradually add sugars, creaming until light and fluffy. Beat in eggs, one at a time. Sift together flour and baking powder. Add alternately with milk and vanilla to creamed mixture. Stir in nuts. Pour into greased and floured 10-inch tube pan. Bake in a preheated 350° oven for about 60 or 75 minutes, just until cake tests done. Cool 10 minutes before taking from pan. Drizzle with walnut glaze.

WALNUT GLAZE

Cream together confectioners sugar and butter; add cream and vanilla. Stir in black walnuts (or English). Drizzle over cake.
YIELD: 1, 10-inch cake

Mrs. George L. Word
(Paige Early)

FLUFFY FLOUR FROSTING

Tastes like whipped cream. Denise's demise; poor old sweet thing . . . .

6 tablespoons instant-blending flour, or 6 tablespoons regular flour and struggle to make it smooth
1/8 teaspoon salt
1 cup milk
1 teaspoon vanilla
1 cup sugar
1 cup sweet (unsalted) butter, slightly softened

In a 1½-quart saucepan, combine flour and salt adding cold milk gradually. Cook over medium heat until very thick, stirring constantly. Remove from heat, and add vanilla; cool. In a large mixing bowl, cream together sugar and butter. Add cooled milk mixture, and beat at high speed for about 5 minutes, scraping bowl sides occasionally. Frost cooled cake, and refrigerate until 1 or 2 hours before serving.
YIELD: 2, 9-inch layers

Mrs. Alan Meckstroth
(Betty Lutz)

CHEESECAKE

Absolutely outstanding! Nice texture; great flavor.

5 whole graham crackers, crushed
3 8-ounce packages cream cheese
6 egg yolks
1 cup sugar
3 tablespoons flour
½ pint sour cream
½ pint half and half
2 teaspoons vanilla
6 egg whites, stiffly beaten

Butter a 9-inch spring-form pan, and sprinkle the sides and bottom with graham cracker crumbs (Use remaining crumbs for top.). In a large mixing bowl, cream the cheese and egg yolks; beat in remaining ingredients except egg whites. Fold in egg whites, and pour into prepared pan. Bake in a preheated 325° oven for 1 hour. Turn heat off, and let stand with the door closed for 15 minutes and then with the door open for 30 minutes. Cool for 6 hours before removing the spring-form pan. Refrigerate.
YIELD: 16 servings

Mrs. Charles J. Roedersheimer
(Alice Murray)

CAKES

FABULOUS CHEESECAKE

Makes its own crust!

1	pound small curd cottage cheese
1	pound cream cheese, softened
4	eggs, slightly beaten
1	tablespoon lemon juice
1	teaspoon vanilla
3	tablespoons cornstarch
3	tablespoons flour
¼	pound butter, melted
1½	cups sugar
1	pint sour cream
1½	cups fresh strawberries, blueberries, or pineapple

In a large mixing bowl, cream together cottage cheese and cream cheese until light and fluffy; beat in eggs. Blend in lemon juice, vanilla, cornstarch, and flour. Add melted butter; beat in sugar, and blend in sour cream. Pour mixture into a greased 9-inch spring-form pan. Arrange a large piece of foil on oven rack to catch drippings. Bake in a preheated 350° oven for 60 minutes. Turn off heat, and leave cheesecake in oven for 2 hours more — do not open oven door. Remove from oven, and remove cheesecake to a serving platter; cover and refrigerate until thoroughly chilled. Cut into small pieces, and serve with fresh fruit.

YIELD: 12 to 14 servings

Mrs. Thomas L. Wagner
(Carmel Schlimm)

CHOCOLATE CHEESECAKE

This is a spectacular and delicious dessert; must be prepared ahead.

CRUST

7	tablespoons butter, melted
2	cups crushed chocolate wafer crumbs
¼	cup sugar
¼	teaspoon cinnamon

FILLING

4	eggs
1½	cups sugar
6	tablespoons unsweetened cocoa
1	teaspoon vanilla
2	8-ounce packages cream cheese, softened
4	cups sour cream

TOPPING

2	ounces semi-sweet chocolate for garnish
1	3-ounce package cream cheese, softened
½	cup whipping cream
4	tablespoons sugar
1	tablespoon Kahlua

Mix together butter, wafer crumbs, ¼ cup sugar, and cinnamon. Press mixture over bottom and partly up sides of a 9-inch spring-form pan; set aside. In a blender, combine eggs, 1½ cups sugar, cocoa, vanilla, and one 8-ounce package of cream cheese. Cover and blend until smooth. Pour about half of the mixture into a large bowl; then add remaining 8-ounce package cream cheese to blender; cover and whirl until smooth. Combine the two mixtures; stir in sour cream, and pour into crust. Bake in a preheated 350° oven for 80 minutes. Cool; cover, and chill for at least 12 hours before serving. Prepare topping shortly before serving. In a mixing bowl, beat 3-ounces cream cheese until soft. Gradually add whipping cream, beating at high speed until mixture is the consistency of stiffly-beaten whipped cream. Gently fold in sugar and Kahlua. Cover and chill until serving time. To prepare chocolate curls, melt chocolate in a heavy saucepan over very low heat. Spread very thinly on a cookie sheet; refrigerate for 15 minutes. Hold the edge of a spatula at right angles to the cookie sheet and start at the edge of the chocolate; push to form a curl. Repeat; refrigerate. At serving time, remove rim, and place cake on a serving dish. Spread cream topping on cake, and garnish with chocolate curls.
YIELD: 16 to 18 servings

Mrs. Arnold I. Schwartzman
(Judith Bassman)

COMPANY CHEESECAKE

A superb cheesecake made unique by its elegant garnish.

1¼ cups graham cracker crumbs
¼ cup butter, melted
¼ cup sugar
5 8-ounce packages cream cheese, softened
1¾ cups sugar
3 tablespoons flour
2 teaspoons grated lemon peel
1 tablespoon grated orange peel
5 whole eggs
2 egg yolks
¼ cup whipping cream
5 canned apricot halves, drained (reserve syrup)
1 8-ounce can pineapple slices, drained and cut into fourths (reserve syrup)
1/3 cup fresh blueberries
1 pint fresh strawberries, rinsed and drained
1 tablespoon lemon juice
1 tablespoon cornstarch
2 tablespoons water

Mix and press the graham crackers, butter, and sugar into a 9-inch springform pan which has been buttered on the sides. In a large bowl, combine the cream cheese, sugar, flour, and lemon and orange peel; add eggs and egg yolks one at a time, beating after each addition. Add cream, and beat until smooth. Pour into crust, and bake in a preheated 500° oven for 10 minutes; reduce heat to 200°, and bake for 1 hour. Remove and cool in the refrigerator. Combine fruit juices to make ¾ cup; add lemon juice, and pour into sauce pan. Stir in cornstarch mixed into 2 tablespoons water, and cook until thickened. Spoon over cake, and garnish with fruit. Arrange apricot halves (one in the center closely surrounded by four). Make a ring of pineapple around apricots. At the outer edge make a rim of strawberries. Sprinkle blueberries all over the top. Enjoy!
YIELD: 12 to 16 servings

Mrs. Lowell Mills
(Susie Taylor)

CHEESE TORTE

You'll think this cheesecake was flown in from New York!

2½	cups vanilla wafer crumbs
½	cup butter, melted
3	8-ounce packages cream cheese, softened
1	cup sugar
5	eggs
1	teaspoon vanilla
¾	pint sour cream (1½ cups)
1	teaspoon vanilla
2	tablespoons sugar
1	10-ounce carton frozen strawberries, thawed
1	tablespoon cornstarch
½	teaspoon lemon juice
1	teaspoon sugar

In a small saucepan, mix vanilla wafer crumbs with melted butter, and press into a 9 or 10-inch spring-form pan. In a large standard-mixer bowl, cream together cheese and 1 cup sugar until light and fluffy. Add eggs one at a time, beating well after each addition (5 minutes after each egg). Add 1 teaspoon vanilla. Pour into prepared pan, and bake in a preheated 350° oven for 35 to 40 minutes, or until set as for pumpkin pie. In a small bowl, mix together sour cream, 1 teaspoon vanilla, and 2 tablespoons sugar. When cake has set, pull out rack (don't remove cake); spoon sour cream mixture over baked cake. Increase oven temperature to 475°, and bake for 5 minutes. Remove from oven, and cool on a rack. In a double boiler, combine all remaining ingredients. Cook and stir over hot water until clear; cool slightly. Spread strawberry glaze on top of cooled cake. Refrigerate 24 hours or overnight. Unspring at serving time.
YIELD: 12 servings

Mrs. Neil F. Freund
(Carole Meyer)

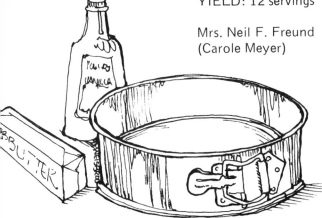

FIVE GENERATION PEACH COBBLER

This recipe contributes to the happiness, health, and longevity
of our family. "Flavor" is enhanced by baking
this luscious stand-by in a heavy crockery dish
equally old and also passed from one loving hand to another.

5 cups fresh peaches,
peeled, pitted, and
sliced
3 tablespoons flour
1¼ cups sugar
1 teaspoon cinnamon
4 to 6 tablespoons
butter

CRUST

1 cup flour
½ teaspoon salt
2 teaspoons baking
powder
2 tablespoons sugar
1/3 cup shortening
1/3 cup milk

Slice peaches into a heavy, greased baking dish measuring approximately 9 inches around and 3 inches deep. Mix together flour, sugar, and cinnamon, and sprinkle over peaches. Dot with butter.

CRUST

Sift together dry ingredients. Cut in shortening until mixture resembles coarse corn meal. Pour milk in all at once, and stir with a fork. Roll dough out on a floured board until it is the size of the baking dish — it will be ¼ to ½-inch thick. Place crust on top of peaches. Bake in a preheated 425° oven for about 30 minutes.
YIELD: 6 to 8 servings

Mrs. George L. Word
(Paige Early)

DARCY'S STRAWBERRIES

Plan an outing to a strawberry patch for a morning of picking.
This seven year old looks forward to the yearly excursion with great
anticipation. Here is her special recipe for your young children.

2 tablespoons powdered
sugar
2 tablespoons strawberry
yogurt
6 whole strawberries
with stems and leaves,
washed

Put powdered sugar and yogurt on a plate. Hold fresh berry by stem and dip into yogurt, then into sugar. Yummy!
YIELD: 1 serving

Miss Darcy Louise Deddens

BAKED CHEDDAR APPLES

Nice change from basic baked apples.

6	large baking apples
¾	cup raisins
1	tablespoon butter or margarine
1	cup sugar
1	cup water
1½	tablespoons milk
1	3-ounce package cream cheese, softened
¾	cup shredded natural sharp cheddar cheese

Core apples and pare a strip from the top of each. Place in an 8 x 8-inch, 1-quart baking dish. Place 2 tablespoons raisins and ½ teaspoon butter or margarine in the center of each apple. Combine sugar and water in a saucepan and cook on medium heat until boiling. Pour syrup over apples and bake uncovered in a preheated 350° oven for 1 hour, basting occasionally with syrup. Meanwhile, in a small mixing bowl, beat cream cheese until smooth. Add milk and beat until fluffy; stir in cheese. Spoon cheese mixture over baked apples. Return to oven for a few minutes. Serve warm.
YIELD: 6 servings

Mrs. William Kasch
(Sonnie Kern)

POT DE CREME

Very rich and chocolaty. Super quick, make ahead.

1	cup half and half
1	6-ounce package chocolate chips
2	eggs
	Dash of salt
1	teaspoon vanilla
	Whipped cream for garnish, if desired

In a small saucepan, scald half and half; remove from heat; set aside. Combine all remaining ingredients in a blender. Blend on low speed for 2 minutes. With motor still on, add scalded half and half; blend 2 more minutes. Pour mixture into 4 pudding cups; cover and refrigerate overnight. At serving time garnish with whipped cream if desired.
YIELD: 4 servings

Mrs. James F. Easton
(Karen Scadura)

AUNT EM'S DATE-NUT PUDDING

Auntie Em lived on a farm and used to make her Date-Nut Pudding around Thanksgiving time. This recipe is about 75 to 100 years old. Syrupy, gooey and oh so rich! Serve in small portions for a tasty luncheon dessert.

1	cup brown sugar
2	tablespoons butter
2	cups flour
4	teaspoons baking powder
1	cup milk
1	cup chopped dates
½	cup nuts, chopped
2	cups brown sugar
3	cups boiling water
1	tablespoon butter
½	pint heavy cream, whipped and sweetened to taste

In a large bowl, cream together brown sugar and butter. Sift together flour and baking powder, and add alternately with milk to the creamed mixture. Stir dates and nuts into the stiff batter. Set aside. Combine 2 cups brown sugar, 3 cups boiling water, and 1 tablespoon butter in a medium-size saucepan; stir and boil for 3 minutes. Pour into well-buttered 9 x 12-inch baking pan. Drop batter by spoonfuls into the hot sauce. Bake in preheated 325° oven for 45 minutes or until golden brown. Serve warm with whipped cream.
YIELD: 18 servings

Mrs. Gelard M. Bechert
(Nan Albers)

DESSERT CUSTARD TOPPING

Use this topping instead of icing for box cakes, brownies, or angel food cakes. Great as the filling for Boston cream pie.

¼	cup butter, melted
2	tablespoons cornstarch
½	cup sugar
2	eggs, or 3 yolks
1	cup milk, scalded, cooled slightly
1	teaspoon vanilla
¼	teaspoon almond extract, optional
½	pint whipping cream, whipped

In a saucepan, mix together butter and cornstarch. Add sugar, eggs, milk, and flavorings. Cook custard over medium heat until very thick (stir constantly with a slotted spoon); cool. Fold in whipped cream. Store any leftover in a covered glass jar.
YIELD: Topping for one cake

Mrs. James C. Medford
(Carolyn Lowe)

246

ALMOND PUFF PASTRY

Excellent with coffee for a morning meeting.

½ cup butter, softened
1 cup flour
2 tablespoons water
½ cup butter
1 cup water
1 teaspoon almond extract
1 cup flour
3 eggs
1½ cups confectioners sugar, sifted
2 tablespoons butter, softened
1½ teaspoons almond extract
1 to 2 tablespoons warm water
Slivered almonds for garnish, optional

In a small bowl, cut ½ cup butter into 1 cup flour. Sprinkle with 2 table-spoons water, and mix with a fork until well-blended. Round into a ball; divide ball in half; pat each half into a 12 x 3-inch strip 3 inches apart on an ungreased cookie sheet; set aside. In a medium-size saucepan, heat ½ cup butter and 1 cup water to a boil. Re-move from heat, and stir in almond extract and flour. Return to low heat, and vigorously stir until mixture forms a ball (about 1 minute). Remove from heat, and beat in eggs all at one time. Divide mixture in half, spread each half evenly and completely over reserved strips. Bake in a preheated 350° oven for 60 minutes, or until topping is crisp and brown. Let cool slightly and glaze. In a small bowl, combine all remaining ingredients, except almonds; mix until smooth. Pour glaze over puffs, and garnish with almond slivers if desired.
YIELD: 2 dozen

Mrs. Bruce A. Triplett
(Leslie Conway)

CHOCOLATE MERINGUE TORTE

A very elegant dessert.

	Paper bags
6	egg whites
¼	teaspoon salt
1	teaspoon vinegar
½	teaspoon vanilla
2	cups sugar

FILLING

1	tablespoon instant coffee
¼	cup boiling water
12	ounces chocolate chips, melted over hot water
1	teaspoon vanilla
1	cup whipping cream, beaten stiff

Cut paper bags or parchment into 5, 9-inch circles; place on cookie sheets. In a large bowl, beat egg whites until almost stiff. Beat in salt, vinegar, and vanilla. Very, very, gradually add sugar, beating until very stiff. Spoon meringue onto paper circles so that the edges are slightly higher than the middle (5 meringues). Bake in a pre-heated 300° oven for 45 minutes. Remove from paper immediately; cool.

FUDGE

Dissolve coffee in boiling water, and add, very slowly, to the melted chocolate. Add vanilla to whipped cream. Slowly add cooled chocolate mixture to whipped cream, beating as you go (Mixture will get runny.). Spoon mixture onto meringue shells. Stack meringues one on top of the other and refrigerate immediately.
YIELD: 10 to 12 servings

Mrs. Richard S. Sutton
(Janet Robinson)

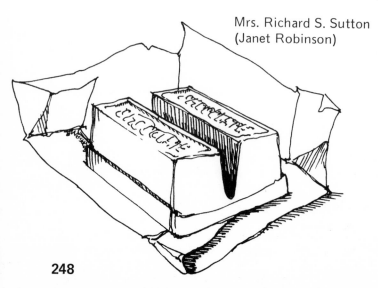

DOBISHE TORTE

Extremely easy and delicious.

1	frozen pound cake (we prefer Sara Lee)
1	12-ounce package semi-sweet chocolate chips
¼	cup boiling water
2	tablespoons powdered sugar
1	teaspoon instant coffee
1	teaspoon vanilla
4	egg yolks
¼	pound butter, melted
2	tablespoons Kahlua, optional
½	teaspoon almond extract
½	cup sliced almonds Whipped cream or ice cream for garnish

Cut pound cake into 4 or 5 layers; set aside. Partially melt chocolate chips in double boiler. Put chocolate chips in blender or food processor; blend for 6 seconds. Scrape and blend again for 6 seconds. Add boiling water, and blend for 6 seconds more. Add 2 table-spoons powdered sugar, dry instant coffee, vanilla, egg yolks, butter, Kahlua, and almond extract. Blend 30 seconds or until smooth. Stack and frost each layer on top and sides. Garnish servings with sliced almonds and whipped cream or ice cream.
YIELD: 6 to 8 servings

Mrs. David R. Bart
(Mary Jo Thurman)

ENGLISH CHOCOLATE TORTE

Rich and chocolaty!

2	cups confectioners sugar
¼	teaspoon salt
2	tablespoons cocoa
½	cup butter, softened
2	egg yolks
1	cup pecans, chopped
1	teaspoon vanilla
2	egg whites, beaten to soft peaks
1	12-ounce box vanilla wafers, crushed

Into a large mixing bowl, sift together confectioners sugar, salt, and cocoa; cream together with butter. Beat in egg yolks, pecans, and vanilla; fold in egg whites. In a buttered 4½ x 8½ x 2½-inch loaf pan, layer crumbs and chocolate mixture; repeat and sprinkle top with crumbs. Cover and refriger-ate for at least 4 hours or overnight. Slice and serve.
YIELD: 8 servings

Mrs. David B. Meeker
(Helen Nelson)

GERMAN CHOCOLATE MINT TORTE

German chocolate cake is the base for this party cake.
It is big, beautiful, and has a super flavor! Time consuming,
but worth every minute. May be made ahead.

CAKE

4	ounces German sweet chocolate (we prefer Baker's)
½	cup boiling water
1	cup butter
2	cups sugar
4	egg yolks
1	teaspoon vanilla
2½	cups sifted cake flour
1	teaspoon baking soda
½	teaspoon salt
1	cup buttermilk
4	egg whites, beaten stiff

FUDGE FILLING

1/3	cup milk
¼	cup butter
6	ounces (1 cup) semi-sweet chocolate bits
1	teaspoon vanilla
2	to 2¼ cups sifted confectioners sugar

Melt chocolate in boiling water. Cool to room temperature. Cream butter and sugar until light and fluffy. Add egg yolks, one at a time, beating well after each addition. Blend in vanilla and chocolate. Sift together flour, baking soda, and salt. Add alternately with buttermilk to chocolate mixture. Beat until smooth after each addition. Carefully fold in beaten egg whites. Grease three 9-inch round cake pans. Line bottoms with waxed paper. Grease again and lightly flour. Divide batter evenly among prepared pans. Bake in a preheated 350° oven for 30 to 35 minutes or until cake pulls away from sides. Cool pans on wire racks for 10 to 15 minutes. Invert onto waxed paper; carefully remove waxed paper liners. Cool completely.

FUDGE FILLING

In a small saucepan, combine milk and butter. Over medium heat, bring just to a boil, stirring constantly. Remove from heat. Add chocolate bits and vanilla. Stir until smooth. Cool to room temperature. Pour filling into a large mixing bowl. Blend in confectioners sugar very gradually (about ¼ cup at a time). Beat filling hard until it thickens. Spread ½ generously over the top of one cake layer. Place a second cake layer on filling; spread generously with remaining filling. Place last cake layer on top.

recipe continues . . .

MINT ICING

MINT ICING

1	envelope unflavored gelatin
¼	cup cold water
1/3	cup creme de menthe, white or green
¼	cup white creme de cacao
2	cups whipping cream, whipped

Soften gelatin in cold water. Heat creme de menthe and creme de cacao together over low heat. Add softened gelatin. Stir until dissolved. Cool completely. Carefully fold whipped cream into the cooled gelatin mixure. Refrigerate 15 minutes. Generously frost the top and sides of cake with mint icing. Cover and refrigerate until serving. Store leftover cake in refrigerator.
YIELD: 16 servings

Mrs. Gerald Westerbeck
(Judy Richardson)

FOUR LAYER CHOCOLATE DESSERT

A light but rich dessert enhanced by the taste of almonds.

¾	cup margarine
2	cups flour
1	cup chopped pecans
1	8-ounce package cream cheese, softened
1	cup confectioners sugar
1	cup whipped topping (we prefer Cool Whip)
3	cups milk
2	4½-ounce packages instant chocolate pudding mix
1	pint whipping cream, whipped
1	4-ounce package slivered almonds, toasted

In a small mixing bowl using a pastry blender, cut margarine into flour. Stir in pecans. Spread evenly on the bottom of a 9 x 13-inch baking dish. Bake in a preheated 300° oven for 20 to 25 minutes; set aside to cool. In another small mixing bowl, beat together cream cheese and confectioners sugar until light. Fold in whipped topping (not whipped cream); spread over cooled crust. In a small mixing bowl, mix milk with the chocolate pudding mixes; beat until thickened. Spread over the cream cheese layer. Spread whipped cream over chocolate pudding. Garnish with toasted slivered almonds. Chill until serving time.
YIELD: 12 servings

Mrs. E. H. Decker
(June Hendrickson)

CHARLOTTE AU CHOCOLATE

**Quick, easy make-ahead that looks like you really fussed.
A sure winner for chocolate lovers.**

2 4-ounce packages German chocolate
3 tablespoons water
3 egg yolks, beaten
2 tablespoons confectioners sugar
2 cups prepared whipped topping
2 egg whites, beaten stiff
12 to 20 whole ladyfingers, split
Prepared whipped topping, for garnish
German chocolate, shaved, for garnish

In a double boiler, melt chocolate over hot water. Blend in water. Remove from heat; cool slightly. Slowly add egg yolks, beating until smooth. Add sugar and mix well. Fold in egg whites. Refrigerate to chill slightly. Fold prepared whipped topping into chilled chocolate mixture. Line sides and bottom of a 1½-quart serving bowl with split lady fingers. Fill the bowl with chocolate mixture. Garnish with more whipped topping and shaved chocolate.
YIELD: 6 to 8 servings

Mrs. Alan L. Edmonson
(Patricia Bieser)

CHIFFON DESSERT

Cool and refreshingly light summertime dessert.

1 package flavored gelatin, any flavor
½ cup sugar
1 cup boiling water
Grated rind of 1 lemon
Juice of 1 lemon
1 13-ounce can evaporated milk, chilled in refrigerator overnight
Food coloring
2 9-inch graham cracker pie crusts, *or* 8 to 10 sherbet dishes

In a small bowl, mix together the first five ingredients. Cool slightly. In a large bowl, whip the cold evaporated milk until firm. Thoroughly fold the gelatin mixture into whipped evaporated milk. Add drops of the appropriate color of food coloring until desired shade is achieved. Pour into prebaked pie shells or sherbet dishes. Refrigerate until serving time.

Mrs. William R. Thompson
(Sally Decker)

CHOCOLATE SOUFFLE

Very rich —

4	egg yolks	In a medium-size mixing bowl, beat
½	cup sugar	egg yolks until light yellow. Add sugar
½	teaspoon vanilla	and vanilla, beating until thickened.
2	squares unsweetened	Continue beating while adding warm
	chocolate, melted	melted chocolate in a slow, steady
4	egg whites, beaten stiff	stream. Gently fold in beaten egg
	but not dry	whites. Refrigerate until serving time.

CHEF'S NOTE: Do not double this recipe.

YIELD: 4 servings

Mrs. David W. Thompson
(Phyllis Kane)

PINEAPPLE FLUFF

Prepare ahead.
This light tasty treat may be served as a dessert or sweet salad.

22	graham cracker squares,	Use your hands to mix together
	rolled fine	cracker crumbs, butter, and sugar.
1/3	cup butter, softened	Reserve ¼ of the mixture. Press re-
3	tablespoons sugar	maining crumb mixture into the
1	10-ounce package	bottom of a 6 x 10 x 1¾-inch casse-
	marshmallows	role dish; set aside. In a small sauce-
½	cup milk	pan, melt marshmallows in milk, stir-
1	7-ounce can crushed	ring constantly over low heat. Refrig-
	pineapple, drained	erate to cool. Fold drained pineapple
½	pint whipping cream,	into whipped cream. Fold whipped
	whipped	cream mixture into the cooled marsh-

mallow mixture. Pour mixture over prepared crust. Sprinkle reserved cracker crumbs over top. Refrigerate until firm. Cut into squares before serving.

YIELD: 6 to 8 servings

Mrs. Jonathan P. Shelton
(Nancy Garst)

GRASSHOPPER SOUFFLE

Very light!

2	¼-ounce envelopes unflavored gelatin (we prefer Knox)
1	cup cold water
½	cup sugar
¼	teaspoon salt
6	egg yolks
½	cup green creme de menthe
½	cup white creme de cacao
3	egg whites
½	cup sugar
2	cups heavy cream, whipped
1	cup heavy cream, whipped and sweetened for garnish
½	to ¾ cup chopped pistachio nuts, optional

Sprinkle gelatin over cold water in a 2½-quart pan. Add ½ cup sugar, salt, and egg yolks. Stir until thoroughly mixed. Place over low heat, stirring constantly, until gelatin dissolves and mixture thickens slightly (about 5 to 10 minutes). Remove from heat; stir in creme de menthe and creme de cacao. Chill, stirring frequently until mixture mounds slightly when dropped from spoon. Beat egg whites in a large bowl until foam has fine bubbles. Gradually add ½ cup sugar, and beat until stiff peaks have hooked tops. Carefully fold gelatin mixture into egg whites. Fold in whipped cream. Make a foil collar extending about 2-inches above the top of a souffle dish that measures 2 quarts to the rim. Tie securely with string. Turn folded mixture into prepared souffle dish. Chill several hours or until firm. Peel foil collar off; garnish with additional sweetened whipped cream and pistachio nuts if desired. Serve in sherbet dishes or on a flat dessert plate. Especially good accompanied with a small, chocolate tea cookie. YIELD: 12 servings

Mrs. Michael W. Craig
(Susan Hockwalt)

STRAWBERRY DELIGHT

Sinfully rich! This has been served with birthday candles to honor special requests in lieu of a traditional cake.

¼ pound butter
2 eggs, beaten
1 pound confectioners sugar
1 11-ounce box vanilla wafers
1 quart fresh strawberries, washed and hulled
1 pint whipping cream, stiffly whipped

Cream together butter, eggs, and sugar. Crumble vanilla wafers by rolling with a rolling pin. Spread half of the crumbs on the bottom of a buttered 8 x 12-inch pan. Spread creamed mixture over this. Layer strawberries on top. Whip cream, and spread over strawberries. Sprinkle with remaining crumbs. Chill for at least 10 hours. Cut into squares to serve.
YIELD: 12 to 15 servings

Mrs. George L. Word
(Paige Early)

FROZEN STRAWBERRY DESSERT

Very different — like an ice cream with crunch.

½ cup margarine
¼ cup brown sugar
1 cup flour
½ cup chopped nuts
2 egg whites
2/3 cup sugar
1 tablespoon lemon juice
16 ounces frozen sliced strawberries, thawed
½ pint whipping cream, whipped

In a saucepan, melt margarine; stir in brown sugar, flour, and nuts. Spread mixture on a greased cookie sheet. Bake in a preheated 350° oven for 20 minutes. Reserve 1/3 of crumb mixture for topping; put remaining 2/3 mixture in the bottom of a greased 9 x 13-inch pan; set aside. In a large mixing bowl, beat egg whites until stiff; slowly add sugar and lemon juice. Beat for 10 to 15 minutes on high speed. Continue beating while adding strawberries. Fold in whipped cream. Swirl mixture in prepared crust, and top with reserved crumb mixture. Freeze until 20 minutes before serving time; cut into squares.
YIELD: 12 servings

Mrs. E. H. Decker
(June Hendrickson)

STRAWBERRY DESSERT

**Light and delicious! A perfect finish
to a summer luncheon; easy to make the night before.**

2	egg whites
	Pinch of salt
¾	cup granulated sugar
1	20-ounce package frozen strawberries (no sugar added; do not drain)
1	9-ounce carton whipped topping (we prefer Cool Whip)
	Fresh strawberries for garnish (optional)
	Fresh mint leaves for garnish (optional)

In a large mixing bowl, beat egg whites with a pinch of salt until stiff. Blend in sugar, 2 tablespoons at a time until very stiff. In a blender, puree the undrained berries. Fold into the egg white mixture; fold in whipped topping. Turn mixture into an oiled 7-cup mold; freeze overnight. At serving time, unmold, and garnish ring with fresh strawberries and mint leaves.

YIELD: 8 to 10 servings

Mrs. L. Keith Wilson
(Aimee Clunet)

BISCUIT TORTONI

Great light dessert for summer. Good after an Italian dinner.

1/3	cup Grapenuts cereal
2	egg whites
2	tablespoons granulated sugar
¼	cup chopped walnuts or pecans
¼	cup chopped maraschino cherries
1	tablespoon maraschino cherry syrup
1	teaspoon vanilla
½	pint whipping cream, whipped
¼	cup confectioners sugar
	Grapenuts cereal for garnish
6	cherries, cut in half

Line cupcake pans with 12 paper liners. Divide 1/3 cup Grapenuts evenly among the 12 paper cups. Beat egg whites until stiff; slowly add granulated sugar. Fold in nuts, cherries, syrup, and vanilla; set aside. Whip cream until stiff, beat in confectioners sugar. Fold whipped cream into egg white mixture. Divide equally among paper cups. Sprinkle a few more Grapenuts on top, and place ½ cherry in the middle of each dessert. Freeze until serving time.

YIELD: 12 servings

Mrs. William R. Thompson
(Sally Decker)

ST. PATRICK'S DELIGHT

Simply delicious — pretty too!

½ cup butter, softened
1 cup flour
2 tablespoons sugar
8 ounces cream cheese, softened
1 cup sugar
2 tablespoons milk
4½ ounces whipped topping (we prefer Cool Whip)
2 3½-ounce boxes instant pistachio pudding mix
3 cups milk
4½ ounces whipped topping (we prefer Cool Whip)

Combine butter, flour, and 2 tablespoons sugar. Flour fingers, and pat mixture into an 8 x 12-inch baking dish. Bake in a preheated 350° oven for 12 to 15 minutes. Remove and cool. Beat together until smooth cream cheese, 1 cup sugar, and 2 tablespoons milk. Fold in 4½ ounces of whipped topping. Spread on cooled crust. In a medium-size bowl, combine instant pudding mix with 3 cups milk. Beat slowly for 2 minutes. Spread on cream cheese mixture. Refrigerate for about 15 minutes or until set. Spread remaining 4½ ounces of whipped topping on top. Refrigerate until serving time. Cut into squares.
YIELD: 12 to 14 servings

Mrs. Harry G. Ebeling
(Martha Bowman)

LEMONDOWN FANCY

Delicious crust; cool and refreshing filling.

1½ cups wheat flakes — do not crush (we prefer Wheaties)
½ cup chopped walnuts
4 tablespoons butter
½ cup brown sugar, firmly packed
3 egg whites
½ cup granulated sugar
3 egg yolks
½ pint whipping cream, whipped
1/3 cup fresh lemon juice

Spread wheat flakes and nuts on an ungreased cookie sheet; bake in a preheated 300° oven for 15 minutes. In a small saucepan, combine butter and brown sugar. Bring to a boil over low heat (Do not burn.). Remove from heat, and stir in wheat flakes and nuts, and mix well. Pat about 2 cups of the wheat flake mixture into a lightly greased 9-inch pie pan. Reserve remaining mixture for topping. In a large mixing bowl, beat egg whites until frothy. Add granulated sugar, 1 tablespoon at a time, beating well after each addition, until thick. In a small bowl, beat egg yolks until thick; fold into beaten egg whites. Fold in whipped cream; fold in lemon juice. Pour onto prepared crust; sprinkle with reserved wheat flake mixture. Freeze until serving time.
YIELD: 8 servings

Mrs. Earl F. Pritchard
(Judy Elliott)

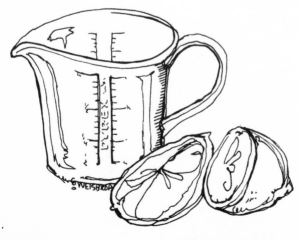

LEMON ICEBOX DESSERT

Very light and creamy; not too sweet. Just right after a heavy meal.

3	egg yolks
½	teaspoon salt
½	cup sugar
¼	cup lemon juice (about 1½ lemons)
3	egg whites
2	tablespoons sugar
½	pint whipping cream, whipped
¾	cup crushed vanilla wafers

Separate eggs. Put yolks in double boiler. Beat yolks with fork; then add salt, ½ cup sugar, and beat well. Stir in lemon juice. Cook over hot water (not boiling) stirring constantly until it thickens on spoon. Remove from fire, and place in refrigerator to chill for 10 to 15 minutes. Beat egg whites. Add 2 tablespoons sugar, and beat until stiff. Fold whipped cream and egg whites into cooled lemon mixture. Put ½ of crushed wafers into bottom of a 9-inch square dish; cover with all pudding mixture; then sprinkle remaining crushed wafers over the top. Cover and put in freezer for 2 to 3 hours. Remove from freezer at least 30 minutes before serving. Cut into 9 squares.
YIELD: 9 servings

Mrs. James C. Snow
(Kathryn Ruddock)

CHOCOLATE SUPER SPEEDER

Light and refreshing.

1	pint whipping cream, whipped
1¼	cups milk chocolate syrup (we prefer Hershey's)
3	tablespoons rum
4	ounces chopped walnuts, or sliced almonds
1	ounce bitter chocolate, grated

In a mixing bowl, beat the whipping cream until stiff. Fold in chocolate syrup and rum. Turn into 6 sherbet glasses or an 8 x 8-inch pan. Freeze until serving time. Garnish with nuts and grated bitter chocolate.
YIELD: 6 servings

Mrs. William B. Howell
(Marcia Hobart)

FROZEN MOCHA-TOFFEE DESSERT

A superb coffee-toffee taste blend.

8	ladyfingers, split
2½	tablespoons instant coffee
1	tablespoon boiling water
1	tablespoon creme de cacao
1	quart vanilla ice cream, softened
1½	cups crushed toffee bars, (we prefer 8 or 9 1-ounce Heath Bars)
½	cup whipping cream, whipped
2½	tablespoons creme de cacao
1	1-ounce toffee bar

Line the bottom and up 2 inches on sides of an 8 or 9-inch spring-form pan with split ladyfingers. Dissolve coffee with boiling water; cool. Stir in 1 tablespoon creme de cacao, ice cream, and 1½ cups crushed candy. Spoon into ladyfinger-lined pan; cover, and freeze until firm. Before serving, combine whipped cream and 2½ tablespoons creme de cacao, and spread evenly over top of ice cream layer. Garnish with additional toffee bar, crushed.
YIELD: 8 to 10 servings

Mrs. William Kasch
(Sonnie Kern)

ICE CREAM PIE

Spanish peanuts add an unusual and delightful touch.

1½	cups graham cracker crumbs
¼	cup peanut butter
3	tablespoons butter, melted
1	12-ounce package semi-sweet chocolate chips
1	cup whipping cream, not whipped
1	teaspoon vanilla
½	gallon vanilla ice cream, softened
¾	cup Spanish peanuts

Mix together crumbs, peanut butter, and butter. Press into 9-inch pie pan. Bake in a preheated 350° oven 8 minutes; refrigerate. In a double boiler, melt chocolate chips over low heat. Add cream in a very slow stream; stir constantly (do not beat). Add vanilla; remove from heat; set aside. Spread ½ of the vanilla ice cream in bottom of chilled crust. Add ¼ cooled sauce; sprinkle ¼ peanuts over sauce; repeat layers. Refrigerate remaining sauce for future use. Cover pie and freeze.
YIELD: 8 servings

Mrs. G. F. Miller, Jr.
(Barbara Wallace)

BUTTERSCOTCH CRUNCH SQUARES

Very rich — a little goes a long way.

1 cup sifted flour
¼ cup oatmeal
¼ cup brown sugar
½ cup butter
½ cup chopped pecans
1 quart chocolate ice cream, softened
1 12-ounce jar caramel or butterscotch sundae topping

In a small mixing bowl, combine flour, oatmeal, brown sugar, butter, and nuts. Pat into a 9 x 13 x 2-inch pan. Bake in a preheated 400° oven for 15 minutes. While still warm, stir to crumble. Cool. Spread ½ of crumb mixture evenly in a 9-inch square pan. Drizzle ½ of sundae topping over crumbs. Spread softened ice cream smoothly and evenly over crumbs and topping. Add remaining sundae topping; sprinkle reserved crumbs over topping; freeze. Cut into squares. YIELD: 16 servings

Mrs. Bruce A. Triplett
(Leslie Conway)

BUTTER PECAN DESSERT

Refreshingly light and tasty.

1½ cups shortbread cookies, crushed
¼ cup butter or margarine, melted
2 3¾-ounce size packages instant vanilla pudding
1¼ cups milk
1 pint butter pecan ice cream, softened
1 4-ounce container prepared whipped topping (we prefer Cool Whip)
3 packages Heath Bars (6 small bars), crushed

Combine crushed cookies and melted butter. Spread in 5 x 9-inch pan and chill. Blend together milk and pudding until thick. Mix in ice cream, beating until fluffy. Spread on cookie mixture. Cover with whipped topping. Sprinkle crushed Heath Bars on top. Chill in freezer at least two hours or overnight. Defrost in refrigerator five hours before serving. YIELD: 6 to 8 servings

Mrs. Hugh Thurnauer
(Eileen Babcock)

SPICED NUTS

Really scrumptious. Careful — these nuts can be habit forming!

1	cup sugar
½	cup water
1	teaspoon cinnamon
¾	teaspoon salt
1	teaspoon vanilla
1	pound pecans or English walnuts

Using a heavy pan, mix together all ingredients, except the nuts. Bring to a boil over medium-high heat. Boil 4 to 6 minutes, or until mixture reaches thread stage (about 240°). Remove from heat. Stir in nuts. Pour onto buttered heatproof platter. Separate nuts; cool at least 1 hour. Store in airtight container.
YIELD: 1 pound

Mrs. James Brown
(Ann Nye Guthrie)

FROZEN CHOCOLATE DESSERT

Outstanding, but rich — serve small portions.

½	cup butter
1	cup shredded coconut (optional)
2	cups graham cracker crumbs
½	gallon ice cream, any flavor
1	cup chopped pecans or walnuts
1	13-ounce can evaporated milk
1	10½-ounce package marshmallows
1	6-ounce package semi-sweet chocolate bits

In a large skillet, melt butter over low heat. Add coconut, and cook carefully until light brown. Remove from heat, and stir in graham cracker crumbs. Set aside ¼ of the crumb mixture. Press remaining mixture into the bottom of a 9 x 13 x 2-inch pan. Place in freezer until firm. Meanwhile, allow ice cream to soften. Spread ice cream over crust, and return to freezer. Add nuts to reserved ¼ crust mixture, and set aside. In the top of a double boiler, combine evaporated milk, marshmallows, and chocolate bits. Cook over low heat until melted. Remove from heat and cool. Spread cooled chocolate mixture over ice cream. Top with crumb-nut mixture. Cover with aluminum foil and freeze.
YIELD: 12 to 16 servings

Mrs. Jonathan Shelton
(Nancy Garst)

CHOCOLATE MINT FINALE

I serve this as my traditional Christmas dessert.

4 tablespoons butter, melted
1¼ cups finely crushed vanilla wafers
1 quart peppermint ice cream
½ cup butter, melted
2 squares unsweetened chocolate, melted
1½ cups powdered sugar
3 egg yolks, well beaten
3 egg whites, beaten stiff
2 to 4 tablespoons chopped pecans for garnish, optional
1 pint fresh strawberries for garnish, optional

In a 9 x 9-inch pan, combine melted butter and wafer crumbs. Set aside 2 to 4 tablespoons of this mixture. Press remaining crumb mixture firmly into bottom of pan to form crust; refrigerate. Soften ice cream, and spread onto crust. Chill in freezer until topping is ready. In a medium-size bowl, mix together melted butter, melted chocolate, and powdered sugar. Add egg yolks. Carefully fold in egg whites. Spread topping over ice cream, and sprinkle with reserved crust mixture and pecans. Cover and freeze until serving time. Cut into squares; garnish with fresh strawberries. YIELD: 12 servings

Mrs. William Pees
(Candy Gray)

ICE CREAM TORTONI

Refreshing, fantastic blending of flavors!

1/3 cup almonds, chopped and toasted
3 tablespoons butter, melted
1 cup vanilla wafers, crushed
1 teaspoon almond extract
3 pints vanilla ice cream, slightly softened
12 ounces apricot preserves

Mix together almonds, butter, crushed vanilla wafers, and extract. Reserve ¼ cup mixture for topping. Sprinkle ½ of remaining mixture over the bottom of a foil-lined 8 x 8-inch pan. Spoon ½ of the ice cream over crumbs. Drizzle with ½ of the preserves. Sprinkle with remaining crumb mixture. Repeat ice cream and preserves layers. Sprinkle with reserved ¼ cup crumbs. Freeze until ready to serve. Cut into squares. YIELD: 9 squares

Mrs. Richard Prigozen
(Roberta Richmond)

DESSERTS

DAIRY FARM VANILLA ICE CREAM

Homemade and hand turned; all ingredients are "real" —
if you can find them! Of course, the ice cream may be prepared
with regular pasteurized milk.

5   eggs
2½ cups sugar
1   quart top cream, or
     whipping cream and
     half and half
     (according to how rich
     you want)
1½ tablespoons real
     vanilla
½   teaspoon salt
     Approximately 1½
     quarts raw whole milk,
     or pasteurized whole
     milk
16 to 20 pounds crushed
     ice
2   pounds rock salt

In a large bowl, beat eggs until light and fluffy. Add sugar gradually, beating well after each ¼ cup addition. Continue beating at high speed until mixture becomes thick and sugar is mostly dissolved. Add cream, vanilla, and salt. Beat at low speed until well blended. Swish a little whole milk in a 1-gallon homemade ice cream freezer can. Pour ice cream mixture into freezer. Add milk up to fill line, or about 2/3 to 3/4 full. Put dasher in place, and turn by hand to mix milk into ice cream mixture; cover. Add ice and rock salt, using 8 to 10 parts ice to 1 part rock salt. Crank for approximately 25 to 30 minutes, or until it is hard to crank. Add more ice and salt as necessary. When ice cream is done, remove ice to a level below the lid; take the lid off, and remove the dasher. Cork the lid, and replace the cover. Then drain the liquid brine. Add more salt and ice to cover the lid (4 parts ice to 1 part rock salt). Cover with newspapers and allow to ripen for 1 to 4 hours before serving. Serve in chilled bowls.
VARIATION: May substitute 1 pint whipping cream or coffee cream and 2% or whole pasteurized milk for the whole milk and cream. This will make ice cream less rich — more like ice milk.
YIELD: 1 gallon

Mrs. Robert L. Deddens
(Ruth Carey)

FRUIT AND BERRY WINE COOLER

This is a great make-ahead summer recipe.
It is a special dessert for a bridge party and is particularly pretty
when served in a cut-crystal bowl.

4 pints of various sher-
   bets (lemon, raspberry,
   orange, lime, etc.) or
   use ½ gallon rainbow
   sherbet
   About 4 cups of fresh
   fruits (blueberries,
   strawberries, red
   raspberries, seedless
   grapes, etc.)
1 11-ounce can manda-
   rin orange sections,
   drained

BERRY WINE SAUCE

1   10-ounce package
    frozen raspberries
1½ cups cranberry juice
¾   cup sugar
3   tablespoons cornstarch
½   cup dry red wine

Make 12 sherbet balls, and place on foil-lined baking sheet. Freeze until hard. Wash and drain fruit. Just before serving, arrange in a large glass bowl, layers of fruit and layers of sherbet balls. Pass Berry Wine Sauce separately and ladle over each serving.

BERRY WINE SAUCE

Bring raspberries and cranberry juice to a boil. Press mixture through sieve to remove all seeds and pulp. Return juice to saucepan. Mix sugar and cornstarch together in small bowl. Add to juice mixture in saucepan. Cook and stir until mixture is thickened and bubbly. Remove from heat, and stir in wine. Cool thoroughly in refrigerator. Serve over sherbet and fruit.
CHEF'S NOTE: Chill the serving bowl in the refrigerator, not freezer. If the glass is too cold, it will frost over during serving.
YIELD: 12 servings

Mrs. Bruce A. Triplett
(Leslie Conway)

CRUNCH DROP COOKIES

A great family cookie. Really tasty flavor and just enough crunch.

2 cups flour
1 teaspoon baking soda
¼ teaspoon salt
1 cup margarine or butter
1 cup brown sugar, packed
1 cup white sugar
2 eggs
1 teaspoon vanilla
2 cups quick-cooking rolled oats
2 cups Rice Krispies cereal
1 cup flaked coconut

Sift together flour, baking soda, and salt; set aside. In a large mixing bowl, cream together margarine, brown sugar, and white sugar until smooth. Add eggs, and beat well. Mix in vanilla; add flour mixture, oatmeal, Rice Krispies, and coconut (Use hands to mix — batter will be stiff.). Drop by teaspoonfuls onto greased cookie sheet. Bake in preheated 350° oven for 12 to 15 minutes, or until done. YIELD: 5 dozen

Mrs. S. Richard Reece
(Ruth Milliken)

LONE RANGER COOKIES

A family favorite since I was a little girl.
Crunchy, healthy, tasty cookie.

1 cup vegetable shortening
1 cup granulated sugar
1 cup brown sugar
3 eggs
1 teaspoon vanilla
2 cups flour
1 teaspoon baking powder
1 teaspoon baking soda
½ teaspoon salt
¾ to 1 cup wheat germ (optional)
¾ to 1 cup corn flakes
1¾ to 2 cups Rice Krispies
1¾ to 2 cups oatmeal

Sift together flour, baking powder, soda, and salt. Set aside. Mix shortening and sugars; add eggs, and mix well. Add flour mixture slowly. Beat in vanilla. By hand, mix in cereals (The more cereal used, the crunchier the cookie. The mixture will be dry.). Drop mixture by spoonfuls onto greased cookie sheet (You may need to press them together with your fingers.). Bake in a preheated 350° oven for 12 to 15 minutes.
CHEF'S NOTE: Use full measure of corn flakes, Rice Krispies, and oatmeal if wheat germ is omitted.
YIELD: 8 dozen cookies

Mrs. Thomas Shulman
(Ellie Arnovitz)

FORK COOKIES

My Mother baked these cookies when I was young.
Good dunking cookies!

1 cup butter or marga-
  rine, melted
1 cup granulated sugar
1 cup brown sugar
2 eggs
2 cups flour
½ teaspoon salt
1 teaspoon baking
  powder
1 teaspoon baking soda
1 teaspoon cinnamon
2 cups quick-cooking
  oatmeal
½ cup coconut

Melt butter; add sugars and eggs. Sift together flour, salt, baking powder, baking soda, and cinnamon. Stir into sugar mixture until well blended. Stir in oats and coconut. Roll into small balls. Place on greased cookie sheet, and press dough with a fork. Bake in a preheated 350° oven for 8 to 10 minutes or until done.
VARIATION: 1 cup chocolate chips or 1 cup raisins may be stirred into dough before baking.
YIELD: 5 dozen cookies

Mrs. Robert James
(Sally Schaefer)

LEMON WHIPPERSNAPPERS

Very light and lemony! Extra quick.

1 18-ounce package
  lemon cake mix
  (we prefer Pillsbury)
1 9 or 10-ounce carton
  whipped topping,
  thawed (we prefer
  Cool Whip)
2 eggs, beaten
½ cup sifted powdered
  sugar

Combine cake mix, whipped topping, and eggs in a large bowl. Stir until well mixed. Drop by teaspoonfuls into powdered sugar (dough will be soft), and roll to coat. Place dough balls 1½ inches apart on a greased cookie sheet. Bake in a preheated 350° oven for 10 to 15 minutes, or until delicately browned. Remove from cookie sheet and cool.
YIELD: about 4 dozen

Mrs. S. Richard Reece
(Ruth Milliken)

HAWTHORN HILL COCONUT MACAROONS

These cookies were always served to the elementary school children who were carollers at Hawthorn Hill (Wright Brothers' home) at Christmas time twenty years ago. My father requested the recipe from the National Cash Register Company for me to use in a 4-H foods demonstration at the County Fair. It was a winner then, and it is still a winner today.

½ cup egg whites (about 4 large egg whites), room temperature
1 cup sugar
2½ cups granulated coconut, or flaked coconut granulated in food processor or blender
1 teaspoon vanilla

Beat egg whites until stiff peaks form when beaters are raised. Add sugar very slowly with beater at medium speed. By hand, fold in coconut carefully. Fold in vanilla carefully. Drop by tablespoonfuls onto a Teflon cookie sheet or a regular cookie sheet covered with parchment or brown wrapping paper. Bake in a preheated 325° oven for about 18 minutes or until light golden in color. Cool slightly before removing from paper with a stiff spatula.
YIELD: about 2½ dozen

Mrs. Robert L. Deddens
(Ruth Carey)

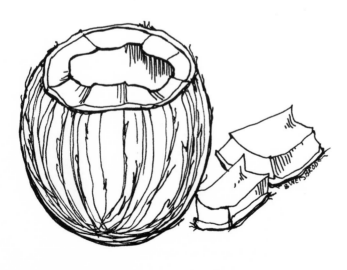

POTATO FLAKE TEA COOKIES

They will never guess the ingredients! The taste is coconut.

½ cup margarine, soften-
ed
1 cup sugar
1 egg
1½ cups potato flakes
(not buds)
1 tablespoon coconut
extract
1 cup buttermilk baking
mix

In a medium-size mixing bowl, cream margarine and sugar. Beat in egg, potato flakes, and 1 tablespoon coconut extract. Stir in buttermilk baking mix. Chill about 2 hours. Form dough into small (marble-size) balls. Press dough with flour-dusted fork onto greased cookie sheet. Bake in a preheated 350° oven for 6 to 8 minutes. Cool cookies for several minutes on cookie sheet. Remove to a cooling rack.
CHEF'S NOTE: Do not double this recipe.
VARIATION: Stir in 1/3 cup frozen French cut green beans, chopped, for a very different chewy little cookie.
YIELD: 90 to 100 small cookies

Mrs. William Keadey
·(Mary Essig)

POTATO CHIP COOKIES

Look good and taste good!
You will be surprised how they seem to melt in your mouth.

1 cup butter, softened
½ cup sugar
1 teaspoon vanilla
1¾ cups flour, sifted
1 cup crushed potato
chips (not too fine)
Granulated sugar for
shaping

In a mixing bowl, cream butter, sugar, and vanilla. Add flour and potato chips. Form into 1-inch balls. Place on cookie sheet. Grease the bottom of a juice-sized glass. Dip the glass into sugar, and press out each cookie. Bake in a preheated 350° oven for 10 to 12 minutes.
YIELD: 4 dozen

Mrs. Bruce Triplett
(Leslie Conway)

269

PEANUT BUTTER COOKIES

*This was my great-grandmother's recipe;
it has a light and delicate flavor.*

1 cup granulated
  sugar
1 cup brown sugar
1 cup shortening
2 eggs
1 teaspoon vanilla
1 cup peanut butter
1 teaspoon baking soda
2 teaspoons baking
  powder
1 teaspoon salt
2½ cups flour

In a large mixing bowl, beat together sugars and shortening. Add eggs one at a time, beating well after each addition. Mix in vanilla and peanut butter. Sift together dry ingredients; stir into peanut butter mixture. Place small teaspoon-sized lumps on greased cookie sheet. Flatten dough slightly with flour-dusted fork. Bake in a preheated 375° oven for about 6 to 8 minutes, or until done.
YIELD: 120, 1¾-inch cookies

Miss Margaret Ann DeMarse

ORANGE COOKIES

These cookies are super delicious — moist, tart, and chewy!

1 cup raisins
1 cup hot water
½ cup margarine
½ cup granulated sugar
½ cup brown sugar,
  packed
1 egg
1 11½-ounce can
  mandarin oranges,
  well drained
2½ cups flour
1 teaspoon baking soda
½ teaspoon salt
1 cup chopped walnuts

Plump raisins by soaking them in hot water for a few minutes. Drain; set aside on paper toweling. In a large mixing bowl, cream margarine and both sugars. Add egg, and beat well. Add drained mandarin oranges, and beat well with electric mixer until oranges are shredded and thoroughly mixed. Sift together flour, baking soda, and salt. Stir into orange mixture, mixing well. Stir in raisins and nuts. Drop by teaspoonfuls onto lightly greased cookie sheets. Bake in preheated 350° oven for 10 minutes; cool.

recipe continues...

ORANGE ICING

2 cups confectioners sugar Undiluted frozen orange juice concentrate, thawed	In a small bowl, mix together powdered sugar and enough orange juice concentrate to make a good spreading consistency. Spread on cooled cookies. YIELD: about 3 dozen cookies

Mrs. S. Richard Reece
(Ruth Milliken)

CHOCOLATE MERINGUE COOKIES

These heavenly, light cookies are the "chocolate addict's" choice.
They are very fragile and do not keep well, but
they don't last long either!

2 egg whites 1/8 teaspoon salt ½ teaspoon white vinegar ½ teaspoon vanilla ½ cup granulated sugar 6 ounces semi-sweet chocolate bits (1 cup), melted, cooled to room temperature 1 cup broken pecans	In large non-plastic mixing bowl, combine egg whites, salt, vinegar, and vanilla. Beat at high speed until thick and foamy. Gradually add sugar, beating at high speed until mixture forms stiff peaks. Carefully fold in the cooled, melted chocolate. Fold in pecans. Drop by small teaspoonfuls about 3-inches apart on a greased cookie sheet (These cookies puff and spread, so give them plenty of room.). Bake in a preheated 350° oven for 8 to 10 minutes (Be certain that oven is preheated.). Watch carefully — the meringue base burns easily. Cool on racks until lukewarm, and then indulge yourself before anyone else discovers them! YIELD: 3 dozen

Mrs. Gerald Westerbeck
(Judy Richardson)

271

RUSSIAN TEA CAKES

Excellent Christmas cookie.

5 cups flour
2 cups sugar
2 cups coarsely ground almonds
1 pound butter
5 egg yolks, beaten
1 teaspoon almond extract

In a large mixing bowl, sift together flour and sugar. Stir in almonds. Cut butter into dry ingredients until texture is coarse. Stir in egg yolks and extract. Pinch off small pieces of dough and roll it into balls. Place on a lightly buttered cookie sheet. Flatten balls with the bottom of a glass dipped in flour. Bake in a preheated 375° oven for 15 minutes, or until golden brown (best baked on second rack from the bottom; watch closely). Frost cooled cookies with tinted butter cream frosting.
YIELD: 8 to 9 dozen

Mrs. C. Stephen Hayes
(Sally Creager)

CHINESE ALMOND COOKIES

Just the thing to serve after a heavy meal — not too sweet.

2¾ cups sifted flour
1 cup sugar
½ teaspoon salt
½ teaspoon baking soda
½ cup butter
½ cup margarine
1 egg, slightly beaten
1½ teaspoons almond extract
Whole unblanched almonds

Sift together flour, sugar, salt, and baking soda. Cut in butter and margarine with pastry blender or low mixer speed until mixture resembles cornmeal. Add egg and almond extract; mix well. Shape dough into 1-inch balls, and place 2-inches apart on an ungreased cookie sheet. Press down to flatten, and press an almond into the center of each. Bake in a preheated 325° oven for 25 minutes or until lightly browned.
YIELD: 4½ dozen

Mrs. Richard Karr
(Mary Frances Wheaton)

GRANNY'S ICED SHORTBREAD COOKIES

This is my most treasured recipe — a tradition as long as I can remember. I serve them with Irish coffee every Christmas Eve, and they look and taste magnificent!

SHORTBREAD

1	pound butter at room temperature (no substitutes)
1	cup superfine granulated sugar
3¼	cups flour

BUTTER ICING

¼	pound butter, softened
1	pound confectioners sugar
1	teaspoon almond extract
2	to 3 teaspoons half and half, or enough to reach spreading consistency

Beat butter well, until light and fluffy. Add sugar and flour gradually. Generously sprinkle flour on a cloth-covered pastry board; knead dough well with your hands. Flour cloth-covered rolling pin and roll dough until about ¼ inch thick. Dip cookie cutters in flour; cut out dough, and place cookies on lightly greased cookie sheet (suggested shapes: star, bell, cross). Bake in a preheated 225° oven for about 1 hour, or until edges of cookie become beige. Cool before icing and decorating.

BUTTER ICING

Mix icing ingredients until smooth. Spread onto cookies. Decorate immediately with gold dragees (little gold balls made of sugar for use in decorating). Store in tin boxes.
YIELD: 4 dozen cookies

Mrs. Charles Ballard
(Patti Davis)

TOFFEE BARS

One of our very favorite cookie bars.

6   to 8 ounces graham crackers
2   cups brown sugar
1   cup butter
½   cup margarine
2   cups chopped pecans or walnuts
2   teaspoons vanilla
1   9-ounce milk chocolate candy bar (we prefer Hershey's)
½   cup semi-sweet chocolate bits

Place graham crackers as close as possible on a 15 x 10½ x 1-inch jelly roll pan. In a small, heavy saucepan, combine brown sugar, butter, and margarine. Stirring constantly to keep from scorching, bring to a boil over medium-high heat. Cook for 5 to 6 minutes. Remove from heat. Stir in nuts and vanilla. Pour brown sugar mixture over graham crackers; spread evenly. Bake in a preheated 350° oven for 8 minutes; cool. In a small saucepan, melt together chocolate candy bar and chocolate bits. Spread over cooled cookies. Place finished pan of toffee bars in refrigerator for 20 minutes (set timer). Remove and cut into squares. Cover and store in refrigerator.
YIELD: 4½ dozen squares

Mrs. S. Richard Reece
(Ruth Milliken)

TURTLE COOKIES

Sweet and elegant cookie.

2   cups flour
1   cup brown sugar
½   cup butter, softened
1   cup pecan halves
¾   cup butter
2/3 cup brown sugar
8   ounces semi-sweet chocolate bits, melted

In a small bowl, mix together flour, 1 cup brown sugar, and ½ cup softened butter. Turn into an ungreased 9 x 13 x 2-inch glass baking dish. Pat firmly and evenly to form a crust. Sprinkle pecan halves evenly over crust. In a 1-quart saucepan, combine ¾ cup butter with 2/3 cup brown sugar.
recipe continues . . .

Cook over medium heat, stirring constantly until entire surface of mixture begins to boil; stir and boil for 1 minute. Spoon hot mixture evenly over pecans and crust. Bake in a preheated 350° oven for 20 minutes, or until entire surface is bubbly and crust is golden brown. Meanwhile, melt chocolate in a small saucepan. Remove pan from oven, and immediately drizzle melted chocolate over surface of cookie. Cool completely before cutting into 1½-inch squares. YIELD: 48 squares

Mrs. William Miller
(Janet Hadler)

PECAN PIE BARS

A rich cookie that definitely satisfies the sweet tooth!

1	18½-ounce package yellow cake mix (reserve 2/3 cup for filling)
½	cup butter, melted
1	egg
½	cup packed brown sugar
1½	cups dark corn syrup (we prefer Karo)
1	teaspoon vanilla
3	eggs
1	cup chopped pecans

Reserve 2/3 cup cake mix for filling. Combine remaining dry cake mix, butter, and 1 egg; mix well. Press into a greased 9 x 13-inch baking pan. Bake in a preheated 350° oven for 15 to 20 minutes or until light, golden brown. Meanwhile, combine 2/3 cup reserved cake mix, ½ cup brown sugar, Karo syrup, vanilla, and 3 eggs. Beat at medium speed for 1 to 2 minutes. Pour filling over partially baked crust; sprinkle with pecans. Return to oven, and bake for 30 to 35 minutes, or until filling is set. Cool; cut into 36 bars.
YIELD: 3 dozen

Mrs. Bruce A. Triplett
(Leslie Conway)

DATE-NUT GOODIES

A very chewy cookie; best when served fresh.

1 cup chopped dates
1 cup chopped pecans
1 cup sifted
confectioners sugar
1 egg white, unbeaten
Colored or white
granulated sugar to
garnish

In a small mixing bowl, combine dates, pecans, and confectioners sugar. Add egg white, and mix thoroughly. Drop by teaspoonfuls onto a greased cookie sheet. Sprinkle with colored or white granulated sugar. Bake in a preheated 350° oven for 10 to 12 minutes or until light brown. Watch carefully — they burn easily. Cool slightly before removing from cookie sheet.
YIELD: about 3 dozen

Mrs. Walter Scott Mills
(Sherry Smith)

DAYTON PASTRY COOKIES

Everyone thinks this must be complicated to taste so good, but it is super easy!

1 cup flour
½ cup butter, softened
¼ cup brown sugar
2 eggs, beaten
1 tablespoon flour
1 teaspoon baking
powder
1½ cups brown sugar
1 cup chocolate chips
1 teaspoon vanilla
1/3 cup confectioners sugar

In a small bowl, mix together 1 cup flour, butter, and ¼ cup brown sugar. Pat mixture into the bottom of a buttered 8 x 9-inch pan. Bake in a preheated 350° oven for 7 minutes. Meanwhile, combine flour, baking powder, and brown sugar. Add eggs; mix well. Stir in chocolate chips and vanilla. After crust has baked for 7 minutes, remove from oven. Add egg mixture, and return to oven for 25 minutes. Sprinkle confectioners sugar over pastry cookies when taken out of oven. Cool before cutting. Refrigerate for 1 hour in pan before serving.
YIELD: 12 bars

Mrs. William Kendell
(Ponnie Childress)

276

SUGARPLUM NUT HORNS

Our favorite Christmas cookie!

¾ pound butter, softened
4¼ cups flour, sifted
3 egg yolks
1 teaspoon vanilla
1 cup sour cream
½ teaspoon salt
1 envelope active dry yeast

NUT FILLING

3 egg whites
1 cup sugar
1 pound walnuts, ground
3 tablespoons pineapple juice

DUSTING-ROLLING MIXTURE

½ cup sugar
¼ cup flour, sifted

Cut butter into flour using a pastry blender. Add remaining ingredients, and mix well. Cover and chill overnight in a non-metal bowl.

NUT FILLING

Whip egg whites with sugar until stiff. Fold in nuts and juice. Set aside.

DUSTING-ROLLING MIXTURE

Sift together sugar and flour, and use to prepare pastry cloth and rolling pin (This dusting-rolling mixture makes a sugary crust.). Warm dough slightly. Divide into 8 equal parts. Roll each into a 10 to 12-inch circle, dusting pastry cloth with the dusting-rolling 'mixture as needed. Cut each circle into 8 pie-shaped wedges. Drop 1 tablespoon of nut filling mixture at the wide end of each wedge. Roll toward the point end, and form a horn or crescent shape. Place on a lightly buttered cookie sheet and bake in a preheated 350° oven until light brown (about 12 to 15 minutes).
YIELD: 64 sugarplum nut horns

Mrs. Charles J. Roedersheimer
(Alice Murray)

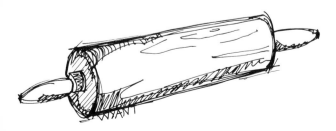

HEAVENLY CREAM SQUARES

Please don't count the calories . . . each bite is a little bit of heaven!

FIRST LAYER

1/3	cup cocoa
½	cup butter
2	cups graham cracker crumbs
½	cup coarsely chopped walnuts
½	cup granulated sugar
1	egg
1	cup flaked coconut
1	teaspoon vanilla

SECOND LAYER

½	cup butter
3	tablespoons milk
2	cups confectioners sugar
3	tablespoons instant vanilla pudding

THIRD LAYER

3	squares semi-sweet chocolate
1/3	cup butter

In a large mixing bowl, mix all the ingredients for the first layer together until well blended; press into a 7 x 11-inch pan. Cover and refrigerate. In a small mixing bowl, beat together all the ingredients for the second layer until well blended. Spread pudding mixture on top of the first layer, and return to the refrigerator. In a small saucepan, melt the chocolate with the butter over low heat. Spread on top of the second layer; refrigerate. When the chocolate is set but still soft, cut into bite-sized squares (This prevents the chocolate from cracking.). Cover and refrigerate until serving time.
YIELD: 40 squares

Mrs. Stephen G. England
(Katherine Benham)

CAPETOWN BROWNIES

Very moist, rich, and chocolaty!

2 eggs
1 cup sugar
½ cup butter
1 teaspoon vanilla
2 squares unsweetened chocolate
½ cup semi-sweet chocolate bits
½ cup flour
1 cup miniature marshmallows
½ cup chopped nuts

Beat eggs. Add sugar and mix well. Melt butter, unsweetened chocolate, and semi-sweet bits together. Cool. Add to sugar and egg mixture. Add vanilla; stir in flour; add marshmallows and nuts. Pour into greased 9 x 9-inch pan. Bake in a preheated 350° oven for 25 to 30 minutes. Cool before cutting.
YIELD: 12 to 16 brownies

Mrs. David C. Hulme
(Christine Hafstad)

BLONDE BROWNIES

A very chewy, rich brownie.

1/3 cup margarine, melted
1 cup brown sugar
1 egg, slightly beaten
1 teaspoon vanilla
1 cup flour
½ teaspoon baking powder
1/8 teaspoon salt
½ cup chocolate chips

In a medium-size bowl, mix together margarine and brown sugar. Add the beaten egg and the vanilla. Sift together dry ingredients, and add to the egg mixture. Pour into a greased 8 x 8-inch pan. Sprinkle ½ cup chocolate chips over the top. Bake in a preheated 350° oven for 20 to 25 minutes.
YIELD: 16 squares

Miss Holly A. Briggs

COOKIES

MERRY CHEESECAKE BARS

Outstanding flavor!

1 cup flour
1/3 cup butter, softened
(no substitutes)
½ cup packed brown
sugar
½ cup chopped pecans
or walnuts

FILLING

8 ounces cream cheese,
softened
¼ cup sugar
1 egg
2 tablespoons milk
1 tablespoon lemon juice
1 teaspoon vanilla

In a small bowl, combine flour, butter, and brown sugar. Blend with a mixer at low speed for 2 to 3 minutes, or until particles are fine. Stir in nuts. Reserve 1 cup of crust mixture for topping. Pat remainder of crust mixture in ungreased 8-inch square pan. Bake near center of preheated 350° oven for 8 to 10 minutes or until lightly browned.

FILLING

In a small bowl, combine all filling ingredients. Beat on low speed with a mixer until smooth. Pour over partially baked crust. Sprinkle with reserved crumb mixture. Return to 350° oven for 23 to 30 minutes, or until golden brown; cool. Cut into bars; store in refrigerator!
YIELD: 24 to 30 bars

Mrs. Bruce A. Triplett
(Leslie Conway)

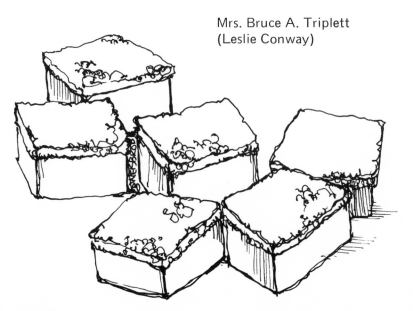

MARSHMALLOW FUDGIES

These are "inhaled" even though they are so full of calories.

CAKE

4	eggs, beaten
2	cups sugar
½	cup flour
1	teaspoon baking powder
3	squares unsweetened chocolate, melted
1	cup butter, melted
1	cup pecans, broken
2	teaspoons vanilla
6	ounces mini-marshmallows

TOPPING

½	cup melted butter
2	squares unsweetened chocolate, melted
1	5-1/3-ounce can evaporated milk
1	cup sugar
1	pound confectioners sugar
1	teaspoon vanilla

In a medium-size mixing bowl, beat eggs and sugar until thick. Sift together flour and baking powder; blend into egg mixture. Mix in all remaining cake ingredients except mini-marshmallows. Spread batter into a well-greased 9 x 13-inch pan. Bake in a preheated 325° oven for 35 minutes, or until done. Cover the hot cake with all of the marshmallows. Pour the hot topping (recipe follows) over the marshmallows.

TOPPING

In top of a double boiler, mix together the first four topping ingredients. Cook, stirring constantly, until sugar is dissolved. Beat in confectioners sugar and vanilla. Pour over marshmallow-covered, hot cake. Wait until the next day to cut into small, 2 x 2-inch squares. Store in tightly covered tin canister at room temperature. YIELD: 3 dozen squares

Mrs. Robert M. O'Hara
(Barbara Nichols)

CANDIED CITRUS PEEL

This is a candy, but it may be used in fruit cake and other recipes calling for candied fruit.

3	large, thick-skinned oranges, or equivalent amount of other citrus fruit
2	cups sugar
1	cup water
1	cup sugar for coating

Wash oranges; cut in quarters, and eat the fruit. Now you are ready to make candy! Remove membrane. Using a serrated knife, scrape oranges slightly to break oil cells; rinse. Cut oranges into ¼-inch wedges. Place in a 3-quart pan and cover with water. Bring to a boil and boil gently for 5 minutes (set the timer). Don't overcook! Drain in a colander. Repeat the 5-minute boil routine 3 times to remove bitter flavor. Drain and lay peel on paper toweling; cover with more paper towels, and press gently to remove excess water. Mix 2 cups sugar and 1 cup water in a sauce pan. Bring mixture to a boil stirring until sugar dissolves. Add drained peel and bring to a boil; gently cook for 10 minutes. Remove from the heat, and when cooled, refrigerate covered saucepan for 8 hours or more. Return to low heat and simmer until most of the syrup is absorbed. Keep heat low to prevent scorching. Remove from heat. Dip peel out of the pan, and roll in granulated sugar. Cool on a rack. Roll again in sugar, and store in a loosely covered container. Keeps well for 3 weeks.

CHEF'S NOTE: Freeze individually on cookie sheet; then place them in a plastic bag for easy access storage.

YIELD: 1-pint candy

Mrs. William Keadey
(Mary Essig)

BAKED CARAMEL CORN

Rich caramel flavor — absolutely divine!

2 cups brown sugar
1 cup butter or margarine
1/8 teaspoon cream of tartar
½ cup light corn syrup (we prefer Karo)
1 teaspoon baking soda
7 quarts popped corn

Combine first four ingredients in a medium-size heavy saucepan. Bring to a boil over medium-high heat, and boil for 4 to 5 minutes; remove from heat. Stir in baking soda until well blended. Pour over popped corn and toss to coat. Arrange on cookie sheets. Bake on top rack in preheated 200° oven for one hour. Stir or turn caramel corn every 15 minutes. Store in airtight containers.
YIELD: 7 quarts

Mrs. Thomas C. Puthoff
(Linda Bates)

CARAMELS

These caramels have become a Christmas tradition in our home, and the children enjoy helping to wrap them. They are great for gift giving.

½ pound butter
1 1-pound box light brown sugar
1 cup light corn syrup (we prefer Karo)
1 14-ounce can sweetened condensed milk
1 teaspoon vanilla
1 cup chopped walnuts, optional

Melt butter in a heavy saucepan. Stir in brown sugar; mix well. Add corn syrup and condensed milk. Cook and stir over medium heat until mixture reaches soft ball stage or 238° on a candy thermometer. Remove from heat; add vanilla. Pour into a well-greased jelly roll pan or a 9 x 13-inch pan. If desired, sprinkle with walnuts. Refrigerate to cool thoroughly. Cut into ½-inch squares, and wrap in waxed paper.
YIELD: about 8 to 9 dozen caramels

Mrs. James Garrison
(Lesli Janacshek)

283

TOFFEE

Simple and quick.

¾ pound butter (no
substitutes please)
½ cup light corn syrup
2½ cups sugar
1 teaspoon salt (if unsalted nuts are used)
2 ounces almonds or
pecans, ground
8 ounce milk chocolate
candy bar, shaved
2 ounces almonds or
pecans, ground

In a heavy, medium-size saucepan, melt butter over medium-high heat. Stir in corn syrup in a steady stream. Gradually add sugar, and stir carefully without getting the mixture high on the sides of the pan. Add salt, if unsalted nuts are used, and 2 ounces nuts. Cook over high heat, stirring constantly, until mixture reaches 290° on a candy thermometer (hard crack). The toffee will be golden yellow in color. Spread the candy about ¼-inch thick on a marble slab or on the backs of two cookie sheets. Put the chocolate on the hot toffee so that it melts. Sprinkle the melted chocolate with 2-ounces nuts. When the candy is cool, crack it into pieces by hitting with a spoon and store in air-tight tin.
YIELD: About 1½ pounds

Mrs. D. J. England
(Dorothy Curry)

CHOCO-MEAL CANDY DROPS

Super easy!

4 tablespoons butter
½ cup milk
2 cups sugar
¼ cup cocoa
¾ cup peanut butter
2 cups quick-cooking
oatmeal

Melt butter in a medium-size saucepan. Stir in milk, sugar, and cocoa. Bring to a boil. Remove from heat. Add peanut butter; stir to melt. Mix in oatmeal. Drop from a tablespoon onto a wax paper-covered cookie sheet. The mixture will seem thin.
YIELD: 2 to 3 dozen

Mrs. Kenneth A. Snowden
(Jenet Kimmel)

BONBONS

These candy cookies are so yummy and rich they are just right after a salad luncheon. Kids love them, too!

3	tablespoons butter
1	cup powdered sugar
1	cup crunchy peanut butter
2	cups Rice Krispies cereal
	About ½-pound white chocolate, for coating cookies

In a small saucepan, melt butter. Add powdered sugar, peanut butter, and Rice Krispies; mix thoroughly. Form into firm 1-inch balls; place on a cookie sheet, and freeze. In a double boiler, melt white chocolate over warm (not hot) water. Roll the balls in the white chocolate to cover them. Remove to waxed paper to cool; cover, and freeze.
YIELD: about 3 dozen

Mrs. Willaim Roberts
(Karen Kreider)

PEANUT BRITTLE

Surprisingly easy!

2	cups granulated sugar
½	cup water
1	cup white corn syrup (we prefer Karo)
3	cups raw (whole) peanuts
1	teaspoon salt
1	teaspoon vanilla
2½	teaspoons baking soda

In a large, heavy pan, combine sugar, water, and corn syrup. Cook over medium heat, stirring occasionally, until 250° on a candy thermometer. Add raw peanuts and salt. Boil over medium heat to 300°, stirring constantly. Remove from heat (work quickly now), and stir in vanilla and baking soda (mixture will foam). Immediately pour, spread, and pull the foamy, hot mixture on a large, buttered marble slab, or use 2 buttered cookie sheets. Cool and break into eating-size pieces. Store in tightly covered tin at room temperature.
YIELD: 2 pounds

Mrs. Stephen Dankof
(Nancy Brundige)

PRALINES

**These will keep for at least three months when stored in an
air-tight container and kept in a cool place.
Great for the holidays!**

1	teaspoon baking soda
1	cup buttermilk
1	cup butter (no substitutes)
3	cups sugar
	Pinch of salt
2	tablespoons light corn syrup (we prefer Karo)
1	teaspoon vanilla
1½	cups pecan halves

In a small bowl, combine baking soda and buttermilk. In a large, heavy pan, melt butter, and swish around the sides of the pan. Using a wooden spoon, stir in the buttermilk mixture, sugar, salt, and syrup. Use a candy thermometer, and cook over medium heat until mixture forms a rather firm ball (I usually cook it until the thermometer reaches 238°.). Stir constantly while mixture is cooking. When the mixture reaches the desired temperature, transfer it to a stainless steel bowl, and stir in vanilla and pecans. Beat with a wooden spoon for about 2 to 3 minutes or until smooth and creamy and color lightens slightly. Working quickly, drop mixture by teaspoonfuls (using two teaspoons) onto waxed paper. Let pralines cool thoroughly before storing in an air-tight container.
YIELD: 50 to 60 pralines

Mrs. Richard C. Shelton
(Louise Wittenmyer)

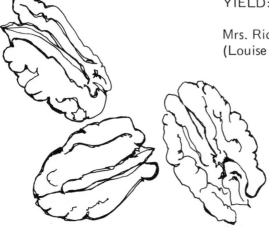

Discover Dayton

The Victory
Theatre

THE VICTORY THEATRE

Boasting a history of both triumphs and disasters, the Victory
Theatre has continued Dayton's performing arts heritage since
1866 — countless theatre luminaries have entertained from the
Victory's stage. Known as the Turner Opera House, Music Hall,
and later the Victory Theatre, the building has survived the
devastation of two fires and a flood. By 1975, the "Faded
Lady" appeared marked for total destruction, but hundreds of
concerned citizens formed the Victory Theatre Association,
dedicated to the preservation of Dayton's only remaining
theatre. In 1978, the Junior League of Dayton, whose Town
Hall Lecture Series began at the Victory, also elected to aid the
"Great Lady" with funds and a dedicated volunteer force. And,
in 1979 the curtain is rising for the third annual theatre season
in an effort to preserve the past to enrich the future.

DISCOVER DINING OUT

What a pleasant discovery Dayton is to connoisseurs of the culinary arts. There are more than a thousand fine dining establishments to be found in Dayton and in the easily accessible areas within the ninety-minute land transport market. Choosing a representative sampling of the wide variety of cuisine and attractive settings offered to the epicurean in the Dayton area presented a formidable task. The Dayton Junior League conducted a survey of our membership to ascertain the restaurants most consistently enjoyed by our members. The restaurants presented here are their choices. Twenty-six fine restaurants generously provided delightful specialty recipes which display the excellence that goes into both the preparation and the presentation of superb food. These and many other fine dining establishments in and around Dayton await your discovery and enjoyment.

CRABMEAT CANAPE LORENZO

1	teaspoon butter
2	chopped shallots
2	ounces fresh chopped mushrooms
2	ounces diced green peppers
8	ounces King Crab
1½	ounces diced pimento
¼	teaspoon English mustard
1	ounce sauterne
¼	cup heavy cream
	Dash cayenne pepper
	Dash of salt
2	egg yolks
	Toast
	Yellow American cheese

Heat butter in saute pan. Add shallots, mushrooms, and green peppers. Saute for a few minutes. Add crabmeat, pimento, mustard, sauterne, and cream. Season to taste. Remove from heat and add egg yolks. Spread mixture on toast. Cover with a slice of yellow American cheese. Cut into 1-inch squares. Place in a buttered serving dish, and heat in a preheated 300° oven for 5 minutes.

CHEF'S NOTE: May be frozen.

VARIATION: This crabmeat mixture may be used to stuff blanched, fresh mushroom caps.

YIELD: 8 servings

SHERLOCK'S HOME
Court House Plaza
Dayton, Ohio 45463

BAKED STUFFED EGGPLANT AND LEMON BUTTER SAUCE

A favorite recipe served in the dining room
of the Dayton Woman's Club.
Included in *Keys To Our Kitchen*, the cookbook published by the
Dayton Woman's Club.

1   large eggplant
1   small eggplant
1   small onion, chopped
¼   cup raw peanuts (the secret ingredient)
½   cup water
8   tablespoons melted butter
1   teaspoon chicken base (LeGout)
    Fine dry bread crumbs
    Chopped parsley
    Paprika

LEMON BUTTER SAUCE

1   cup butter
    Juice of 2 lemons
1   tablespoon finely chopped parsley

Cut a lengthwise slice off the large eggplant, and scoop out center, leaving the shell intact for serving. Peel the smaller eggplant, and cut into small cubes. Cook eggplant with the onions, peanuts, water, butter, and chicken base until tender. Thicken with bread crumbs. Fill the shell with the cooked mixture; put it in a baking pan, and bake in a preheated 350° oven for 15 to 20 minutes, or until the eggplant turns brown on top. Sprinkle with buttered crumbs, chopped parsley, and paprika. Return to the oven until crumbs are brown. Serve with Lemon Butter Sauce.

To make Lemon Butter Sauce, cream butter, and add the lemon juice and parsley. Chill before serving. Makes about 1 cup of sauce.
YIELD: 8 servings

DAYTON WOMAN'S CLUB
225 North Ludlow Street
Dayton, Ohio 45402

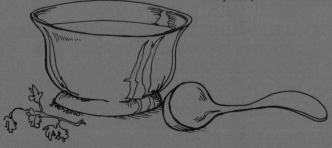

POTATO CHEESE SOUP

**"This is our favorite soup at 1776 Inn.
We have many requests for the recipe."**

2½	pounds frozen steak fries	Simmer covered potatoes with water, bouillon, onion salt, pepper, and
1	quart water	paprika for 8 to 10 minutes, or until
5	chicken bouillon cubes	potatoes are very soft; whip smooth.
1	tablespoon onion salt	Blend in condensed soup and milk;
½	teaspoon pepper	heat through. Add cheese; cook and
½	teaspoon paprika	stir until melted. Salt to taste.
1	25-ounce can condensed cream of celery soup	YIELD: 2½ quarts
8	cups milk	1776 INN
1¼	pounds process American cheese, shredded	U. S. Rt. 42 North
	Salt, to taste	P. O. Box 1776
		Waynesville, Ohio 45068

MAURICE DRESSING

**"This dressing is used on our Maurice Salad
and our Elder-Beerman Salad Sandwich.
You may serve this dressing on a chef's salad or a julienne salad."**

1	tablespoon finely grated onion	Mix together onion, parsley, and salad dressing using an electric mixer.
1	teaspoon finely grated parsley	Gradually add Instant Blend to thin to desired consistency.
1	pint salad dressing Instant Blend (imitation cream), for thinning	YIELD: Approximately 1 pint
		ELDER-BEERMAN STORES CORP. Court House Plaza Dayton, Ohio 45463

PEASANT SALAD

1	head lettuce, bite-size pieces
¾	cup chopped celery
1	green pepper, chopped
8	ounces fresh spinach, torn
2	medium red onions, sliced
6	hard-boiled eggs, sliced
1	10-ounce package frozen peas, not cooked
2	tablespoons sugar
1	teaspoon salt
½	teaspoon white pepper
1	pint Miracle Whip
6	ounces cheddar cheese, grated
½	cup crumbled crisp fried bacon

In a large bowl, mix together lettuce and celery. Layer all remaining ingredients over lettuce and celery in the order listed. Cover and refrigerate for 8 hours. Toss together just before serving.
YIELD: 8 servings

THE PEASANT STOCK
RESTAURANT
424 East Stroop Road
Dayton, Ohio 45429

SCHIAVONE'S FAMOUS MEATBALLS

Old family recipe used in restaurant.

2	pounds ground beef
1	cup dry bread crumbs
¼	cup oil
2	eggs, well beaten
½	cup grated Romano cheese
2	cloves garlic, minced or crushed
1	cup finely minced fresh parsley
½	teaspoon salt
2	teaspoons black pepper

In a bowl, combine all ingredients. Mix well, and form into balls. Fry in oil until brown.
YIELD: 6 to 8 servings

SCHIAVONE'S
CASA MIA RESTAURANT
8401 Claude Thomas Road
Franklin Square
Franklin, Ohio 45005

COOK A "PINE CLUB" STEAK AT HOME

The most important thing to remember in cooking steak is to get the finest quality meat. It doesn't have to be "prime," but you do have to know how to select "choice" cuts. The meat should be pink, not red, and the fat should be chalk-white and not have any yellowish tint to it. You don't have enough heat in your broiler to cook a steak like we can with our commercial equipment, but these instructions will help you to overcome this handicap.

Take a sheet of cooking foil, and turn the edges up to make a pan effect. Perforate the foil to allow grease to run out (Place a second sheet of foil on the broiler rack below the cooking area to catch the drippings.). A medium-rare steak should be broiled very close to the burner. A 1-inch steak takes about seven minutes on one side and five minutes on the other side for a perfect medium-rare serving.

Pour melted butter over the cooked steak, and serve on a preheated plate. A little salt or other seasoning added after cooking, while the steak is still hot, will also add to the flavor.

PINE CLUB
1926 Brown Street
Dayton, Ohio 45409

BREAST OF TURKEY ON BROCCOLI MORNAY

8	large broccoli spears
3	tablespoons butter
3	tablespoons flour
1	cup scalded milk (do not boil)
1	teaspoon salt
1/8	teaspoon white pepper
¼	cup grated cheddar cheese
8	large slices white turkey meat
	Bread crumbs
	Grated Parmesan cheese
	Paprika

Cook broccoli spears in lightly salted boiling water for 5 to 8 minutes, or just until done. In a small saucepan, melt butter, and add flour; mix well. Add milk, salt and pepper, and simmer for 2 to 3 minutes. Add grated cheddar cheese; stir until melted. Cover broccoli spears and turkey slices with cheese sauce; sprinkle with bread crumbs, Parmesan cheese, and paprika. Bake in a preheated 350° oven for 10 to 15 minutes, and serve.
YIELD: 4 servings

NEIL'S HERITAGE HOUSE
2189 South Dixie Drive
Dayton, Ohio 45409

SALMIS DE CAILLES AUX ANANAS

(Quails with Fresh Pineapple and Curacao)

1	large ripe pineapple
8	quail
	Salt and pepper
	Butter
2	ounces carrots, diced
2	ounces celery, diced
2	ounces onions, diced
½	pound mushrooms, quartered
1	sprig of thyme
1	bay leaf
6	ounces dry white wine
3	ounces Madeira
1½	ounces Curacao
1	cup veal stock
1½	ounces sweet butter
1½	ounces Curacao

Cut off both ends of the pineapple; cut the pineapple in 4 equal slices. With a melon-ball cutter, hollow out each quarter of pineapple without piercing the bottom. Reserve the pineapple balls and the juice. Cut the quail in two, and remove the backbones (Reserve the backbones, necks, giblets, and liver to add to the sauce.). Season the quail with salt and pepper. Saute them in butter, browning them; remove the quail. Add the vegetables, thyme, and bay leaf, and cook for five minutes. Remove the excess butter. Place the quail back in the skillet. De-glaze with the wine, Madeira, and 1½ ounces of the Curacao. Add the reserved pineapple juice and the veal stock, and bring to a boil. Cover the skillet, and cook in a preheated 375° oven for 15 minutes, or until done. Remove the quail; place them in the pineapple rings. Add the pineapple balls; keep hot. Reduce the sauce, and strain through a fine strainer. Thicken the sauce with 1½-ounces sweet butter (Do not boil.). Add the rest of the Curacao. Pour the sauce on the quail.
YIELD: 4 servings

LA MAISONNETTE
114 East Sixth Street
Cincinnati, Ohio 45202

BRAISED LAMB SHANKS

4   lamb shanks, 15 to
16-ounces each
Salt and pepper
3   tablespoons vegetable
fat (we prefer Crisco,
etc., to butter or
margarine)
1   large onion, peeled
and diced
1   cup cut fresh
mushrooms, cut in
halves or quarters
¾   cup sliced celery, cut
in 1-inch by ¼-inch
slices
1   red turnip, peeled,
and cut in 1-inch by
¼-inch pieces
3   tablespoons tomato
paste
5   tablespoons flour
¼   teaspoon black pepper
2   cloves fresh garlic,
minced
½   cup Burgundy wine
1/8   teaspoon rosemary
leaves, finely chopped
1   pinch thyme leaves
1   bay leaf
6   cups good lamb stock
(or 1, 10¾-ounce can
beef consomme
thinned with 1 can
water)
Salt to taste
Fresh chopped parsley
for garnish

Season lamb shanks with salt and pepper. Heat fat in heavy braiser, and brown lamb shanks on all sides. Add onion, mushrooms, celery, and turnips; brown. Stir in tomato paste; add flour; brown lightly. Add rosemary, thyme, bay leaf, garlic, and pepper; add Burgundy wine. Add six cups seasoned lamb stock; cover braiser, and braise lamb shanks in 325° to 350° oven for 1 to 1½ hours, or until done. Skim off fat occasionally. Taste and add salt or pepper if necessary. Arrange lamb shanks on plate; cover with sauce, and sprinkle with fresh chopped parsley.
YIELD: 4 servings

GOLDEN LAMB INN
27 South Broadway
Lebanon, Ohio 45036

VEAL AFRICAN

12	2-ounce portions tender veal (top round, filet or loin)
	Salt and pepper
6	bananas, peeled and cut in half
	Flour
3	tablespoons cooking oil
	Toasted coconut
	Fresh chopped parsley
	White rice

Pound veal down, using meat mallet. Season with salt and pepper. Roll veal around half of a peeled banana, and fasten with a toothpick. Dust lightly in flour, and saute in frying pan until lightly browned, using oil. Remove toothpicks. Put in a casserole dish; cover with curry sauce (recipe follows) and bake at 350° degrees for 10 minutes. Garnish with coconut and parsley. Serve with white rice.

CURRY SAUCE

1	medium onion, chopped
¼	teaspoon dry mustard
½	cup butter
1	apple, sliced
2	tablespoons flour
1¼	teaspoons curry powder
½	teaspoon mace
2½	cups chicken broth
½	cup coconut

To make Curry Sauce, combine onion, dry mustard, butter, and apple in a large saucepan, and simmer slowly for 8 minutes. Add flour, curry powder, and mace. Cook for 4 minutes. Add broth, and simmer for 45 minutes. Add coconut; simmer 15 minutes, and strain.

YIELD: 6 servings

DAYTON RACQUET CLUB
Winters Bank Tower
Second and Main Streets
Dayton, Ohio 45402

BRACIOLETTE CI VITELLO

STUFFING

1	pound bread crumbs
¼	cup sweet basil
6	eggs, lightly beaten

BECHAMEL SAUCE

2	tablespoons butter
2½	tablespoons flour
1	cup boiling milk
½	teaspoon salt
½	cup water

In a bowl, mix together all stuffing ingredients; set aside. Prepare Bechamel sauce: in a saucepan, melt butter; stir in flour. Remove from heat, and stir in boiling milk, salt, and water. Return to heat, and boil for about 2 minutes. Remove from heat, and set aside.

Recipe continues . . .

VEAL

2	pounds veal cut into 8 slices from the leg or shoulder	
	All-purpose flour	
6	tablespoons butter	
1	large garlic clove, chopped	
6	fresh parsley sprigs, leaves only, chopped	

Pinch of salt
Pinch of freshly ground black pepper

8 slices of prosciutto, (Italian ham)
24 slices Swiss cheese
2 tablespoons olive oil

Layer the following on each slice of veal: 1 slice of prosciutto, 1 covering of stuffing, and 3 slices of Swiss cheese. Roll veal and skewer. Lightly flour and brown in butter, oil, and all remaining seasonings. Remove and place in casserole. Add Bechamel sauce, and bake for one hour at 375°.
YIELD: 8 servings

ANTONIO'S ITALIAN &
AMERICAN RESTAURANT
28 West Franklin Street
Centerville, Ohio 45459

VENISON STEAKS

4 8-ounce boneless venison steaks (well trimmed)
Salt and pepper to taste
4 ounces butter
4 medium shallots, finely minced
1 cup Burgundy wine
1 pinch thyme
1 cup brown sauce
1 tablespoon currant jelly
1 tablespoon sour cream
Chanterelles or mushrooms, optional

Season venison steaks with salt and pepper. Melt butter in saute pan, and allow pan to get very hot. Place steaks in pan, and saute to desired degree of doneness. Remove steaks from pan; add minced shallots to butter, and brown lightly. Add Burgundy wine and thyme, and allow liquid to reduce until somewhat thickened. Blend in currant jelly and brown sauce; allow to come to a slow boil. Over low heat, blend in the sour cream, and serve over steaks. If desired, saute chanterelles or mushrooms, and place over the top of steaks before sauce is poured over. Serve steaks with glazed apples and Brussels sprouts.
YIELD: 4 servings

THE INN
4120 Far Hills Avenue
Dayton, Ohio 45429

PEKING DUCK

Duck, about 5 pounds
3 tablespoons molasses
  or honey
½ tablespoon white
  vinegar
1 cup boiling hot water
3 tablespoons sweet bean
  paste
20 scallions, 2-inches long
20 mandarin pancakes
  (or soft burritos)

Clean outside of the duck; pat dry. Mix together molasses, vinegar, and hot water to make a syrup-like mixture. Hang the duck by the neck, and pour boiling water over the surface several times (This will prevent the skin from shrinking.). Pour the syrup mixture all over the duck (not inside). Suspend the duck in a cool, airy place for several hours, until it is dry. Use charcoal-type oven, or a kettle-type grill. Hang duck for even roasting. Roast at high heat for about 20 minutes and then at low heat for 20 minutes (kettle-type grill; turn every 20 minutes until done). Turn frequently; the skin will be golden brown and crisp. Slice skin and meat into thin pieces. Put some bean paste, 1 scallion piece, and 1 or 2 pieces of duck on each pancake. Roll up, and eat with fingers.
YIELD: 4 servings

PEKING INN
101 West Franklin Street
Centerville, Ohio 45459

EASY BEARNAISE SAUCE

Excellent with broiled meats.

¼ cup tarragon vinegar
2 teaspoons dried
  tarragon
1/8 teaspoon white pepper
2 tablespoons minced
  shallots
3 egg yolks
1 cup melted butter

Put egg yolks in blender. In a saucepan, combine vinegar, tarragon, pepper, and shallots. Reduce over high heat to one tablespoon. Remove from heat; add to egg yolks in blender. Slowly blend in melted butter. Cover and keep warm until serving time.
YIELD: 1 cup

THE STOCKYARD'S INN
1065 Springfield Street
Dayton, Ohio 45403

FLOUNDER STUFFED WITH ZESTY CRABMEAT

½ onion, finely chopped
½ green pepper, finely
   chopped
3 stalks celery, finely
   chopped
   Butter
½ teaspoon salt
   Pinch of pepper
1 pound crabmeat
½ teaspoon dry mustard
1 egg
12 ounces mayonnaise,
   (we prefer Hellmans)
20 saltine crackers
24 to 28, 3 to 4-ounce
   filet of flounder
   Butter
   Paprika

Saute onion, green pepper, and celery in butter with salt and pepper. Pick shells from crabmeat (very important). Add dry mustard to crabmeat; add egg, mayonnaise, and vegetables to crabmeat. Add saltines; mix well. For each serving, place 1, 3 to 4-ounce filet of flounder on a tray. Add 2½ to 3-ounces of the crab mixture. Cover with another 3 to 4-ounce filet; cover lightly with butter. Sprinkle with paprika. Bake for 10 to 12 minutes at 450°.
YIELD: 12 to 14 servings

OAKWOOD CLUB
2414 Far Hills Avenue
Dayton, Ohio 45419

QUICHE LORRAINE A LA JACQUES

2   10-inch pie shells
6   ounces bacon, diced
6   ounces ham, diced
1   small onion, diced
2   green onions, diced
¼   cup chopped parsley
1   ounce butter
4   ounces Swiss cheese,
    diced
4   ounces Gruyere cheese,
    diced
4   ounces grated
    Parmesan cheese
1½ pints milk
4   whole eggs, lightly
    beaten
    Dash of salt and white
    pepper
¼   teaspoon fresh ground
    nutmeg

Line 2, 10-inch pie shells with pie or puff pastry dough (or use frozen raw pie shells). Saute bacon, ham, onions, and parsley in hot pan with 1-ounce butter for 4 to 5 minutes. Drain off extra fat from bacon. Spread Swiss, Gruyere, and Parmesan cheeses on the bottoms of the pie shells; then add the sauteed ingredients. Pour the milk, eggs, salt, pepper, and nutmeg over the sauteed mixture. Bake in a pre-heated 300° to 325° oven for 30 to 40 minutes. Cut each quiche Lorraine pie into 4 pieces. Serve hot.
YIELD: 8 servings

JACQUES RESTAURANT
Court House Plaza
Dayton, Ohio 45463

SWISS CHEESE CROQUETTES

Serve with "Tomato Sauce."

3	ounces margarine
4½	ounces flour
¼	teaspoon salt
	Dash of cayenne
2	eggs
¾	cup hot milk
1½	pounds Swiss cheese, finely grated
	Flour for dusting
	Egg batter (1 egg lightly beaten)
	Bread crumbs for coating
	Deep fat for frying

TOMATO SAUCE

2½	ounces butter
2	tablespoons finely chopped onions
1	tablespoon finely chopped green pepper
1½	ounces cornstarch
½	cup cold water
1½	quarts canned tomatoes
1	tablespoon salt
1½	ounces granulated sugar

STOUFFER'S TOP OF
THE PLAZA
RESTAURANT
E. Fifth & S. Jefferson St.
Dayton, Ohio 45402

Melt margarine; then add flour, salt, and cayenne, and beat to combine. Cook over medium heat, stirring frequently for 3 to 5 minutes. Transfer the mixture to a mixing bowl. Add eggs gradually, beating at high speed; continue beating for about 5 minutes, or until well blended. Add hot milk while beating on high speed; continue beating for 5 to 8 minutes until smooth; add grated cheese, and beat enough to distribute cheese evenly. To form croquettes, weigh mixture into 2-ounce portions and shape into cylindrical croquettes 2¾-inches long and 1½-inches wide. Place on a tray; cover and refrigerate overnight. Roll croquettes in flour to coat lightly; shake off excess. Dip in egg batter, and drain. Roll in bread crumbs. Deep fat fry at 350° for 2 minutes. Drain on absorbent paper. Serve immediately.

TOMATO SAUCE

Melt butter; add onions and green peppers, and saute for five minutes (until just tender). In a separate container, dissolve cornstarch in cold water. Add dissolved cornstarch, canned tomatoes, salt, and sugar to the sauteed vegetables. Cook over medium heat, stirring occasionally to break up tomatoes, for 5 to 8 minutes (until starch taste disappears and mixture has thickened).
YIELD: 4 servings
        1½ quarts sauce

CHEESE SOUFFLE

Serve with a melted hot cheese sauce, and garnish with a strip of crisp bacon.

½	pound margarine
½	pound flour
1	quart milk
1	tablespoon salt
½	teaspoon white pepper
¾	pound Old English cheese, shredded
14	egg yolks
14	egg whites

Melt margarine in a large saucepan, and blend in flour. Gradually stir in milk. Cook, stirring constantly, until mixture boils and thickens. Add seasonings, and cool slightly. Beat egg yolks until thick and lemon colored. In a separate bowl, beat egg whites until stiff. Add yolks to slightly-cooled milk mixture. Add cheese, stirring until cheese is melted; fold in beaten egg whites. Turn into a greased 8 x 10-inch casserole dish. Set pan in hot water. Bake in a preheated 325° oven for about 1 hour, or until golden brown.
YIELD: 8 servings

RIKE'S DINING ROOM
Second & Main Streets
Dayton, Ohio 45402

OLD FASHIONED CREAM PIE

1	9-inch pastry shell, unbaked
1	cup brown sugar, packed
½	cup flour
1	pint half and half
½	teaspoon vanilla
	Nutmeg
	Cinnamon
	Butter for dotting

Mix, directly in pie shell if you desire, brown sugar, flour, half and half, and vanilla. Sprinkle with nutmeg and cinnamon; dot with butter. Bake in a preheated 325° oven for 40 to 45 minutes, or until set.
YIELD: 6 servings

LITTLE COUNTRY SCHOOL HOUSE
S. R. 571
West Milton, Ohio 45383

APPLE COBBLER FLAMBE

A Grand Finale original!

Pie dough, enough for
a 2-crust pie
1 cup butter, whipped,
or ¾ cup stick form
1 cup sugar
Juice of one lemon
(no seeds please)
3 apples, peeled, cored
and sliced
½ cup pecans, small
pieces
½ cup raisins
¼ cup Grand Marnier
Ice cream, enough for
4 balls (tennis ball
size), vanilla or
cinnamon
Powdered cinnamon to
garnish
¼ cup 151 proof rum

Using 4, 10-ounce souffle dishes, or other oven-proof dishes, make 4 individual pie crusts (straight sides if possible). Bake, cool, and remove from dishes. In a large skillet, melt butter; add sugar, lemon juice, apples, pecans, and raisins. Cook, uncovered, until very hot, bubbly, and thickened. Add Grand Marnier, and stir well. Meanwhile, place crust on serving dishes (individual plates or bowls) with a large scoop of ice cream in each shell, and sprinkle cinnamon on each. When apple mixture is ready for flaming, warm 151 proof rum and ignite. Pour gently into apples, and move the pan back and forth slowly to combine flavors. Spoon apple mixture into shells on top of ice cream. Serve immediately. Please enjoy!
YIELD: 4 servings

GRAND FINALE
3 Sharon Road
Glendale, Ohio 45246

BANANA BREAD

1 cup sugar
½ cup butter
3 ripe bananas
2 eggs
2 cups sifted flour
1 teaspoon baking soda
¼ teaspoon salt

Cream together sugar and butter. Add bananas and eggs; beat well. Sift together flour, baking soda, and salt; add to batter. Pour into a greased loaf pan, and bake in a preheated 350° oven for 1 hour.
YIELD: 1 loaf

WEST MILTON INN
136 North Miami Street
West Milton, Ohio 45383

L'ARMAGNAC CHEESECAKE

1   pound cream cheese
¾   cup sugar
1   orange
1   lemon
¼   cup Armagnac brandy
¼   cup Grand Marnier
2   pints heavy cream
½   cup sugar
1   tablespoon pure vanilla
1   Genoise cake, or yellow cake, ½ x 9-inch round

Mix cream cheese and sugar together until smooth. Grate rind of orange and lemon; then add the squeezed orange and lemon juice plus the Armagnac brandy. Mix until smooth, and add the Grand Marnier. In a separate bowl, whip heavy cream, sugar, and vanilla until stiff. Fold whipped cream into cream cheese mixture. Place a ½-inch thick layer of Genoise cake (or yellow cake) on the bottom of a 9-inch spring-mold pan. Pour the prepared ingredients into the mold pan, and refrigerate for at least 2½ hours. Remove from the refrigerator right before serving, and decorate to your own liking (Our cheesecake is topped with whipped cream flowerets and orange segments.). YIELD: 14 servings

L'ARMAGNAC RESTAURANT
121 South Sixth Street
Columbus, Ohio 43215

GLAZED BANANAS

2   eggs, beaten
3   cups brown sugar, packed
1   cup evaporated milk
1   tablespoon white vinegar
    Chopped peanuts for garnish
4   to 5 bananas, sliced

In a saucepan, combine eggs, brown sugar, and evaporated milk. Bring to a boil; add vinegar. Remove from heat, and chill thoroughly. Arrange sliced bananas in a serving dish. Spoon cold sauce over bananas, sprinkle with peanuts, and serve.
YIELD: 1-quart sauce

THE APPLE TREE
2189 State Route 235
Xenia, Ohio 45385

STRAWBERRY MOUSSE

1½ pints fresh strawberries
½ cup sugar
1/3 cup water
1 envelope gelatin
½ cup egg whites
¾ cup whipping cream
½ cup sugar (for egg whites and whipping cream)
1½ ounces strawberry liqueur
2 ounces Kirschwasser

Combine ½ cup sugar, water, and strawberries in a saucepan, and bring to a boil. Simmer for approximately 8 to 10 minutes while crushing the strawberries with a wire whip. While strawberries are simmering, whip egg white (gradually adding the sugar) until stiff, and put aside in refrigerator. Whip whipping cream (adding the remaining part of the sugar), and put it aside in the refrigerator. When strawberries are cooked, place saucepan in a bowl of ice to chill. While strawberries are still somewhat warm, combine strawberry liqueur and Kirschwasser in a coffee cup (or similar container); stir gelatin into liqueur, and mix into the strawberries, until gelatin is dissolved. Now continue chilling the strawberries until cool. Fold egg whites and whipped cream into the strawberries, and chill in refrigerator.
YIELD: 10 to 12 servings

KING COLE RESTAURANT
Winters Bank Tower
Second & Main Streets
Dayton, Ohio 45402

PARAGON SUPREME

A summer cooler.

½ ounce vodka
½ ounce blackberry brandy
½ fresh banana
½ ounce grenadine
1 ounce orange juice
1 ounce pineapple juice

Blend with crushed ice. Garnish with banana slice and a cherry.
YIELD: 1 serving

THE PARAGON RESTAURANT
797 Miamisburg-Centerville Road
Dayton, Ohio 45459

TOWN HALL

For the past twenty-four years, the Junior League of Dayton, Ohio, has sponsored a highly successful Town Hall Lecture Series. The Dayton Town Hall Lecture Series is proud to be regarded by booking agents and speakers as one of the largest and most successful Town Hall series in the country.

In the past twenty-four years, the profits from the Town Hall series have enabled the Junior League of Dayton, Ohio, to return over $500,000 to the community in the form of various projects. The community's tremendous support of Town Hall enables the Junior League to continue fulfilling their commitment to the ever-changing needs of the Dayton community.

To give an additional entertaining chapter of cuisine to the cookbook, some of the past Town Hall celebrities have enthusiastically and graciously submitted their favorite recipes. We thank them for their delicious contributions to our cookbook, and we hope that you enjoy their extra finesse in gourmet cooking.

RECIPE FOR A HAPPY MARRIAGE

"I ran into this at a wedding shower given by the most sentimental 'groupies' I know — newswomen! It accompanied a bottle of champagne gaily tied with ribbon, and this recipe was attached . . . ."

"Always keep a bottle of champagne on
ice for special occasions.
Do not wait for special occasions!"

YIELD: 2 happy people

LIZ CARPENTER
Formerly Executive Assistant to Vice
President Lyndon B. Johnson and
Press Secretary and Staff Director to
Mrs. Johnson.

WHAT'S JEWISH COOKING?

Before you can even begin to understand authentic Jewish cooking, you must be inducted into the secrets of traditional grandma cooking, made up more of ritual than recipe, and a far greater accountability for what came out rather than what went in. No book which specifies exact ingredients can convey to the modern woman all of the very inexact alchemy, hardly even written down ("just watch"), passed from generation to generation to fill the home with nose-boggling aromas, choking sweet smoke, soul-searching smog, pungent air pollution, far more meaningful and memorable than any printed set of instructions could ever conjure up.

You can tell a modern woman how to make soup, but you can't tell her (because Mama never told) how you get it to the temperature of molten lava, so hot that swallowing it makes smoke rings come out of your ears (If you tried to quench the fire in the gut by drinking cold water, you ended up percolating.). Today we also work on the assumption that soup is liquid. Wrong again. Mama's was solid. I myself saw many a spoon stand up in the middle of the soup, then go limp as a noodle.

In an age of food processors, it is hard to go back to Mama's hand chopping of chicken livers. My mother, single handedly, chopped four wooden chopping bowls into the livers. It gave the food body, even splinters.

There was no such thing as meat cooked rare. All meat was cremated (The sight of blood made Papa nauseous. "What's this? A kitchen or an operating room?").

To say to Mama that some doughy delight came out fluffy was an insult, not a compliment. A single pancake weighed more than the plate it was put on. When cold, it could be used as a hockey puck. Her meatballs did melt in the mouth, like she said, but hardened again in the stomach, like we said. Were it not for the fact that everything was lubricated with chicken fat, nothing would move down the gullet.

Calories, of course, didn't count. My mother thought that they were holes in the teeth. Anybody who weighed less than 200 pounds was put on the critical list. Our skinny doctors (the ones who predicted a cholesterol grave for us) died regularly. We lived on, and waddled our way to their funerals.

Mama's baking was not instant but instinct. She just "felt" how much flour it needed, how much salt it needed, how much sugar it needed, then proceeded to embellish it by putting into it what it "might" need. Anything that was loose in the closet might go into the cake: dates, nuts, fruits, honey, cinnamon, and some almonds for decoration across the top. When was it ready? If you could still lift it out of the oven, it wasn't. It had to weigh like a man-hole cover and smell like a forest fire.

Most often Mama made her own dough. She'd take everything off the round dining room table, spread a tablecloth, make a mountain of flour in the middle with a crater on top, put some water and eggs into the crater, and then start kneading with her hands. When the mass developed some consistency, she would spread it with a rolling pin, add a little flour, more rolling pin, a little more flour, a little more rolling pin. The little mountain had become a live self-expanding round bed spread that spread and spread over the edges of the table into drapes that hung almost down to the floor. At the last second Mama would gather up all the loose ends and shape them into a challeh (traditional white bread) with a braid on top — just like my sister's. She then shellacked the whole job (except for my sister) with a chicken-feather brush, dipped in the whites of raw eggs. She also made little challehs for each of the children. To each his own.

I did not, from the start, have any intention of seriously discussing traditional Jewish cooking. Through all my kidding I hope we can catch some of the incense of tradition — not just a tradition of food, but a tradition of love through food, the wonderful sacramental sharing of the blessings of the earth amongst the people of the earth.

No drug on earth has yet been invented which will "send me," or "turn me on," as much as the song-filled, love-filled, heart-filled, heart-burning concoctions of the traditional mama. If I ever get to taste "L.S.D.," I know I will probably say, "It's not like Mama used to make."

To your good health!

SAM LEVINSON — Teacher, humorist, and author.

DOWN(S') HOME STAFF-OF-LIFE

"This is so basic that something like it can be found in several books on bread. What can make it uniquely yours is the care that goes into the selection of flour (many health food stores have proper flour) and the attitude, mood, and mental processes that accompany the labor of the baker (I listen to music when I bake, and I imagine the flavor to be affected by the choice of what I listen to.)."

2	cups milk (whole, warmed to 115°F)
1	package dry yeast
2	tablespoons sugar
1	tablespoon salt
¼	cup melted butter
5	to 6 cups white flour (should be unfiltered, unbleached, unprocessed)

In a large mixing bowl, dissolve the yeast in about ½ cup of the warm milk. Put the rest of the milk in the warmed mixing bowl, and add the sugar, salt, and butter. Stir in the flour (all but about a cup), and continue stirring until thick, adding some flour if necessary, but saving some flour for hands and board while kneading. When the dough begins to leave the sides of the bowl, turn it out on a floured board and knead it for 10 minutes or so, until a finger poke comes back (as though dough is slightly rubbery). Clean bowl, and butter sides; put dough in; turn greased side up; cover with a damp cloth, and allow to rise in a warm (75° to 80°), draft-free place until double in size. This will take 1½ hours or more. Punch the dough once to deflate and drive off excess carbon dioxide; knead some more, and divide and shape into 2 loaves. Put each loaf into buttered bread tins and allow to rise again (again about double size). Slash loaf tops, and put in oven. Bake in a preheated 400° oven for 45 minutes, and when it looks like loaves of finished homemade bread, remove and take out of pans to cool. Eat and rejoice!

YIELD: 2 loaves

HUGH DOWNS
Announcer of many well-known television shows and former host of the *Today Show*.

TANGY DIP AND VEGETABLE HORS D'OEUVRES

"Our guests, all diet concious,
appreciate the serving of low-cal tidbits!"

TANGY DIP

½	pint sour cream
2	tablespoons mayonnaise
1	large pod pressed garlic
1	tablespoon seasoning salt
½	teaspoon dill weed
½	teaspoon prepared mustard
½	teaspoon freshly ground pepper
	Raw vegetables

Blend all until smooth and creamy. Suggested raw vegetables to dip: sliced fresh mushrooms, cherry tomatoes, flowerets of cauliflower, carrot sticks, celery sticks, red and green bell pepper strips, kohlrabi or jicama strips, and green beans.
YIELD: 6 to 8 servings

ART LINKLETTER
Radio and television personality and author of the best seller *Kids Say The Darndest Things.*

CHEESE LOG

"With my compliments . . . . "

½	pound American processed cheese spread (I prefer Velveeta)
½	pound cream cheese
½	pound pecans
2	cloves garlic, crushed
	Chili powder
	Crackers (I prefer Ritz)

Mix American processed cheese spread and cream cheese together. Put through meat grinder with crushed garlic. Put pecans through grinder and mix with the cheese. Put all together through grinder. Shape into a cylinder. Put chili powder on waxed paper and roll cheese log over it until it is well coated. Wrap, secure, and chill. Slice and serve on crackers.

JAMES W. SYMINGTON
Former Congressman from Missouri and former Chief of Protocol of the United States.

APPLESAUCE

"Not being a cook, I am extremely limited in this area. The one thing I do love to make is very simple and I think delicious."

1	large bag McIntosh apples, 8 to 10 large
1	6-ounce can concentrated frozen orange juice
3	orange juice cans water

Peel, core, and dice a bag of McIntosh apples (They are thin-skinned and the easiest to peel.), and put them in a large pot to slowly boil. Add one tin of concentrated frozen orange juice with the directions of three tins of water. NO SUGAR. That is it, and I hope you enjoy it.

LILLIAN GISH
Renowned actress who has performed in movies, on television, and on stage.

NOODLE & SPINACH RING

"This is the recipe I have chosen for your cookbook. I enjoy it and I hope your readers will enjoy it too. Good luck with your cookbook and thank you for thinking of me."

1	8-ounce package noodles
1	10-ounce package frozen chopped spinach
1/3	cup bread crumbs
1	cup grated American cheese
2½	cups milk
4	eggs, slightly beaten
1	teaspoon salt
1	teaspoon worcestershire sauce

Cook noodles in salted water. Drain. Cook spinach in ½ cup salted water *only* until thawed. Drain well. Alternate layers of noodles, spinach, crumbs, and cheese in a buttered 2-quart ring mold. Combine all other ingredients; pour over noodles. Bake in pan of hot water in preheated 350° oven for about 45 minutes.
YIELD: 6 servings

ANN LANDERS
Syndicated columnist whose advice is read by millions.

308

SPINACH CASSEROLE

"Our daughter gave this recipe to my wife on a recent visit we made to her and her family. Normally I don't like spinach; in fact, I wrote a couplet: Children eat spinach/Inach by inach. But, I like this recipe."

2   10-ounce packages frozen chopped spinach, thawed and well drained
½   envelope onion soup mix
1   8-ounce carton sour cream
2   tablespoons grated Parmesan cheese
    Buttered bread crumbs

Mix all ingredients together except bread crumbs, and pour into an 8 x 8-inch pan. Top with buttered crumbs. Bake for 30 minutes in a preheated 350° oven.
YIELD: 4 to 6 servings

RICHARD ARMOUR
Educator, humorist, and author of several books and a syndicated feature in *Family Weekly*.

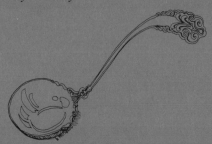

ZUCCHINI SOUP

"A summer marvel! I collect recipes wherever I go."

5   or 6 zucchini, cut into small pieces
1   medium onion, chopped
1½   teaspoons curry powder
3   cups chicken broth
1   cup heavy cream
½   cup milk
    Seasoning salt to taste, 1 teaspoon or more (I prefer Lawry's)
    Chives to garnish

In a large soup kettle, simmer the first 4 ingredients until the zucchini is tender. Put in a blender or a food processor and puree. Add cream, milk, and salt. Chill thoroughly and correct seasoning. Garnish with chives.
YIELD: 6 to 8 servings

CELESTE HOLM
Academy Award winning star of stage, screen, and television.

POLLY BERGEN'S CHILI

3   cloves garlic, minced
      Cooking oil
6   large onions, finely
      chopped
6   large green peppers,
      finely chopped
6   pounds ground round
      or chuck
5   16-ounce cans Italian-
      style tomatoes
4   to 6, 16-ounce cans
      kidney beans, drained
2   6-ounce cans tomato
      paste
      Salt and pepper to
      taste
2   teaspoons wine vinegar
5   whole cloves
3   bay leaves
4   tablespoons chili
      powder, or more to
      taste
4   drops tabasco sauce,
      or to taste
      Sugar
2   teaspoons cumin

In a large roaster, saute garlic in oil and remove. Saute onions and peppers until golden; remove and drain. Add meat to oil; separate with a fork, and cook until all meat is grey in color. Drain off accumulated oil. Add onions and green peppers to the meat; mix well, and then add all of the remaining ingredients. Cover and simmer over low heat for 1 hour. Simmer uncovered for another hour. Remove cloves and bay leaves before serving. YIELD: 25 servings

POLLY BERGEN
Recording and television star, award-winning actress, author, and business-woman.

PHILLI CHILLI

**Not counting the chopping time,
this can be ready to eat in 20 minutes.**

1	cup vegetable oil (I prefer Wesson)
1	pound ground sirloin
1	entire garlic root, chopped fine
3	large onions, chopped
1	green bell pepper, chopped bite size
1½	teaspoons garlic salt
1½	teaspoons onion salt
1½	teaspoons chili powder
1	teaspoon tabasco sauce
1	teaspoon seasoning salt (I prefer Lawry's)
½	cup chopped parsley (dehydrated or fresh)
5	16-ounce cans kidney beans, drained (I prefer S & W)
1	20-ounce can tomatoes, cut up bite size

Heat oil in large pot. Lightly brown meat, and make it small, bite-size pieces with a pancake turner. Add garlic and onion toward the end of the meat-browning process. Drain excess oil; add all remaining ingredients in order listed. As soon as it is hot, it is ready to serve; however, it enhances the flavor to keep it on the lowest possible simmer for an hour or even longer. If "your" simmer makes it bubble or too hot, use asbestos pads over heat. This chili should be served with garlic bread.
YIELD: 12 servings

PHYLLIS DILLER
The internationally famous comedienne.

TUNA CASSEROLE

1	cup shell macaroni
½	cup chopped onions
¼	cup chopped green pepper
3	tablespoons vegetable oil
	Flour
1	10¾-ounce can condensed cream of chicken soup
1½	cups milk
1	7-ounce can tuna, drained
2	tablespoons chopped almonds

Cook macaroni; saute onion and green pepper in oil. Mix flour with cream of chicken soup; add milk. Mix all ingredients; turn into casserole, and sprinkle the chopped almonds on top. Bake uncovered in a preheated 350° oven for 30 minutes.
YIELD: 4 servings

NORMAN VINCENT PEALE
Clergyman, editor of *Guideposts* magazine, and author of *The Power of Positive Thinking.*

ROAST HAM IN BLACKBERRY WINE SAUCE

1	teaspoon dry mustard
1	10-pound ham
4	6-ounce cans papaya nectar
1	bottle blackberry wine
1	cup orange juice
1	teaspoon ground cloves
½	cup kumquat juice
2	tablespoons apricot jam
6	tablespoons brown sugar
1	tablespoon coarsely grated orange rind
	Large whole cloves, for garnish

Sprinkle mustard over bottom of a deep roasting pan. Remove rind from ham with a sharp knife, and place ham on an adjustable rack in the pan. Pour papaya nectar over the ham. Roast in a preheated 300° oven, basting every 10 minutes for about 1½ hours. Turn ham over halfway through cooking time so underside browns. While ham is roasting, combine blackberry wine, orange juice, ground cloves, kumquat juice, apricot jam, brown sugar, and grated orange rind in heavy enamel saucepan. Bring to boil. When ham has roasted 1½ hours, remove from oven. Score the fat on the top of the ham and make a design with the whole cloves. Roast another hour, basting with a little of the wine mixture every 10 minutes, until deeply browned (If ham is not browning, raise temperature to 350°.). If pan drippings are cooled first, the fat will rise to the top and be easily removed. Serve remaining wine mixture hot as sauce.

DAVID SUSSKIND
Award-winning producer and director of theatre, movies, and television.

BETTY ROLLIN'S 5-MINUTE LAMB

1	5-pound leg of lamb
2	tablespoons vegetable oil
2	tablespoons soy sauce
1	tablespoon Dijon mustard
1	teaspoon rosemary
¼	teaspoon thyme
¼	teaspoon sage
¼	teaspoon pepper
¼	teaspoon salt
	Garlic, slivered

Remove lamb from refrigerator one hour before roasting. Preheat oven to 350°. Remove outer fat covering from lamb. In a small bowl mix together all remaining ingredients except garlic slivers. Smear mixture over lamb. Using a pointed knife, make slits and insert garlic slivers under skin. Roast, fat side up, on a rack in an uncovered pan. Roast 20 to 30 minutes per pound (160° to 180°).
YIELD: 8 servings

BETTY ROLLIN
NBC news correspondent and author of the sensitive book *First You Cry*.

MATZO LE POULET SCHMALTZ SUPREME (FRIED MATZO)

"This recipe dates back to the Royal House of the Czar Nicholas in Kiev, Russia, early 20th century. It was one of the favorite recipes of Rasputin and was supposed to add strength to his libido for his nightly missions to the ladies of the court."

6	Matzos (I prefer Manischevitz)
4	eggs
	Water
	Salt and pepper to taste
	Schmaltz (rendered chicken fat)
	Onions, chopped

Soak matzos in warm water to soften. Beat eggs with a little water until they are fluffy. Add salt and pepper. Put soft matzo (water drained) in egg mixture. In a large skillet, heat chicken fat until hot. Add onions, and matzo-egg mixture. Fry until golden brown on one side; turn, and fry until golden brown. Serve immediately (Temperature used is same as scrambled eggs.).

DR. EDGAR BERMAN
Surgeon, consultant to the United States Government, and author of *The Solid Gold Stethoscope*.

EDITOR'S NOTE: In lieu of rendered chicken fat, use butter or margarine. Fried matzo could be served with syrup or jelly for breakfast or brunch.
YIELD: 4 servings

BEEF & CHICK-PEA STEW

1½   pounds beef stew meat
2   tablespoons flour
1   teaspoon paprika
1   teaspoon salt
¼   teaspoon pepper
1/8   teaspoon cloves
2   tablespoons olive oil
1   large onion, chopped
2   cloves garlic, crushed
2½   cups beef broth
1   16-ounce can chick peas, drained
Noodles

Coat beef with flour, paprika, salt, pepper, and cloves. Brown in oil in a Dutch oven; remove meat. Add onion and garlic to drippings and saute until tender. Return meat and add broth. Cover and simmer for 1 hour, or until meat is tender. Stir in chick peas, and simmer 10 more minutes. Serve over noodles.
YIELD: 5 servings

PETER DUCHIN
Pianist, conductor, and composer, recognized as one of America's best-known orchestra leaders.

CHICKEN CASSEROLE

"A chicken casserole that is easy to prepare . . . and a delight to eat!"

1   3½-pound chicken, trussed
2   tablespoons butter
1   tablespoon oil
2   onions, finely chopped
2   carrots, finely chopped
½   cup chicken broth
½   teaspoon salt
Freshly ground black pepper
1   teaspoon marjoram
1   tablespoon cornstarch dissolved in 2 tablespoons cold water
2   tablespoons finely chopped parsley

Brown chicken, breast side down — first, in hot combined butter and oil. Remove the chicken. Saute the vegetables in the same butter and oil for 3 minutes until softened. Place chicken on bed of vegetables in a casserole. Add the broth, salt, pepper, and marjoram. Cover and cook in a preheated 350° oven for 50 minutes. Remove chicken and cut into serving pieces. Stir the cornstarch mixture into the pan juices, and stir over a low heat with a wire whisk until the sauce has thickened. Replace chicken pieces and garnish with parsley.
YIELD: 4 servings

JUNE WEIR
Fashion News Director of *Vogue* Magazine.

CHICKEN McKINLEY

"This recipe has been served in a cabin in McKinley Park,
on a boat in Glacier Bay, and often in our home in Anchorage."

12	chicken thighs, or 6 thighs and 6 drum-sticks, or 6 thighs and 4 breast halves, or 6 breast halves
1	10¾-ounce can condensed cream of chicken soup
½	soup can water
1	cup mayonnaise Juice of ½ lemon
1	tablespoon curry, or more if desired
1	to 2 cups corn flakes, lightly crushed

Place chicken pieces in flat casserole dish; place all remaining ingredients (except corn flakes) in blender and blend until mixed well (about 5 seconds). Pour sauce over chicken; sprinkle with 1 to 2 cups corn flakes. Cover and bake in a preheated 425° oven for 45 minutes. Uncover and bake 15 minutes longer. Serve with rice or barley and a salad or a green vegetable.
YIELD: 4 to 6 servings

LOWELL THOMAS, JR.
Former State Senator, Lt. Governor of Alaska, author, and lecturer.

RICE WITH VERMICELLI

"I was raised in a big family. Both of my parents were from Lebanon, and it was chicken and rice every Sunday, the big dinner after church."

1	cup vermicelli or thin spaghetti, broken into 1-inch pieces
4	tablespoons butter (½ stick)
5	to 6 cups chicken broth or water
2	cups raw rice (washed and drained)
1	tablespoon salt
½	teaspoon cinnamon
½	teaspoon pepper
½	teaspoon allspice Dash of ground cloves
1	cup pine nuts or slivered almonds Butter

Brown vermicelli lightly in melted butter over low heat. Stir continuous-ly. Heat broth or water. Mix rice and all seasonings with browned vermicelli. Stir in broth; bring to a boil — watch that mixture does not boil over. Reduce heat to low; cover and steam until rice is tender and all liquid absorbed. Lightly brown pine nuts or almonds in butter. Serve rice on a platter; cover with nuts.
YIELD: 6 servings

HELEN THOMAS
Journalist and president of the White House Correspondents' Association.

BARBARA WALTERS' MOTHER'S STUFFED CABBAGE ROLLS

"The secret is extremely simple — chili sauce and grape jelly!"

3   **pounds lean ground chuck**
2   **teaspoons salt**
¾   **teaspoon pepper**
2   **teaspoons celery salt**
½   **cup catsup**
2   **eggs**
½   **cup crushed, unsalted crackers**
2   **heads (2-pound size) green cabbage**
6   **quarts boiling water**
3   **cups chopped onion**
2   **cups chili sauce**
1   **cup grape jelly**
¼   **cup water**

In a large bowl, combine ground chuck, salt, pepper, celery salt, catsup, eggs, and crushed crackers. Mix with hands just until mixture is well combined. Cut out and discard hard center core of cabbage. Place cabbage in a large kettle. Pour boiling water over it; let it stand until leaves are flexible and can be removed easily from the head — about 5 minutes (If necessary, return cabbage to hot water to soften inner leaves.). Using a ¼-cup measure, scoop up a scant ¼ cup of the meat mixture. With hands, form into rolls, 3-inches long and 1-inch wide, making about 28 rolls in all. Place each meat roll on a drained cabbage leaf; fold top of leaf over meat; then fold sides, and roll up into an oblong. Continue rolling remaining meat rolls and cabbage leaves. In the bottom of a lightly greased 12 x 11½ x 2¼-inch roasting pan, spread chopped onion evenly. Arrange cabbage rolls in neat rows on top of onion. In a 2-quart saucepan, combine chili sauce and grape jelly with ¼ cup water; heat over medium heat, stirring to melt jelly. Pour over cabbage rolls. Cover pan tightly with foil. Bake in preheated 375° oven for 2 hours. Remove foil; baste rolls with sauce; bake, uncovered, 40 minutes longer, or until sauce is thick and syrupy and cabbage rolls are glazed. Serve with sauce spooned over rolls.
YIELD: 28 cabbage rolls, 14 servings

BARBARA WALTERS
Newscaster, writer, and television producer, as well as co-host of the *Today Show* and *ABC Evening News*

SWEET POTATOES

"My recipe may be too simple. At any rate here it is."

Sweet potatoes

Place sweet potatoes in their jackets in the ashes of a fire.

CHEF'S NOTE: Of course, it would be good to add corn on the cob, watermelon, maple-nut ice cream, and a first class cup of coffee. All the best!

LOWELL THOMAS
World-famous broadcaster, explorer, voice of *Movietone News,* and developer of Cinerama.

CORN ON THE COB — MAINE STYLE

"This is not really a recipe — it is more of a how-to-do-it suggestion. I learned it from a Maine guide while at Lake Kennebago near Rangely, Maine, when I was there fishing the lakes and steams."

Cold water
Shucked and cleaned
corn on the cob
Butter
Salt and pepper

Fill a large pot with cold water. Put the corn in cold water; turn on heat. Let water come to a boil, and then remove the pot from the heat. Salt to taste. You may leave the ears in the water as long as you wish — they will not deteriorate (You may even leave the remainder overnight — heat up when ready to eat more. You will have crisp kernels, not the soggy ones that result from dropping corn in boiling water as so many people do.). It's easy and simple! Serve with butter, salt, and pepper.
YIELD: As much as needed

FRANK BLAIR
Journalist and newscaster, best known, perhaps, for his appearances on the *Today Show.*

317

BASQUE OMELET

1	cup chopped onion
1	clove garlic, pressed
1	tablespoon salad oil
3	medium tomatoes
½	teaspoon sea salt
1	teaspoon dried basil
	Freshly ground black
	pepper to taste
1	medium tomato
1	California avocado
6	eggs
½	teaspoon sea salt
2	tablespoons margarine

Saute onion and garlic in oil in saucepan over low heat. Peel and chop 3 tomatoes; add to onion mixture and cook, stirring occasionally, for 5 minutes. Season with ½ teaspoon salt, basil, and pepper. Cover and keep warm. Slice remaining tomato. Halve, peel, and slice avocado. Beat eggs with remaining salt in bowl until light and fluffy. Melt margarine in 9-inch skillet over low heat. Add egg mixture and cook until bottom is set. Spoon tomato sauce mixture over omelet and cook to desired doneness. Top with tomato and avocado slices. Serve immediately.
YIELD: 6 servings

JEANE L. DIXON
Advocate of extrasensory perception, author, lecturer, and columnist.

CREME CARAMELLE

	Granulated sugar
	Water
2	eggs
1½	cups milk
3	tablespoons granulated sugar
1	teaspoon vanilla

Put about ½-inch of sugar in a saucepan. Cover with water until the water is only 1/8-inch over sugar. Boil over medium heat until the color of caramel — watch carefully (takes 15 to 18 minutes). Divide this into the bottoms of 5 oven-proof custard cups — *not* buttered. Beat eggs with milk; add 3 tablespoons sugar and vanilla. After caramelled sugar is hard, strain milk mixture unto cups. Line pan with brown paper. Fill pan ¾ full of water, and put cups in. Bake at 350° for 35 to 45 minutes. Test with knife — if it comes out clean, the custard is done.
YIELD: 5 servings

HUGH SIDEY
Ranked as one of the nation's top journalists, he is *Time* Magazine's Washington Bureau Chief.

MAMA'S CAKE

"Even today I have a picture of Mama in my kitchen, looking over my shoulder just as she did when I was eight years old."

My kitchen seems friendly today,
Warm.
Perfumed with vanilla.
Mama is making a treat —
Her cake.
It's simple,
Not a fancy one like the lady down
The street —
Who gave me a piece of hers
Yesterday.
But her kitchen didn't seem to
Smell as sweet —
Nor did I have the pleasure
Of watching her make it.

I'm watching Mama.
I smell our sweet kitchen.
Mama is here —
I'm near Mama,
And guess what —
Not only will I get some of the
Finished product,
She'll let me run my small
Fingers
Around the bowl —
To get the leavings,
What didn't get in the pan.

I like the kitchen.
I like Mama's cake.

Reprinted by permission of Pearl Bailey, from PEARL'S KITCHEN Copyright 1973, by Pearl Bailey.

PEARL BAILEY
Known as "America's Ambassador of Good Will," her career has encompassed the entire show-business spectrum.

TRAIL MIX

"Always keep this nutritious and delicious snack close at hand
in bowls about the house, in bags in the car,
in pocket or purse at school or work — NIBBLE!"

Equal parts of:
Almonds
Sunflower seeds
Pumpkin seeds
Peanuts
Sesame seeds
Raisins
No salt

In a very large bowl, combine equal parts of all ingredients.
YIELD: 1 ton!

DR. LENDON H. SMITH
Television personality, author of many pediatric-care books, and columnist for *McCall's* magazine.

USING A FOOD PROCESSOR: GENERAL HINTS

The Steel Blade

The most important thing to remember is DO NOT OVER-PROCESS — it's always surprising how fast these machines do the job. To prevent over-processing, use the ON-OFF system. Turn the machine on for just one second, then off to check the contents. Often, only two or three of these one-second bursts will give the desired results.

When preparing dough or batters for cakes and cookies, it is especially important to avoid overprocessing, as this can result in a very tough product. Add the flour and baking powder last, and process it only long enough to incorporate it into the mixture. Adapting recipes for use in your food processor is easy if you remember this.

In chopping if you want to obtain medium-size pieces, put one-inch chunks into the work bowl and process in two or three short bursts. If you want finely minced pieces, put larger chunks in the work bowl and process for a longer time.

To grate lemon, orange, or grapefruit peel, put strips in work bowl with a small amount of sugar and process until you have the desired consistency (Be sure to subtract the amount of sugar used from the amount needed to complete the recipe.).

In making pie dough put shortening or butter (preferably frozen), salt, and flour in work bowl and process briefly until it looks like small peas. Then, with machine running, pour ICE water through the feeding tube until a ball of dough forms and rides on top of the blade. If you use three times the amount of flour as shortening and enough ice water to make a ball, you will always have perfect pie crust. Chill, then roll between sheets of waxed paper, put in pie pan, and chill again if time permits.

Save bread crumbs in a plastic bag in the freezer, then process with herbs, seasoned salt, or grated cheese, and return to the freezer. Just pour out as needed to top casseroles — no need to thaw.

Make your own garlic salt by processing fresh garlic cloves and kosher salt with a bit of fresh parsley and a dash of paprika. Just add ingredients and mix until it smells and looks right. Store in the refrigerator. This is also good with herbs to use in salad or vegetable dishes, and it makes a super Christmas gift!

The Slicing Blade

Whenever possible, fill the feeding tube to capacity for even slicing. If only one item is being sliced, force it to the right side of the feeding tube with the pusher as the direction of the cutting disc will help keep it in an upright position.

If you wish to make small julienne strips, slice first, then place the slices on edge in the feeding tube and slice again.

To slice meat for an oriental stir-fry, use partially frozen meat — it will hold its shape better.

Use the slicing blade to prepare cabbage for cole slaw, as the shredding disc makes the pieces too small.

The Shredding Blade

When shredding cheeses, make sure they are as firm and cold as possible, and do not force them into the blade, as this can cause the machine to jam and stall.

Shred iceberg lettuce for tacos, and keep some on hand for sandwiches. It's delicious this way, neat to eat, and children like it. It also keeps surprisingly well.

The Plastic Blade

For tasty salad dressings, remember the same three to one ratio as pie crust, only this time use three times as much oil as vinegar. Add salt, pepper, and herbs to taste, and vary with Dijon mustard, lemon juice, cheese, and fresh parsley. You'll never use the bottled dressing again!

When making mayonnaise or hollandaise, add a chunk or two of ripe, fresh avocado to the mixture for a subtle taste treat.

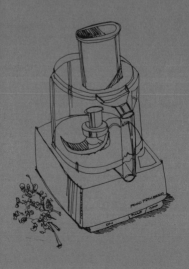

MICROWAVE COOKING GUIDE

Microwave cooking is an increasingly popular means of preparing food because it is timesaving both in cooking time and clean-up time — cooks can prepare freezer-to-table meals in a matter of minutes. This section does not contain specific recipes for microwave use but rather contains some tips and guidelines which we hope will help you to experiment successfully and to have fun with your microwave.

The microwave can do most of the things that a conventional range can do: boil, sear, fry, steam, bake, roast, and more, but the microwave can complete the processes in about one third the time. The moisture molecules in the food absorb energy and vibrate rapidly, causing friction within the food. No general adapting guide is possible since recipes vary so greatly; however, the microwave cook needs to remember that food content, density, temperature, quantity, and placement all affect the cooking process. For example, foods with high sugar or fat content cook fastest; those with high moisture levels cook faster than those with low moisture levels. Foods at room temperature cook faster than chilled or partially frozen foods, and solid foods, such as meats, take longer to cook than porous ones like breads. Also, foods such as cheese, eggs, mayonnaise, condensed milk, cream, sour cream, oysters, scallops, and mushrooms should *not* be cooked on high — use a medium setting to avoid popping and poor results. Variations in cooking times can also occur with changes in voltage levels in a home: peak usage hours mean lower levels of voltage and longer cooking times. Use similar recipes in your microwave cookbook as guides to your experimenting; and, when you are in doubt about cooking time, choose less time rather than more — you can always process the dish for a few seconds longer. Have fun with your microwave; try some of our ideas!

APPETIZERS AND SNACKS

Prepare most appetizers ahead of time and reheat on high.

Soften cheese by heating on medium setting for 1 minute.

Freshen stale potato chips or crackers by microwaving on high for 30 to 45 seconds for 2 cups.

Warm lemons, oranges, or limes for 30 seconds on high for more juice and flavor.

Soften raisins, dried apricots, prunes, etc., using 1 tablespoon of liquid (water, brandy, etc.) per cup of fruit. Microwave for 1 minute on high; let stand.

BEVERAGES AND SOUPS

Heat a mug of water for two minutes on high and then add instant coffee or tea or a tea bag. For a quick, fresh glass of iced coffee or tea, just pour over ice!

Store leftover coffee in the refrigerator and reheat in a cup or mug — no bitter taste.

Make condensed soups in the bowls by dividing water and contents evenly, stirring, and heating (2 to 3 minutes).

Make instant soup in a mug by heating all ingredients on high for 2 to 2½ minutes.

BREADS

Yeast bread dough rises on lowest setting with dish set in water in 1/3 to 1/2 the usual time.

Bread will not brown when cooked in a microwave.

Biscuits don't do well in a microwave.

Fill dishes only half full for quick breads as they expand greatly!

Microwave quick breads on a low setting for all but the last few minutes; finish baking on high. Quick breads will be moist on top when finished — do not overcook.

Freshen breads, rolls, or cookies by wrapping them in a napkin and microwaving on high for 10 seconds.

CONDIMENTS AND PRESERVES

Get that last little bit out of a jelly or honey jar or a ketchup bottle by microwaving for 5 to 10 seconds on high.

Soften brown sugar by wrapping it in a damp paper towel and microwaving for 10 seconds per cup on high.

VEGETABLES

Use very little water to cook vegetables — they will keep their color and nutrients.

Cover vegetables and stir midway through the cooking process for more even cooking.

Put butter, salt, and seasonings in the bottom of the dish.

Rinse peas and beans, and no more water is necessary.

Undercook vegetables by two to three minutes as they will continue to cook while standing. Overcooking will cause dehydration and toughness. Keep covered.

Prick any vegetables with skin (potatoes, etc.) before cooking.

Cook vegetables on high unless they are in a sauce or contain mushrooms.

Cook frozen vegetables in the box or pouch if desired, but mix them midway through the cooking process (Approximately 10 to 12 minutes total cooking time for most frozen vegetables — see carton.).

Blanch vegetables on high in small bunches.

Some sample times are as follows:

Asparagus	1-inch pieces	4 cups	¼ cup water	1½-quart casserole 4½ minutes
Broccoli	2-inch pieces	1 pound	1/3 cup water	1½-quart casserole 6 minutes
Cauliflower	flowerets	1 medium	½ cup water	2-quart casserole 6 minutes
Corn off the cob	——	4 cups	no water	1½-quart casserole 4 minutes
Corn	6 ears	——	no water	8 x 12-inch dish 5½ minutes
Peas, shelled	——	4 cups	¼ cup water	1½-quart casserole 4½ minutes
Snow peas, washed	——	4 cups	1 tablespoon	1½-quart casserole 3 minutes
Spinach, washed	——	1 pound	no water	2-quart casserole 4 minutes

GRAINS

Make hot cereal in the bowl by microwaving measured ingredients for 1 minute, 10 seconds on high (10 to 15 seconds longer if you like it thicker); stir and serve!

MEATS

Meats shrink less in a microwave than in a conventional oven.

Meats with high fat content (pork, lamb, etc.) cook faster than others — watch carefully.

Since microwaved food continues to cook after being removed from the oven, the meat temperature should be less than when removing it from a conventional oven (rare — 120°; medium — 140°; well done — 160°). Let meats stand 10 minutes after being removed from oven before serving.

Wrapping meat in plastic wrap will defrost it faster.

Always thaw meat *before cooking.*

Add *no salt* to meat until after it has cooked.

Marinate tougher cuts of meat before microwaving.

For rare hamburgers that aren't cold inside, sear outsides in a skillet on the stove and then heat through in the microwave.

POULTRY

Cook most whole poultry uncovered.

Thaw birds before roasting. For turkeys figure 2 minutes per pound on high first and then 3 minutes per pound on low (defrost).

Figure 9 minutes per pound for roasting poultry (slightly longer for a heavy turkey).

Cook poultry breast side down for the first half of the cooking time.

Put no salt on the outside of the bird; put salt inside the cavity.

Keep stuffing loose for microwaving.

Put thicker parts to the *outside* when cooking pieces.

Don't cook giblets in a microwave — they'll be tough.

Cook any bird over four pounds on high for the first half of the cooking time and then on medium (roast) for the remainder.

Fourteen pounds is the maximum size bird for the microwave (at least 1-inch between bird and oven on all sides).

Turn any bird over 10 pounds three times during cooking.

Standing time is especially important for large birds (10 to 15 minutes).

SEAFOOD

Fish cooks quickly, so be careful not to overcook. One pound of whitefish, sole, perch, etc., cooks in 6 to 7 minutes on high.

Fish is done if it flakes when pricked near the center with a fork.

Do not reheat fish — it tends to get tough.

Tuck thin ends of filets under to allow for more even cooking.

Cook fish covered to retain moisture.

Cook fish on high unless it is in a sauce (except for oysters, clams, scallops, and snails — they tend to pop, so use a medium setting).

Cook shellfish in the shell (6 to 7 mintues for 8-ounces) if desired. Partially loosen from shell before cooking.

SAUCES

Sauces don't get lumpy or stick to the bottom of the pan when cooked in a microwave!

Cook sauce in a container at least twice the size of the sauce amount.

Stir thoroughly before cooking and one or two times during the cooking process.

One cup of white (or brown) sauce cooks in 3 to 3½ minutes on high; 2 cups cook in 5 to 6 minutes.

EGGS AND CHEESE

Do not cook eggs and cheese on high — both will get tough and rubbery.

Pierce yolks or they will explode.

Do not reheat cooked eggs unless they are chopped — they can explode.

Do not cook eggs in their shells.

When substituting cheeses be sure to select one of the same type called for.

Use a medium setting for most cheese dishes. Cheese fondue or other recipes with extremely high cheese content do better on low.

CAKES

Angel food cake won't work in a microwave!!

Microwave cakes do not fall.

Watch time carefully as cakes can easily overcook and become dry.

Only fill containers ½ full of batter as microwave cakes increase greatly in volume (as with quick breads) — make an extra cake or cupcakes out of leftover batter.

Line cake pans with wax paper for easy removal.

Use styrofoam cups to make rings for paper cupcake liners.

Heavier cakes (applesauce, etc.) turn out best.

Grease but do not flour cake pans (The flour will adhere to the cake!).

Round pans work best for even baking.

Bake layers individually (9-inch layer approximately 7 minutes on low, then 3 to 4 minutes on high).

Cakes will be moist on top when finished.

COOKIES

Bar cookies, such as brownies, do better than individual cookies, which tend to spread out.

Begin cooking bar cookies on a medium setting and finish on low to complete cooking of center.

Commercial refrigerator cookies won't work in a microwave.

PIES AND PASTRIES

Heat pie a la mode without melting the ice cream! Microwave for 15 to 20 seconds on high.

Microwave frozen pies in 15 minutes!

Add a little yellow food coloring as you mix pie crusts to give them a better color since they don't brown in a microwave.

Build crusts higher than for a conventional oven as they will bubble.

MISCELLANEOUS DESSERTS

Flaming desserts are easy — heat ¼ cup brandy for 10 to 15 seconds; pour over dessert; light immediately.

Make crepes ahead and fill with fruit and then warm quickly.

Heat sugared, whole strawberries for a moment to intensify flavor.

Do not bake popovers in a microwave as the crust will not form properly.

Soften chocolate squares in the wrappers — 30 to 45 seconds on high for one square.

MICROWAVE OVEN

WINE GUIDE

It has been said that the addition of wine to a meal makes the difference between eating and dining. While nothing can replace a Coke with a burger and fries, anyone who spends time planning and preparing a meal should be aware of the special ambiance, the air of "special occasion," that a bottle of wine adds. The children seem quieter, the meal more relaxed, and the cook far more rewarded for her efforts if a meal is savored rather than gobbled.

Traditionally, certain wines accompany certain dishes, and wine snobs tend to be very strict on this subject. The old rules of red wines with red meats and white wines with fish or fowl are sound — the result of centuries of experiment. The delicacy of a dry white wine would be overpowered by a beef stew or roast just as surely as a heavier more robust red Burgundy would eliminate the delicate flavor of a finely-spiced veal or chicken dish. When more than one type of wine is to be served with a meal, serve the lighter wines first; for example, a Chablis with the appetizer or soup and a red Bordeaux with the steak or roast — the heavier wines tend to dull the taste buds for the more delicate white or rose wines. Clearly, the heavier the meal the heavier, more full-bodied the wine served.

Everyone has heard of the sky-high prices offered for special vintage years of rare wines. It is important to note that all wines do have life expectancies. When you purchase a bottle or a case of wine, the vintner supposed that you would be drinking it within a certain time. White wines should be consumed within two to three years; reds, since they are more robust, will remain sound six to ten years; however, there are exceptions. If you are purchasing wine in quantity, do check with your wine merchant as to how long the wine can be stored. All still wines that have been bottled a year or more are likely to throw some sediment, especially the deeper-colored, full-bodied red wines. If there is some sediment, the wine should be decanted so that the sediment remains in the original bottle. Once decanted, the wine will taste just as good as if there had been no sediment.

For the selection of glasses, the glass should be clear, not opaque or tinted, in order to show the brilliancy in color of the wine. Metal goblets should not be used, for they seem to give a metallic taste to the wine. A good all-purpose wine glass is a clear-stemmed six to nine-ounce capacity glass, which can be used to serve all wines including sparkling dessert wines. For table and sparkling wines fill to about five ounces; for appetizer and dessert wines fill with two to three ounces. Wine glasses are usually placed at the right in the table setting. If more than one wine is to be served, the glass for the first wine is placed farthest to the right, and no more than three wine glasses should be in front of each guest at any one time.

The storage of wine is very important. Wine can be expensive, and just as you care for your other investments, you must care for wine, too. All bottles of wine should be laid down. This insures that their corks remain moist and prohibits air from coming in contact with the wine. The temperature of storage should be as constant as possible, and the ideal is from 50-55° F. Always store your sparkling wines nearest the floor, then still whites, and on top still reds. The storage area shoud be designed so that the disturbance of wines is minimal.

SERVING TEMPERATURES

Champagne and Sparkling	35° F	One hour in cracked ice or in refrigerator
Still White and Rose Wines	50° F	One-half hour in cracked ice or one hour in refrigerator
Still Reds	70 to 75° F	Stand bottle up for one to two hours in the dining room before serving—opened

Below is a general glossary of wines and the foods with which they marry most successfully. But, almost any wine merchant, vintner, or cook will hasten to add that the individual is the best judge, and personal preference always comes first. In other words, drink what you prefer.

WINES

AMERICAN	IMPORTED	FOODS
RED WINES		
Cabernet Sauvignon	Bordeaux — Medoc	Steak, Roasts,
Pinot Noir	St. Emilion	Stews, Game,
Gamay Beaujolais	St. Julien	Chops, Casseroles,
Zifandel	Spanish Rioja	Spaghetti
Barbera	Burgundy — Beaujolais	
Burgundy	Pommard	
Chianti	Chambertin	
Petit Sirah		
ROSE WINES		
Grenache Rose	Tavel Rose	Ham, Pork, Lamb,
Rose de Cabernet	Anjou Rose	Veal, Poultry
Gamay Rose	Cotes de Rhone	
Vin Rose	(light red)	
WHITE WINES		
Pinot Chardonnay	Pouilly Fuisse	Poultry, Soups,
Grey Reisling	Vouvray	Fruits, Fish,
Chenin Blanc	Sancere	Shell Fish
French Colombard	Muscadet	
Chablis	Pouilly Fume	
Johanisberg Riesling	Bordeaux Blanc	
Gewurztraminer	Sauterne	
Sauvignon Blanc	Graves	
Semillon	German Rieslings	
Sauterne	Alsation	
DESSERT WINES		
Ruby Port		Fruit, Nuts, Cheese,
Tawny Port		Cake, Cookies
APPETIZER WINES		
All Sherries		Soup
Vermouth		
Champagne		All Foods

330

COOKING WITH WINE

Just as a bottle of wine lends elegance and festivity to a meal, the addition of wine in the cooking process adds a flavor and character to certain dishes that couldn't be had otherwise. Seasonings provide flavors that may overpower the flavor of the food; wine, on the other hand, brings out the basic food flavors and blends them with its own flavor.

A simple marinade of equal parts sherry and soy sauce, perhaps spiced with garlic, is perfect for either steak or chicken that's headed for the grill. The same marinade can be brushed on hamburgers that are to be grilled or fried. Simmer frozen carrots in sauterne and butter, and compare the aroma and taste with carrots you've simply boiled or steamed in water. Add a tablespoon or two of sherry to a can of pea or tomato soup. How about adding a touch of sherry to top a grapefruit and broiling the grapefruit several minutes? Casseroles and stews improve their flavors and aromas with the addition of ¼ cup of wine. Bundt cakes or pound cakes improve when sherry replaces part of the liquid called for in a recipe. Remember, too, you are adding only the flavor of the wine — the alcohol evaporates during the cooking.

A good dry white wine or a rose makes an excellent all-purpose cooking wine. The dry reds are good, but they darken certain dishes. They are more compatible with stews, minestrone, and roast meats. Commercial cooking wines are available (The difference between a drinking and a cooking wine is the addition of salt. Legend has it that salt was added as a deterrent to thirsty cooks in the days when many people had household help.). Again, the basic rule of cooking with wine boils down to personal preference — if you enjoy drinking a particular wine, you'll enjoy that same flavor if you use that wine as part of your recipe.

There are many libraries devoted solely to wine, its production, varieties, and uses. One can find authorities who will praise imported wines over American wines and vice versa. For the occasional consumer, it should be noted that as in everything, you get exactly what you pay for. If you purchase a reliable, well-known brand, chances are you'll be satisfied.

"Life affords no finer example of a happy marriage than good food mated with good wine." — F. Scott Fitzgerald

Vail K. Miller, President
Heidelberg Distributing Company

Nationally famous nature centers, museums, and historical buildings are only a few of the fascinating points of interest waiting to be discovered by Dayton's residents and visitors. The Dayton Chamber of Commerce has devised a "Discover Dayton Tour" highlighting thirty-one of the city's numerous sights. Each numbered point of interest corresponds with the numerals on the map. We invite you to discover how beautiful Dayton is.

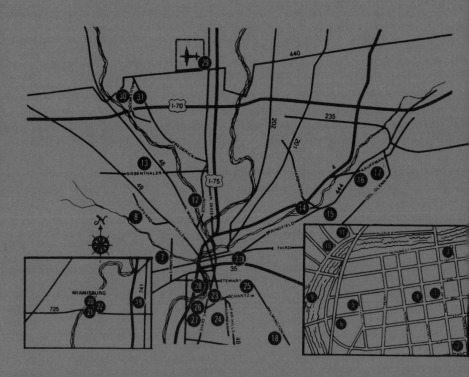

Reprinted by permission of the Dayton Area Chamber of Commerce

POINTS OF INTEREST MAP

1. Courthouse Square
2. Dayton Convention Center
2a. Oregon Historic District
3. Miami Conservancy District
4. Dayton Municipal Building
5. County Government Plaza
6. Sinclair Community College
7. Paul Laurence Dunbar House
8. United Theological Seminary
9. Soldiers Monument
10. Masonic Temple
11. Dayton Art Institute
12. Dayton Museum of Natural History
13. Benjamin Wegerzyn Garden Center
14. Dayton Hydrobowl
15. United States Air Force Museum
16. Wright Brothers Memorial
17. Wright State University
18. Defense Electronics Supply Center
19. Cox Arboretum
20. Miamisburg Civic Center
21. The Market House
22. Miamisburg Mound
23. Sugar Camp, NCR Corporate Education Center
24. Hawthorn Hill
25. University of Dayton
26. Deeds Carillon
27. Carillon Park
28. University of Dayton Arena
29. Amateur Trapshooting Association
30. Aullwood Audubon Farm
31. Aullwood Audubon Center

ART COMMITTEE CHAIRMAN
Gracey Weisbrod (Mrs. Alfred)

COVER DESIGN
Molly Cammerer (Mrs. Richard) Nora Murray (Mrs. George)

CONTRIBUTING ARTISTS
Molly Cammerer (Mrs. Richard) Alice Roedersheimer (Mrs. Charles)
Nancy Dankof (Mrs. Stephen) Beverly Todd (Mrs. D. Bruce)
Rebecca Meeker (Mrs. David) Gracey Weisbrod (Mrs. Alfred)
Barbara Wyant (Mrs. Jonathan)

DISTRIBUTION COMMITTEE CHAIRMAN
Carol Devery (Mrs. Kieran)

DISTRIBUTION COMMITTEE
Kathy Anderson (Mrs. Richard) Susie Mills (Mrs. Lowell)
Laurie Laine Blank Linda Nevin (Mrs. Robert)
Mary Brattenberg (Mrs. Richard) Lynn Olive (Mrs. Ben)
Susan Castle (Mrs. Charles) Linda Puthoff (Mrs. Thomas)
Deborah Drury (Mrs. David) Alice Roedersheimer (Mrs. Charles)
Lesli Garrison (Mrs. James) Elizabeth Sava (Mrs. Samuel)
Bonnie Boyles Geiger Joyce Sutherland (Mrs. Charles)
Donna Hawkins (Mrs. Jerry) Edythe Taylor (Mrs. Robert)
Judy Hershberger (Mrs. Terry) Beverly Todd (Mrs. D. Bruce)
Judy Hohman (Mrs. Roy) Amy Trowman (Mrs. Bruce)
Chris Hulme (Mrs. David) Barbara Weprin (Mrs. James)
Sally James (Mrs. Robert) Jo Ann Williams (Mrs. John)
Kiki Lesley (Mrs. Michael) Paige Word (Mrs. George)
Rebecca Meeker (Mrs. David) Barbara Wyant (Mrs. Jonathan)
Rosalie Miller (Mrs. James) Sue Zulanch (Mrs. Donald)

INDEX COMMITTEE CHAIRMAN
Sue Elling (Mrs. Stephen)

INDEX COMMITTEE
Ruth Deddens (Mrs. Robert) Katherine England (Mrs. Stephen)
Linda Puthoff (Mrs. Thomas)

LAYOUT CHAIRMAN
Louise Shelton (Mrs. Richard)

PROMOTIONS COMMITTEE CHAIRMAN
Carolyn Medford (Mrs. James)

PROMOTIONS COMMITTEE ASSISTANT CHAIRMEN
Ardith Hamilton (Mrs. Alexander) Phoebe Shaw (Mrs. Harry)
Jane Setzer (Mrs. Frederick, Jr.) Judy Lebensburger (Mrs. Kenneth, Jr.)

PROMOTIONS COMMITTEE
Mary Brattenberg (Mrs. Richard) Susie Kennett (Mrs. David)
Amy Gibson (Mrs. Gregory) Meredith Levinson (Mrs. James)
Darlene Gutmann (Mrs. Max) Niel Lorenz (Mrs. Geoffrey)
Mary Hawn (Mrs. Paul) Linda Patterson (Mrs. Dennis)
Barbara Hohman (Mrs. Russell) Peggy Woods (Mrs. Donald)
Angie Karas (Mrs. Gregory)

PROOFREADING COMMITTEE CHAIRMAN
Sue Elling (Mrs. Stephen)

PROOFREADING COMMITTEE ASSISTANT CHAIRMAN
Carole Taylor (Mrs. David)

PROOFREADING COMMITTEE

Laurie Laine Blank
Margot Clutter (Mrs. William)
Lesli Garrison (Mrs. James)
Dede Geidner (Mrs. Charles)
Amy Gibson (Mrs. Gregory)
Ann Krintzline (Mrs. Bill)
Connie Mereness (Mrs. D. R.)
Janet Metcalfe (Mrs. Steven)
Barbara Miller (Mrs. G. F., Jr.)

Linda Puthoff (Mrs. Thomas)
Kay Roberts (Mrs. John)
Elizabeth Sava (Mrs. Samuel)
Susan G. Stayton
Edythe Taylor (Mrs. Robert)
Virginia vonReichbauer (Mrs. William)
Barbara Weprin (Mrs. James)
Susan Wilson (Mrs. James)

RESTAURANT COMMITTEE CHAIRMAN
Peggy Mayhew (Mrs. William)

RESTAURANT COMMITTEE

Ellen Hansman
Cynthia Karas
Jane Kemmerer

Sonnie Kasch (Mrs. William)
Patricia Wilke (Mrs. Patrick)
Peggy Woods (Mrs. Donald)

SPECIAL FEATURES

CREATIVE WRITERS

Sue Elling (Mrs. Stephen)
Katherine England (Mrs. Stephen)
Sandra Folkerth (Mrs. S. L.)
Harriet Hawkins (Mrs. James)

Julie Hughes (Mrs. Gene)
Sherry Petersen (Mrs. Ronald)
Sally Thompson (Mrs. William)
Judy Westerbeck (Mrs. Gerald)

TESTING COMMITTEE CHAIRMAN
Sally James (Mrs. Robert)

TESTING PARTIES CHAIRMAN
Mary Karr (Mrs. Richard)

TESTING PARTIES ASSISTANT CHAIRMAN
Nancy Schooley (Mrs. C. Hyland)

FOOD CATEGORIES CHAIRMEN

Vickie Baumann (Mrs. Herwig)
Pam Cagle (Mrs. Stephen)
Annette Casella (Mrs. Eugene)
Maria Castleman (Mrs. P. Stanley)
Carol Devery (Mrs. Kieran)
Donna Hawkins (Mrs. Jerry)
Barbara Hohman (Mrs. Russell)
Ann Hughes (Mrs. Donald)
Ginny Koon (Mrs. Richard)
Judy Lebensburger (Mrs. Kenneth)

Chris McClure (Mrs. Stephen)
Carole McLaughlin (Mrs. Richard)
Betty Meckstroth (Mrs. Alan)
Barbara O'Hara (Mrs. Robert)
Laura Overholzer (Mrs. James)
Karen Roberts (Mrs. William)
Patricia Wilke (Mrs. Patrick)
JoAnn Williams (Mrs. John)
Peggy Woods (Mrs. Donald)

TYPING COMMITTEE CHAIRMAN
Annette Casella (Mrs. Eugene)

TYPING COMMITTEE ASSISTANT CHAIRMEN
Brenda May (Mrs. Donald)   Linda Puthoff (Mrs. Thomas)

TYPING COMMITTEE

Katie Brown (Mrs. Edgar)
Susan Castle (Mrs. Charles)

Sara Gatenbee (Mrs. Robert, Jr.)
Chris Hulme (Mrs. David)

The Junior League of Dayton, Ohio, Inc. would like to thank its members and their friends who contributed so much to this book.

Nancy Jackson Adkins
Rebecca Stuart Albery
Patricia Moran Allen
Anne Smith Almoney
Geneva Ferguson Amburgey
Kathy Krug Anderson
Margy Todd Anderson
Dorothy DiGeorgia Antolini
Katherine Carey Augustine
Barbara Welsh Austin
William H. Austin
Ruth Eason Axsom
Linda Kline Babel
Pat Hocker Baird
Eleonore Hanson Balbach
Patti Davis Ballard
Mary Lou Pointer Balsom
Frances Gantt Balta
Joan Feulner Barry
M. J. Thurman Bart
Mary Granson Battenberg
Vickie Overholzer Baumann
Catherine Luken Bayley
Ruth McBride Bayley
Darlene DaPore Bayman
Nan Albers Bechert
Nan Roettig Becker
Kathy Smith Bell
Luz Belvo
Emily Verwold Benham
James Ellsworth Benham
Natalie Theobald Bettcher
Kathleen Tehan Biegel
Helen Elsner Blakeney
Liselott Schloerd Blank
Deanne Evenhouse Bolt
Elesa Bieser Boos
Eva Bilski Bothmann
Althea Busch Bowers
Merea Miley Bowman
Bonnie Hughes Bozorgi
Pat Farley Brady
Betty Laufman Brainard
Mary Waldo Bredeson
Holly A. Briggs
Nancy Bowers Briggs
Carol Millonig Brinkman
Corinne Crabill Broad
Ann Nye Guthrie Brown
Katie Bates Brown
Sara Shelton Browner
Patricia Weyer Buckley
Patricia Holland Byrnes
Pam Shough Cagle
Molly Wall Cammerer
Nancy Ferneding Campbell
Eloise McLaughlin Carey

Annette Dix Casella
Susan Ohmer Castle
Maria Preonas Castleman
Sandra Myers Chamberlin
Virginia Stout Cheslock
Patricia Jones Clark
Ann Michael Claypoole
Margot Urschel Clutter
Elizabeth McBride Clymer
Rebecca Busch Collins
Sallie Morris Collins
Kathleen Emerson Compton
Judy Giddings Cook
Margaret Fogt Cothern
Cheryl Burcham Cotner
Bobbe Dailey Coyne
Ellen Virginia Coyne
Linda Augaitis Coyne
Kaye Battenfield Cragg
Susan Hockwalt Craig
Karen Folz Crawford
Julia Razor Czechowski
Nancy Brundige Dankoff
Sharon Dant
June Hendrickson Decker
Lynn Hagerup Decker
Darcy Louise Deddens
Marcia Kramer Deddens
Robert Lawrence Deddens
Ruth Carey Deddens
Marilyn Accardi Dehner
Patty L. Delony
Margaret Ann DeMarse
Jane Deuser
Carol Stefan Devery
Carol Williamson Dickerson
Mary Healey Donnelly
Deborah Herman Drury
Janet Fanning Dues
Karen Scadura Easton
Martha Bowman Ebeling
Patricia Bieser Edmondson
Carol Kleinhenz Eisert
Stephen Richard Elling
Sue Struble Elling
Jan Franklin Elsasser
Dorothy Curry England
Katherine Benham England
Stephen G. England
Doris Battles Ewing
Gretchen Glick Falknor
Kathleen Hughey Fellers
Sally Willey Fisher
Florence Eardly Flanagan
Jackie Hawkins Florence
Sandra Long Folkerth
Janet Spencer Franklin

Kelly Kuhl Franz
Margaret Loomis French
Carole Meyer Freund
Mary Dillon Gallagher
Lesli Janacshek Garrison
Sara Hart Gattenbee
Bonnie Boyles Geiger
Brenda Bailey Gerding
Amy Gamble Gibson
Gerald L. Gibson
Manja Moore Gibson
Muriel Markel Goodman
Barbara Bennett Greer
Martha Boyd Gresham
Veronica Toth Gronek
Mary Slife Guenin
Sandra Owen Gunlock
Darlene Weller Gutmann
Rosemary Doerr Gutmann
Jill Wasson Hallows
Ardith Paul Hamilton
Ellen Hansman
Nancy Dilts Hardy
Marjorie Rothley Harrington
Elizabeth Haswell
Donna Odom Hawkins
Harriet Beardsley Hawkins
Mary Moore Hawn
Jane Sever Haywood
Phyllis Fraser Heck
Bonnie Bright Heikes
Sandra Oberschlake Hemm
Lisa Herbert
Ann Blanford Herr
Phyllis Walsh Hilgeman
Mary VonderHarr Hinger
Peg Boyer Hoagland
Berit Stolpe Hodgkinson
Barbara Hosic Hohman
Judy Hoeltke Hohman
Susie Headley Holloway
Home Economics Class of
  Alter High School
Roberta Ryan Hook
Jane Hoyne Hosty
Mary Stephens Houpis
Marcia Hobart Howell
Mary Lou Hoopman Hudson
Ann Sutherland Hughes
Judy Loeffel Hughes
Christine Hafstad Hulme
Susan Lowell Hulme
Shirley Harshman Humerick
Nancy Schoedihger Hurley
Betty Luedcke Huter
Robert C. James
Sally Schaefer James

Ann Prindle Johnson
Susan Johnson
Waddie Burchwell Johnson
Sandra Wood Johnston
Margaret Wilson Jones
Pam Leech Kahown
Angie Kalkas Karas
Mary Frances Wheaton Karr
Marjorie Geiger Kasch
Sonnie Kern Kasch
Cynthia M. Kaufmann
Katherine W. Kavanaugh
Mary Essig Keadey
Jill Reeder Kendall
Ponnie Childress Kendell
Susy Lamar Kennett
Mary Sue Hanson Kessler
Janet Cummings Klosterman
Ginny Waite Koon
Edla Armstrong Kramer
Dorothy Elder Kuhns
Carol Lamar Kuntz
Gay Miller Lady
Marjorie Bailey Lange
Linda Disinger Laughter
Ann Wiley Leakas
Judy Lewis Lebensburger
Kiki Huber Lesley
Catherine LeSourd
Laraine Kanner Levine
Catherine Petro Licata
Henrietta Clunet Light
Litton Systems, Inc.
Julie Stayton Long
Marilyn Shute Lorenz
Niel Phillips Lorenz
Emelia Zazvorka Lutz
Helen Daley Macbeth
Antoinette D. Makarewicz
Linda Helton Maleske
Marie Arno Mann
Patty Harris Martin
Jana Lowe Matthews
Brenda Amburgey May
Peggy Walker Mayhew
Maude VanMeter McAfee
Eleanor C. McCann
Ann Gordon McClure
Chris Brewer McClure
Barbara Becker McLaughlin
Carole Kiser McLaughlin
Marilyn Janning McLaughlin
Marthel R. McLaughlin
Suzanne Lukawitz McMahan
Ruth Cummings Mead
Alan Meckstroth
Betty Lutz Meckstroth
Carolyn Lowe Medford
James C. Medford

Bette Smith Medlen
Barbara Perry Meeker
Helen Nelson Meeker
Rebecca Bottomley Meeker
Marjorie Wagnon Mellor
Barbara McClure Melton
Lynn Wagner Merrill
Geraldine Bishop Meyer
Susan Vallo Meyer
Barbara Parkin Miller
Barbara Wallace Miller
Carol Vontz Miller
Janet Hadler Miller
Rosalie Schottenstein Miller
Ruth Gambill Miller
Vail K. Miller
Sherry Smith Mills
Susie Taylor Mills
Ann Focke Mischler
Karen Kwenski Mitchell
Mitzi Benham Mittlestead
Katherine Koenig Mosier
Nora Wall Murray
Hildy Brokop Nellis
Barbara Baldwin Neroni
Edythe Engle Nesmith
Linda Fox Nevin
Gail Decker Newsome
Marie S. O'Donnell
Sue Edwards Oertel
Barbara Nichols O'Hara
Cheri Huber Ohmer
Deborah Ohmer
Lynn Johnson Olive
Lorna Young Osborne
Linda Bruggeman Otte
Dora McWilliams Overholser
Laura Heywood Overholser
Beth Maloney Paolino
Mary Ann Hawker Parker
Melanie Parker
Nancy Logan Parker
Linda Epstein Patterson
Sharon Rafferty Patterson
Virginia Conklin Peck
Candy Gray Pees
Ronald Petersen
Sherry Hess Petersen
Diane Kitzerow Phillips
Carol Crabill Pohl
Melinda Terry Pohl
Myrtle Ledet Potter
Carol Good Powell
Constance Burg Powers
Beverly Lowe Pratt
Nancy Peters Preising
Rita Fanget Price
Roberta R. Prigozen
Julia Smith Prijatel

Judy Elliot Pritchard
Virginia Joplin Pugh
Donna Stearns Puthoff
Linda Bates Puthoff
Thomas C. Puthoff
Ruth Milliken Reece
Jack Rekstis
Karen Kreider Roberts
Jane Baehr Robinson
Gerry Anne Cronin Rocco
Alice M. Roedersheimer
Lois Huston Ross
Barbara Stanek Russ
Myrtie C. Rutledge
Linda Shields Rutmann
Chris Derby Saunders
Elizabeth Tsourounis Sava
Mary Clunet Sawtelle
Sandra LeGault Sawyer
Elspeth Hummel Schantz
Susan West Schantz
Wendy Broad Scholl
Nancye Sherk Schooley
Connie Adams Schriber
Mary Ann Grzech Schuler
Jill Greene Schultz
Mary Allan Schumacher
Judith B. Schwartzman
Louise Babcock Scott
Patti Krygier Scott
Diana Prugh Sebaly
Kay Eutsler Selke
Jane Miller Setzer
Carol Hardey Shafer
Phoebe Crouch Shaw
Elaine Haywood Shawhan
Louise Wittenmyer Shelton
Nancy Garst Shelton
Ruth Shannon Shelton
Sheila Donnachie Shelton
Catherine Wray Shepherd
Alice Holden Sheridan
Kathryn H. Sherman
Theresa Newlin Sherow
Celia Spiegelman Shulman
Ellie Arnovitz Shulman
Ann Harlamert Simms
Judy Moorhead Slanker
Mary E. Marshall Smith
Kathryn Ruddock Snow
Jenet Kimmel Snowden
Linda Amann Snyder
Margaret Sorauf
Lillian Harvey Stacy
Mrs. Walter Starz
Diana Headley Stein
Pam Swartzel Stephens
Betty Burr Steward
Susan Gowdy Stickel

CONTRIBUTORS

Alice Gilbertson Stone
Sandra Smith Strom
Mary Lou Thompson Struble
Joyce Jehl Sutherland
Janet Robinson Sutton
Pamela Dunlop Swaim
Elma Carey Talbot
Mae Stacey Talley
Carole Fitzpatrick Taylor
David R. Taylor, Jr.
Dawn Young Taylor
Judy Bell Terry
Barbara Butt Thomas
Judy Anderson Thomas
Sally Decker Thompson
Phyllis Kane Thompson
William R. Thompson
Jo Thurman
Eileen Babcock Thurnauer
Cornelia Ernst Tinkler
Barbara Gabler Todd
Beverly Wyatt Todd

Leslie Conway Triplett
Mary Wilson Trostel
Robyn Bowman Tsaloff
Judy Fanning Turner
Harriet Epstein Velevis
JoAnn Zieroff Vincent
Virginia D. vonReichbauer
Elizabeth Manier Wack
Carmen Schlimm Wagner
Suzanne Canny Wagner
Susan Katterjohn Walker
Barbara Berg Wasmund
Bette Barlett Weinheimer
Gracey Potter Weisbrod
Rosemary Dahlen Welsh
Barbara Beerman Weprin
Barbara Davis Weprin
Lillabel Hill West
Tina Player West
Judy R. Westerbeck
Agnes Hempfling Wheeler
Corrine Piepenbring White
Koto Usuda White

Nancy Wilcox White
Delores Lowicki Whitney
Mary Kay Bradley Wick
Sara Gerhart Wieland
Patricia Settle Wilke
Evelyn Force Willey
Jo Ann Ferrante Williams
Sue Seifert Williams
Frances Keehn Williamson
Aimee Clunet Wilson
Jeanne Thomas Wilson
Natalie Wilson
Susan Amann Wilson
Mary Jane Bolender Wise
Shannon Spoon Wise
Peggy White Woods
Paige Early Word
Elizabeth Petty Wright
Barbara Jones Wyant
Joyce Canney Young
Diana Hawkins Ziegler
Nancy Hattersley Zorniger

METRIC CONVERSIONS

1 ounce (dry)	=	28.3 grams (g)
1 pound	=	0.45 kilogram (kg)
1 teaspoon	=	5.0 milliliters (ml)
1 tablespoon	=	15.0 milliliters (ml)
1 fluid ounce	=	30.0 milliliters (ml)
1 cup	=	0.24 liter (l)
1 pint	=	0.47 liter (l)
1 quart	=	0.95 liter (l)
1 gallon	=	0.004 cubic meter (m^3)
1 peck	=	0.009 cubic meter (m^3)
1 bushel	=	0.04 cubic meter (m^3)

* * *

1 gram (g)	=	0.035 ounce
1 kilogram (kg)	=	2.2 pounds
1 milliliter (ml)	=	0.2 teaspoon
		0.07 tablespoon
		0.03 fluid ounce
1 liter (l)	=	4.2 cups
		2.1 pints
		1.1 quart
1 cubic meter (m^3)	=	264.0 gallons
		113.0 pecks
		28.0 bushels

WHEN YOU KNOW	YOU CAN FIND	IF YOU MULTIPLY BY
ounces (dry)	grams	28
pounds	kilograms	0.45
ounces (liquid)	milliliters	30
pints	liters	0.47
quarts	liters	0.95
gallons	liters	3.8

WHEN YOU KNOW	YOU CAN FIND	IF YOU MULTIPLY BY
grams	ounces (dry)	0.035
kilograms	pounds	2.2
milliliters	ounces (liquid)	0.034
liters	pints	2.1
liters	quarts	1.06
liters	gallons	0.26

TEMPERATURE

degrees Fahrenheit	degrees Celsius	5/9 (after subtracting 32)
degrees Celsius	degrees Fahrenheit	9/5 (then add 32)

1 calorie = 4.18 joules (j)

INDEX

340

INDEX

346

INDEX

354